TRANSFORMATIONS
OF
CIRCE

TRANSFORMATIONS
OF
CIRCE

The History of an Enchantress

JUDITH YARNALL

UNIVERSITY OF ILLINOIS PRESS
Urbana and Chicago

This book is printed on acid-free paper.

"Temptation" (translated by Brenda Walker and Andrea Deletant) is reprinted from *Life Sentences: Selected Poems,* by Nina
Cassian, edited by William Jay Smith, by permission of Nina
Cassian and W. W. Norton & Company, Inc. Copyright © 1990
by Nina Cassian.

Library of Congress Cataloging-in-Publication Data

Yarnall, Judith, 1940–
    Transformations of Circe : the history of an enchantress / Judith
Yarnall.
        p.   cm.
    Includes bibliographical references and index.
    ISBN 10: 0-252-02063-4 (cloth). — ISBN 10: 0-252-06356-2 (pbk. : alk.
paper).
    ISBN 13: 978-0-252-02063-6 (cloth). — ISBN 13: 978-0-252-06356-5 (pbk. :
alk. paper).
    1. Circe (Greek mythology) in literature. 2. Literature—History
and criticism. I. Title.
PN57.C52Y37   1994
809'.93351—dc20   93-14024
                                                              CIP

For Julia, Katherine, and Anna

Where love reigns, there is no will to power; and
where the will to power is paramount, love is lacking.
The one is but the shadow of the other.

—C. G. Jung

Temptation

Call yourself alive? Look, I promise you
that for the first time you'll feel your pores opening
like fish mouths, and you'll actually be able to hear
your blood surging through all those lanes,
and you'll feel light gliding across the cornea
like the train of a dress. For the first time
you'll be aware of gravity
like a thorn in your heel,
and your shoulder blades will ache for want of wings.
Call yourself alive? I promise you
you'll be deafened by dust falling on the furniture,
you'll feel your eyebrows turning to two gashes,
and every memory you have—will begin
at Genesis.

—Nina Cassian (translated from
the Romanian by Andrea Deletant
and Brenda Walker)

Contents

Illustrations

Acknowledgments

It is a pleasure to thank everyone who contributed to and supported this book. Philip Ambrose, Robin Schlunk, and Jean Davison of the Classics Department at the University of Vermont taught me as an auditor in their Greek classes and helped me acquire the foundation necessary for beginning this study. Mary Davison of the English Department at McGill University knowledgably guided my investigation while it was taking on its earlier form as a doctoral thesis, supporting my overall point of view and making me aware of many invaluable sources. Financial support from the Friends of McGill enabled me to explore my initial intuitions by traveling to temple sites in Greece and Turkey. At a later stage in the project, Johnson State College very generously provided a grant for production of the photographs that illustrate this book.

My family of friends in Vermont and Montreal sustained me while I was working on this investigation; to them I am especially grateful. Annemarie Curlin, Anthony Grimaldi, Martha Rivera, Wolfe Schmokel, and Phyllis Stanley acted as translators, making sources available to me that otherwise would not have been accessible. June Trayah of the Bailey-Howe Library at the University of Vermont and Catherine Mongeon, who handles interlibrary loan at the John Dewey Library at Johnson State College, aided my researches with consistent skill and good humor. Dialogue with Bill MacDougall, Henry Finney, and, especially, Diana Henderson helped me to strengthen the individual chapters to which they gave careful critical readings. Barbara McManus, of the College of New Rochelle, read several earlier versions of the manuscript; her vision of what this book could be helped it to assume its final shape. My editor, Ann Lowry, gave me excellent assistance throughout the publication process.

Finally, I thank Julia Alvarez and Paolo Vivante, dear friends and muses, for the inspiration they have given me; their contributions to this book are nonspecific but immeasurable.

Introduction

Stories also have stories. Circe's begins in the *Odyssey,* on the island of Aiaia that Homer dreamed for her, in the chambers of the palace where she richly entertained Odysseus and in her sty full of sailors turned pigs. Or perhaps it began much earlier, in tales of a woman or goddess of prodigious powers that were recited around hearthfires and in the banquet halls of kings. We shall probably never know at what moment, in what era, Circe the enchantress first took on deed and shape.

What we can know for certain—what Western literature attests to—is her remarkable staying power once she has emerged from the mists of prehistory. She appears briefly in Virgil's *Aeneid* as the ruler of a promontory where the air vibrates with the howls of chained and enraged beasts—a place to be avoided at all costs. Slightly later, more sedately, she turns the symbolic wheel that governs incarnation, the endless series of births and deaths, in Neo-Platonic allegory. She is the fair witch who lounges on a bed of rose petals in Spenser's Renaissance bower of bliss, waiting for virile young lovers to appear and offer themselves for her delectation. Or the lovelorn, rejected enchantress of seventeenth-century drama and ballet, who finally comes to realize that all her magic counts as nothing compared to the greater magic of enjoying and retaining a man. In James Joyce's *Ulysses* she appears as Bella Cohen, the businesswoman-cum-whore who presides over a house where possibilities proliferate like exotic blooms in the midst of Dublin's Nighttown. And in the work of recent women writers, Eudora Welty and Margaret Atwood in particular, she is a strong-voiced, clear-eyed, solitary figure who speaks out knowingly about her powers and their limits. Circe herself, in the twists and turns of her story through the centuries, has gone through far more metamorphoses than those she inflicted on Odysseus's companions, who had merely to suffer and endure the transformation from man to beast to man.

This book is a survey of Circe's metamorphoses and of what they indicate about the cultures and eras that produced them. Her longevity as a presence in Western literature suggests that she is an archetypal character, one who appears again and again as an expression of a basic human experience, fear or desire. She is an image (and I follow Jung in this hypothesis) generated by a node of energy or a patterning process in our collective unconscious that demands expression. Specifically, Circe offers an image of the strong woman who has power to give shape and form: someone we all experienced once, while we were waiting to be thrust out into this world. Because she acts upon adults, exclusively adult males, and not developing fetuses, she also acts as a dramatic reminder of our original, and in some sense constant, plasticity and helplessness. No matter what century or work Circe appears in, she is associated with our bodily vulnerability and has power over that—a power that is often presented as sexual allure.

Attitudes toward Circe and her powers, as will be apparent in the chapters to follow, differ widely from Homer's time to that of other ancient writers, from the Renaissance to the twentieth century. These different versions of Circe's myth can be seen as mirrors, sometimes clouded and sometimes clear, of the fantasies and assumptions of the cultures that produced them. To ask fiction and poetry to serve as evidence for social history, for how people actually went about the outward business of their daily lives, is to tread upon shaky intellectual ground. But to look to works of the imagination for signs of how people feared and dreamed, and protected themselves from their fears and dreams, is to embark upon a far more promising search, one in keeping with the very nature of myth, fiction, and poetry.[1]

When we first encounter Circe in Homer, she is part of a myth that has already been given literary treatment, worked into epic poetry. The *Odyssey* is the foundation text of this study, but it is highly doubtful whether it contains the original Circe. Artists—particularly artists like Homer who collect, shape, and burnish the legends of their people— do not create from airy nothings. They work with what is already there: in daily life, in dreams, in stories that have been told before. How, then, did Circe originate? How does any myth begin? The first of these questions I address in chapter 2, which explores the affinities of iconographic details connected with Homer's character with those used in ancient goddess religions. As for the second, I follow Mircea Eliade, Phillip Wheelwright, and Joseph Campbell in believing that myth begins existentially, as a response to mystery.[2] A myth is a symbolic narrative that is flung out like a life preserver from the collective psyche toward a phenomenon that it does not understand and yet cannot avoid addressing. Most basically, this mystery is life itself, the experience of waking up in a world that is overwhelmingly, shimmeringly *present.* The creation myths of every culture address this huge and basic perplexity, while a host of more focused myths confront parts of it.

I say "address" instead of "explain" because the task of myth is not to explain away mystery by making it accessible to reason and logic, but rather to provide a means of relating to it, so that the tribe or culture is not forced into retreat. The form of narrative, with its reliable sequentiality, provides such a word-by-word means—just as the sound of the storyteller's voice in the firelit darkness must once have reassured both audience and self of the effectiveness of human presence.

Implicit in this conception of myth is the assumption that the story develops at the interface between psyche and outward reality. Echoes of history, of events that actually occurred, may thus well be found in symbolized, transmuted form in myth. Having read and believed the *Iliad* as a boy, and accepting Homer's geography as true, Heinrich Schliemann staked his life's fortune on his conviction that an obscure hill in northwestern Turkey was Troy. He was perhaps lucky to be proved right. Lying just beneath the surface of several chapters of this book, and occasionally protruding into its argument, is my considered but unproven theory that the Circe-Odysseus myth as it is found in Homer addresses the shift from goddess religions to the Olympian pantheon, and from the matrilineal to patriarchal organization of society, which occurred at some time in Mediterranean and Aegean prehistory. Lacking a written record other than the problematical one of the *Odyssey* itself, supported by archaeological evidence that often remains teasingly ambiguous, this hypothesis may not convince the unconverted. Yet if it is true, it gives the encounter of Circe and Odysseus a very large foreground, one particularly relevant to our time when prerogatives of gender-based power are again shifting and eroding.

Once a myth is formed and recorded, it becomes an artifact of cultural imagination and thus subject to historical inquiry as well as to endless reforming by individual writers and artists, many of whom also draw from their own wells into the collective unconscious in order to recreate it. Jung's theory that the deepest stratum of our psyches is roughly the same in all of us is attractive because it accounts for the often striking correlation of imagery between myths ("the world's dreams," according to Joseph Campbell), imaginative literature, and our individual nighttime dreams. It is also compelling because Jung insists on the interconnection between psyche and body (or spirit and flesh, in the rhetoric of Christianity) that has so often been denied in Western culture. As he puts it, "The unconscious is the psyche that reaches down from the daylight of mentally and morally lucid consciousness into the nervous system that for ages has been known as the 'sympathetic.' This does not govern perception and muscular activity . . . but . . . maintains the balance of life and, through the mysterious paths of sympathetic excitation, not only gives us knowledge of the innermost life of other beings but also has an inner effect on them."[3] He sees us as connected with each other psychically because we resemble each other physically, carrying the same basic genetic codes. To Jung, the collective unconscious is objective reality, with all its attendant authority. Yet he is reluctant to recognize a complementary authority and reality in that which exists and occurs outside of the psyche. In this respect my conception of myth—as symbolic narrative resulting from a confrontation of the inner and outer worlds and not just from projection—differs in emphasis from his.

I have avoided using the terms "anima" and "anima figure" to describe Circe in this study, though to orthodox Jungians surely Homer's Circe, with her power to reduce a man to squealing, rooting helplessness or to inspire him to range beyond his former boundaries, to find his soul's direction in the midst of chaos and the kingdom of death, must appear as an anima figure par excellence. To Jung, the anima is "the archetype of life itself," the mysterious female figure who guards the gateway to a man's collective unconscious and who must be confronted by any male seeking psychic wholeness.[4] She is the contrasexual element within himself, just as the animus (which Jung associates with rationality and assertive will) is the contrasexual element within a woman. He links the feminine with Eros and the masculine with Logos: a dualism and assumption that goes back at least to Plato's time and that has been used historically (though not by Jung) to discount women's spirituality and intelligence.[5] For this reason, together with the Jungian tendency to view the collective unconscious as the primary objective reality and thus to conflate the anima figures of male mythmakers, writers, and dreamers with the feminine as it is actually lived and experienced by women, I have been wary of anima rhetoric, finding it more clouding than clarifying. It is more helpful to think of Circe simply as an archetypal woman of power, whose potency is grounded in her disturbing ability to give form to flesh and blood, than as an anima figure. She is as compelling to modern women seeking to explore the range of their own natures as she has been to male poets and dreamers in the past.

Insofar as myth is archetypal, it is timeless, eternal. Yet myths are also, inescapably, productions of time. They are artifacts of the imagination, of the cultures and eras that give new, distinctive twists to their narrative shape. Margaret Atwood's Circe—who asks Odysseus "Don't you get tired of saying Onward?"—tells her story in a salty, knowing, disillusioned voice whose tones are those of recent feminism. Joyce's, who has no story of her own (a deficiency she shares with almost every other Circe imagined by a male writer), plays upon Leopold Bloom's sexual masochism like a virtuoso, like the turn-of-the-century femme fatale she emphatically is. Calderón's seventeenth-century Circe, a Counter-Reformation temptress whom he forthrightly renames "Sin," uses her abundant sexuality to deflect Ulysses from his quest for salvation. Her actions provide the clearest example of an allegorical scenario that had been impressed upon the myth for centuries, one structured upon the Platonic and Augustinean assumption that what pleasures the body hurts the soul. And Homer's Circe? She is a goddess who dwells in a "sacred house," like Artemis at Ephesus or Aphrodite at Paphos or Demeter at Knidos—like the numerous female divinities of the ancient world who prevailed before godhead was restricted by sex. Circe as protean enchantress mirrors her times and provides us, if we carefully examine her changes, with insight into the guiding assumptions of those times. Her myth has acted as a magnet particularly for what writers of different eras have had to say about the relationship of sexuality, with all its possibilities for vulnerability and power, to human nature as a whole.

In the following chapters I organize my investigation chronologically, in order to follow the sequentiality of Circe's meta-story. The only departure from this order occurs in chapter 2, which explores Homer's possible sources for the Circe-Odysseus myth after I have retold that myth in chapter 1. For reasons of both drama and homage, it seemed wise to let Homer have the first word. Four chapters in all are devoted to the ancient world and two (one exclusively on Spenser) to the Renaissance—times when the myth proved particularly compelling to writers and artists. Its fascination lingered through the seventeenth century, during which Circe and Ulysses appeared in a variety of dramatic works ranging from light court entertainments to sacramental *auto.* Chapter 7 focuses upon these plays and also contains a brief discussion of Milton's Eve in *Paradise Lost,* who—though she is not named Circe and never reduces men to pigs—seemed too relevant to the themes of this study to ignore completely. During the Enlightenment, the Circe myth, along with many others, was discounted or ignored while Western culture conducted its love affair with reason. My investigation therefore jumps two hundred years to the late nineteenth century, when Circe's sinister, dark-edged beauty began to be stroked upon Pre-Raphaelite and salon canvases; this eighth chapter also examines in considerable detail the carnival of suddenly unrepressed sexuality that is Joyce's Nighttown chapter in *Ulysses.* The final chapter explores the work of current women writers, who probe the consciousness and voice behind the seductress facade and thus restore to the enchantress a balance, a depth of presence, rarely found in her since Homer's time.

Archetypal stories are magnetic stories, drawing upon our deepest desires and fears, tempting critics as well as artists to obsess and distort. Often Circe's least sensitive, most dogmatic interpreters have been most influential in setting her image. The Homeric allegorists, for instance, who wrote several commentaries on the myth in the centuries following Plato and who were perhaps the first literary critics, were also the first to commit a great critical sin. By ignoring evidence that did not fit their theories—the whole last half of the myth as it appears in the *Odyssey*—they created a Circe who is a caricature of Homer's. Their example is admonitory. I have taken the principle of examining not just the character or image, but the image within the text as a whole as a guideline. Though Circe and her howling beasts occupy only fifteen lines of the *Aeneid,* for instance, my discussion of her presence in the poem covers several pages and explores the ways in which she is expressive or symptomatic of Virgil's treatment of the feminine. Myths are complete stories that address mystery; even when they are set within polished literary works they ask of the critic a similar concern with wholeness.

Myths also demand a respect for their origins, for the awesome perplexities that prompted them. Though she is herself the veteran of many transformations, the archetypal core of Circe's power remains unchanged: she is the female figure who possesses the ability to *transform,* to give shape to others or to take it away. She offers both debasement and deliverance, a new life in the flesh. How artists and thinkers of different eras have responded to the profoundly ambiguous allure of this promise is the substance of this book.

1

Homer's Story

Circe emerges from and recedes into mystery. Her presence is made known, just before she first appears in book 10 of the *Odyssey*, by the most insubstantial of signs, hearthsmoke and the piercing lilt of her song. When she walks away from Odysseus for the second and final time in book 12, she disappears on a path leading up among dawnlit trees. In between, while she shares the poem's narrative foreground with its hero, her presence takes on definiteness and force, but never surrenders its dangerous tinge of the enigmatic. Who is she? Why does Homer accord her a position of great importance? For unmistakably, she dwells at the core of the *Odyssey*, at the center of its central section: that part bracketed by the Telemachiad and the return to Ithaca that tells of the hero's adventures among unknown peoples and seas. Circe is far more than just another member of this section's exotic cast; she becomes, as Joseph Campbell has remarked, Odysseus's mystagogue, instructing him in the details of his way.[1] She does not appear until he is thoroughly lost, and she does not disappear until he has regained some sense of his bearings and of the dangers to come. The story of their encounter is thus pivotal to his direction and to the poem as a whole. What follows is a retelling of Homer's story, with close attention to some of the details of his phrasings.

Odysseus and his men beach their ship on Circe's island, Aiaia,[2] because they have no choice. Hungry and driven by need to replenish their stores, mourning for comrades who have just been brutally murdered by the Cyclops and Laistrygoneans, they are understandably fearful of what will come next. In this condition, stripped of his usual vigor and self-possession, Odysseus would hardly seem fit for yet another adventure, particularly for one that will prove to be an archetypal encounter between the sexes. In the world of the *Odyssey*, however, the most desperate moments are frequently the most auspicious.

Odysseus, who is narrating this story to the assembled nobility on Nausicaa's island of Phaiacia, tells them immediately that Circe is a "dread goddess of human voice" (*deine theos audéessa*),[3] the daughter of Helios by the ocean nymph Perse and sister of "baleful" Aietes. The descriptive phrase implies that Circe occupies an unusual ontological niche. Although a divinity, of another order of being and power than that of mortals and therefore a presence to be feared, she is nevertheless accessible for she speaks our tongue. She is no Olympian, accustomed to lofty heights. Her island, as Odysseus later tells us (12.3–4), is close to "where the dwellings and dancing floors of early-born Dawn are, and the rising places of the Sun."[4] The old Greek name for Asia Minor, Anatolia, is derived from *antolai,* this word for rising places; this fact, combined with her kinship to Aietes, who in the Argonaut legends figures as king of Colchis on the eastern shore of the Black Sea, strongly suggests that Circe's island is somewhere in that region.[5] In Homer's time the Pontus or Black Sea was the edge of the known world; its shores were thought to be populated by wealthy, barbarous, shamanistic Scythians and by their Amazon neighbors. With its aura of magic and gold, this region seems appropriate to Circe, daughter of Helios the sun god. On her mother's side, too, Circe's lineage is elemental. Connected by heritage with the great energies of sea and light, it is small wonder that she herself should possess the power to loosen the bonds of form, to transform.

But Odysseus, in telling the Phaiacians of Circe's background, gets ahead of himself; when he first lands on Aiaia he knows nothing of her or her powers. All he sees when he climbs a rocky lookout is a puff of smoke ascending from the island's thickly wooded center. Thoroughly disoriented, having no choice but to explore, he shakes lots with his men and sends the winner, his captain Eurylochos, off with a scouting contingent while he himself remains with their ships. Eurylochos and his men weep as they set forth, for they have learned by now to expect the worst.

What they find is an establishment that blends the stately with the sinister. Circe's home is made of stone polished smooth on all sides, a labor-intensive building material found nowhere else in the *Odyssey* and appropriate to the status of a Mycenaean king or a divinity. When Odysseus refers to this house as a *hiera domata,* a sacred palace (10.426, 445), he is not flattering or exaggerating. Homer never questions Circe's authenticity as a goddess or her right to live like one, though he gives her character some human shades. He refers to her with forms of the word *thea* thirteen times in book 10.[6]

The unusual menagerie roaming Circe's grounds is disconcerting to Eurylochos and his men. Tamed wolves and mountain lions rise up to fawn on them, like dogs begging for scraps. Monsters—*pelora*—Odysseus later calls them. The word is strong, used elsewhere only for Scylla and Polyphemos; it expresses the Greek horror at seeing the order of nature overturned. Yet Odysseus refrains from implying that these creatures were formerly human. That interpretation comes only from Eurylochos, when, after refusing to enter Circe's house, he reports back to Odysseus in terror. "She will make all of you into swine or wolves or lions," he says (10.432–33), and he goes on, with a boldness born of fear, to accuse Odysseus of rashness, of wantonly causing the death of his men.

Should we believe Eurylochos on this point? Certainly the predominant inclination of Homer's readers has been to do so. Yet an acquaintance with goddess worship in ancient Anatolia and Greece raises cause for doubt. One of the most common elements of this religious iconography, as will be discussed in the next chapter, was the goddess of wild things flanked by heraldic predators, particularly by leopards and lions. Her ability to calm the most dangerous and deadly of beasts was taken as a sign of her awesome power.

As the wary Greeks approach Circe's dwelling, they are lured by the sound of her singing as she sits weaving shining, ambrosial fabrics on her great loom. Eurylochos calls her voice *liga,* meaning shrill or piercing (10.254)—the word Homer uses most commonly to describe the wails of the Trojan women. The same word is used for the playing of Demodocos, the harper at the Phaiacian court, whose music brings tears to Odysseus's eyes. It connotes an emotionally piercing quality, suggesting that Circe is truly and poignantly of human voice. Listening to her from a distance, the Greeks wonder whether she is goddess or woman (10.228, 255), an ambiguity they decide to investigate.

Circe welcomes them, seating them on her comfortable chairs and offering them a brew that they drink immediately, concocted of grated cheese, barley meal, fresh honey, and strong Pramnian wine, to which she has added a pinch of a "vile drug" that robs them of human form. Then she raises her wand, her *rhabdos,* and herds the newly made swine to her sty. Her transformative magic seems to reside in the drug rather than the rod, which may well be an ordinary driver's stick.[7] Yet because this moment illustrates more clearly than any other female dominance over the male, the *rhabdos* has come to seem potent, a symbol of phallic powers improperly assumed. A Greek amphora now in Berlin shows a seated Circe with raised rod in hand, compelling a naked sailor who turns round, abashed, to discover his small, curled tail (figure 1). The *rhabdos* here is clearly an instrument of power.

All this time Eurylochos has hung back, wary but ignorant of the extent of the catastrophe. When he later tells of his companions' disappearance, Odysseus determines to go after them. He is intercepted on the forest path by Hermes, who suddenly and magically presents himself. God of wayfarers and adventurers, Hermes is the only Olympian to venture into those scenes of the *Odyssey* that occur beyond the pale of human civilization. His intervention here seems prompted by affinity rather than by the express command of Zeus; he is Odysseus's great-grandfather (though Homer makes nothing of the fact) and the two share a streak of cunning.[8] Hermes, associated as he is with journeys, windfalls, and male sexuality, is the perfect divinity to prepare Odysseus for his role in the drama awaiting him. He gives the hero an herb, a countercharm called "moly" in the language of the gods, which he pulls up from the ground beneath them. It has a white, milky flower and a black, tenacious root.[9]

Just as the moly will overcome the evil drug, the *pharmakon kakon,* so, Hermes tells Odysseus, his own prowess with his sword will overcome Circe's wand. She will then command him to share her bed. He must not spurn her, Hermes is careful to emphasize, though first he must make her swear a great oath to work no further harm.

The meeting between Circe and Odysseus is charged with recognition. Protected by the moly, Odysseus does not hesitate to drain the golden cup that she holds out to him. Circe also has been prepared for the encounter by Hermes. When Odysseus appears she knows him by his power to withstand her transformative magic and calls him by name. "Some steady will must be in your breast," she exclaims (10.329), attributing his heroic firmness to a consciousness lodged near his heart.[10] When he holds his bronze sword above her head, feigning intent to kill, she slides down and takes his knees in a ritualized gesture of surrender.

Figure 1. Circe, on Greek amphora found at Nola. Courtesy of the Antik-ensammlung, Staatliche Museen zu Berlin-Preussischer Kulturbesitz.

This is the posture that Priam had adopted when he came to ask Achilles for Hector's body and that Phemios, the harper at Ithaca, is later to assume as he begs Odysseus for his life. It is not her life, however, that Circe asks for; even with Hermes' help, Odysseus would not be capable of killing an immortal. The challenge, the play of power here, has far more to do with attraction than fear. When Circe speaks she assumes an intimacy, gracefully measuring her words: "Let us mount our bed, so that we may mingle in lovemaking / and trust each other in friendship" (10.334–35). Odysseus accepts this invitation to pleasure and good faith, though first he has her swear the oath. *Perikalle* Homer calls her bed, a word meaning literally "beautiful all around" that he elsewhere applies to the loveliest gifts of nature, such as harbors and rivers and olive trees.[11]

From this point on in Homer's version of the myth, Circe uses her formidable powers beneficently. Trust rather than perfidy follows from their lovemaking. Circe never lies to Odysseus, as Aphrodite does to the Trojan Anchises when she claims to be a mortal woman as she is seducing him.[12] Nor does Circe threaten him with impotence or any other bodily harm. Odysseus is one of the very few men in myth or literature who mingles sexually with an immortal goddess and does not later suffer for his presumption.

After this interlude Odysseus remembers his purpose. True captain that he is, he refuses to partake of the sumptuous food set out by Circe's housekeeper, or to drink the wine the beguiling forest and water nymphs who act as her handmaids have ladled from a silver krater into golden cups. Nourishment will not pass his lips, he says, until his men are restored to their proper forms. Circe obliges, smearing an antidotal ointment on their skins that makes the bristles fall away. The men at once become younger than they were before, taller, and more handsome (10.395–96). What could be more creaturely than the sound that is wrung from within them as they are released to human shape? "A passionate cry emerged from all," Homer writes (10.398), "and the walls resounded terribly."[13] As the men are restored to themselves and greet Odysseus, Circe too seems to take on humanity. The passage ends with a line that elegantly and succinctly suggests the power of emotion to bind together the most disparate of lives in the intensity of a moment: "And the goddess herself took pity" (10.399).

Then the easeful days of the Greeks upon Circe's isle begin. During the winter season when navigation is dangerous, they restore themselves in Circe's halls amidst an abundance of rich meats, honeyed wines, and sensuous pleasures. Gentled perhaps by love, Circe is no longer referred to in book 10 as "dread goddess of human voice," but rather as *dia the-aon,* "divine among goddesses" (10.400, 455, 503), an epithet also used for Calypso and Athene and, in the parallel form of *dia gynaikon,* for Penelope. Discourse between the goddess and her lover now takes on a heightened courtesy and gravity, she addressing him as "hero" or "god-born son of Laertes, Odysseus of many wiles" and he replying *potnia,* "Lady." In some lost versions of the myth, Odysseus is so satisfied that he stays with Circe for years, fathering one or several children by her, including a son Telegonos who years later seeks him out and kills him by mistake.[14] Homer does not mention any children born of their union, but he does suggest unmistakably that Odysseus forgets about Ithaca while on Aiaia.

When "the long days had come to completion"—that is, when the best sailing weather of the year had come round with the summer sol-stice—Odysseus's men tap him on the shoulder to remind him of their destination. The language here (10.472), highly unusual for subordinates addressing a leader, gives the measure of their exasperation. *Daimonie,* they call him—an untranslatable term used for a person doing some-thing so abnormal or incomprehensible as to imply a state of posses-sion. The word mixes bewilderment with a tinge of insult; it is the one Odysseus is later to choose for Penelope, when, after he has killed all the suitors and been bathed and graced by Athene, she still withholds her recognition. Ordered by his men to remember Ithaca, his earth and fatherland, Odysseus comes back to himself at once and begs Circe to send him homeward. On their "flawless" bed he grasps her knees. The gesture of surrender thus becomes balanced, mutual.

She grants his request unhesitatingly, saying that she does not wish him to remain in her house against his will. Whether it is merely be-neath her dignity to content herself with a half-willing lover, or wheth-er she actively cares for Odysseus enough to wish him to accomplish his destiny apart from herself, must remain unknown, for Homer does not hint at her motives. She gives Odysseus his freedom and her help without complaint or reserve. Unlike Calypso, she has not a trace of possessiveness.

Once the spell of pleasure between Odysseus and Circe has ended, she again takes on some of her dread aspect. Her affinities with the Un-derworld are revealed when she tells Odysseus that it is necessary for him to go there in order to seek out the counsel of Tiresias. He reacts as would any mortal—with fear and despair—for he interprets her instructions as a death warrant. He knows, no doubt, that no human being save Heracles has come back from the house of Hades alive. Yet her directions reassure him, for in telling him what animals to sacrifice both at the mouth of the Erebos and back home in Ithaca, she seems to assume that he will live to return. It is left to him to break the news of this terrible journey to his men, who are so full of terror that they shed "mighty tears" and loudly tear at their hair. Book 10 ends with Circe reassuming the remoteness and sufficiency unto herself that are her prerogatives as a goddess. Veiled, wrapped in a finely woven, silvery cloak, she passes by Odysseus and his men unseen. When they get to the shore they discover her gifts, a black ewe and ram whose blood they will use to summon the dead.

Where is the palace of Hades? As Homer tells it, the entrance to the Underworld lies on the other side of Oceanos, the circular river that bounds the world, close by the lands of a mysterious people called the Cimmerians.[15] With the help of a vigorous breeze sent by Circe, the Greeks arrive after one day and night of sailing. After Odysseus fulfills her detailed instructions—digging a pit; pouring libations of milk, honey, wine, and clear water; scattering barley; and last, letting the dark blood of the animals stream into the hollowed ground—the shades swarm up. They are attracted particularly by the blood, the life-substance they need in order to speak. The first to appear is that of Elpenor, one of their own number, who died when he fell off Circe's roof upon awakening from a drunken sleep on his last morning on the island. He begs Odysseus to return to Aiaia, so that he may receive cremation and proper rites. Circe's reappearance in the narrative is thus assured. When Tiresias appears, his advice to Odysseus, though necessary, is more moral than practical. Its essence is simple: restrain yourselves, do not eat the Oxen of the Sun. Although he reassures Odysseus that he, at least, will return to Ithaca, Tiresias does not give him specific sailing directions or a tally of the dangers he must pass on the way.

That kind of useful nautical advice comes from Circe, whose powers of prophecy prove exceedingly accurate. After Odysseus and his men have returned to her island, built Elpenor's pyre, and allowed it to burn to embers, she comes down to the shore to welcome them. She holds out her usual generous quantities of meat and wine, speaking with a teasing, perhaps affectionate tone. *Sketlioi,* she calls them, "unflinching ones"

... *disthanées,* "twice-diers" (12.21–22). The stalwart ones, well sated, fall asleep at nightfall and at that time Circe draws Odysseus aside with a human and intimate gesture. Lying beside him, she questions him about "each thing," about all the terrors and wonders he has seen, behaving in her curiosity exactly as Penelope will later during their first night of reunion in the olive bed. His answers assure her that he has duly passed through the ordeal she has imposed upon him; in response, she rewards him with more information.[16] She recites several of the dangers still to come—the Sirens, Scylla and Charybdis, the Oxen of the Sun—and tells him how to avoid or cope with each.

Her message is very much about the boundaries of heroism. When Odysseus wants to know how to fight off Scylla, she again teasingly addresses him as *sketlie* and asks if he must always engage in battle. All his bronze-sworded valor, she says, will be powerless against this immortal monster. The best course for him and his men will be to bend to the oars, flee. The exchange is minor, occupying only a few lines, but it beautifully illustrates the perspective, constant in Homer, against which the glory of heroism is seen. Her divine knowledge makes military prowess appear as a limited thing.

At dawn the Greeks take to their ship and Circe heads upland, away from the shore. There are no goodbyes. Whatever kindness and intimacy has developed between her and Odysseus recedes with her into the unknown.

This, then, is Homer's version of the story. What does it all mean?

This question is not as straightforward as it seems. To interpret Homer is to embark upon an enterprise fraught with risks, chief among them the possibility of distorting with one's own cultural and personal biases a myth that is complete and compelling as presented. My late twentieth-century, feminist biases—toward the equality and complementarity of the sexes, toward a consciousness as informed by intuition and the senses as it is by reason, toward the emergence of synthesis from seemingly intractable dualisms—color my understanding of the Circe-Odysseus myth as surely as those of the ancient allegorists and Renaissance poets and mythographers attracted to this story marked theirs. To think otherwise would be naive, to consider myself exempt from a dialogic process of reading that stretches through centuries.

Beyond the somewhat avoidable risk of distortion induced by bias, however, the reader who seeks meaning in Homer faces another difficulty. For in a sense, to interpret Homer at all is to violate his mode of imagining, which is at every turn clear and immediate, presenting and accepting the wondrously varied sensuousness of life, elevating human experience through the repetitions of ritual rather than by the transcendence of abstraction. In Homer there *is* virtually no abstraction, for the requisite vocabulary had not yet developed. Our inclination to regard meaning as truth distilled from, somehow purified of, experience is irrelevant to a reading of the *Odyssey*, where the event and its significance are one. Whatever meanings are to be found in this myth of Circe and Odysseus, must, if true to the spirit of the poem, evolve naturally from its accretion of narrative detail and from the *entirety* of its structure. Loyalty to the wholeness of the myth and to that of the work in which it is found can also act as a salutary curb upon the tendency of bias to pull the interpreter astray. A major problem with many later interpretations of Circe is that they sever rather than honor the wholeness of her myth.

An appropriate way, then, to begin a search for this myth's significance is to notice what place its story occupies within the structure of the *Odyssey* as a whole. Odysseus's adventures in the Unknown—that is, in the mysterious realm that lies beyond the pale of human civilization—are bracketed by the Telemachiad and by his return. Populated by giants and enchantresses who evoke immense pleasures and fears, this territory of the Unknown suggests all that is untamed, unexplored, scarcely understood; it finds its most convincing modern analogue in the barely charted territory of the psyche. Pressed to define what couldn't be defined, Carl Jung once retorted that "the unconscious is not this thing or that; it is the Unknown, as it immediately affects us."[17] In this part of the *Odyssey* the sea, an ancient emblem of unfathomable natural forces beyond human control, is supremely important. It supports Odysseus and his men as they careen from one adventure to another at the mercy of winds, and it threatens to engulf the Ithacan when he alone survives shipwreck. The danger for Odysseus is that his immersion in the Unknown will be complete, that he will be overwhelmed by roiling seas and surrender his individual identity to the elements.

"Ego's archetype is the Hero," James Hillman remarks.[18] Certainly a quicksilver, resourceful consciousness, always alert to opportunities for self-preservation, is the hallmark of this particular hero. As Homer never tires of telling us, Odysseus is *polymetis*, possessed of abundant shrewdness. But his egocentric intelligence alone is not sufficient to bring him back to Ithaca, the dear remembered land, the kingdom of the familiar and the recognizably human that is normative for him. Ithaca is his destiny, the place where he belongs. At heart he is a most domestic hero, whose quest is not to achieve glory or aim for the stars: it is merely to return and put his house in order. His sojourn among the presences of the Unknown both delays this destiny and prepares him for it, by enlarging his conscious knowledge of the great forces that surround and penetrate the fragile boundaries of civilized life.

Of the ten episodes that comprise this phase of his wandering (the Lotos-Eaters, the Cyclops, Aeolos, the Laistrygoneans, Aiaia, Hades, the Sirens, Scylla and Charybdis, the Oxen of the Sun, Calypso), those involving Circe stand at the very center. It takes Odysseus a long time to reach her; he must be thoroughly lost before he does. When he finds her, she mediates for him most of the remaining dangers of the Unknown.[19]

Specifically, what Odysseus loses before his encounter with Circe is his faith in the efficacy of his own unaided will. This faith has been beaten out of him by a series of failures and disastrous successes. The sack of Ismaros—a predatory venture to which Odysseus gave his full consent, although he disapproved of his men's loitering and carousing afterwards—is followed by a retaliatory seastorm sent by Zeus, which blows his ships drastically off their course toward Ithaca. His blinding of Polyphemos, seemingly his most clever trick, also comes back to haunt him. In a brilliant pun on his own name, he had told Polyphemos that his eye had been gouged out by Nobody, *outis*. When he was safely beyond the range of the Cyclops's hurled boulders though, Odysseus could not resist the temptation to assert his ego, to take credit for this masterly piece of underdog's aggression. Shouting his true name, he enabled Polyphemos to call down the wrath of Poseidon, the Cyclops's father, upon his head. The incident with Aeolos's bag of winds again illustrates the failure of Odysseus's will to restrain—this time to restrain his men (as on Ismaros, and in the Oxen of the Sun incident to come). They open the bag, thinking it contains gold, and let loose the gales that blow them toward the Laistrygoneans. In each case the will to control is overcome by the sheer force of appetite: for pleasure, for glory, for wealth. The Laistrygoneans, those avatars of rapaciousness, reflect a dynamic already disastrously at work within Odysseus and his men.

It is a thoroughly disoriented Odysseus, injured in the ego virtues of confidence and pride, who takes the path through the forest toward Circe's house. Without the moly, which comes from completely outside himself and functions as the Homeric equivalent of grace, he would presumably be no match for her. She is initially a powerful antagonist, embodying more than any other character in the *Odyssey* the power and allure of the primordial feminine. The cup or krater or bowl (Homer is not specific on this point) that she holds out to Odysseus and his men is a vessel of transformation, like the womb. It is a containing structure that models interior space, a symbol that, as Erich Neumann points out, signifies the archetypal essence of the feminine.[20]

The concept of transformation itself, which Jungians associate with the individuation process through which the psyche attains wholeness, and which is often used generally to describe personal or spiritual growth, was once associated primarily with women because of the changing processes of their bodies. Neumann writes of "blood-transformation mysteries" such as menstruation, pregnancy, and childbirth, that were regarded by primitive peoples with awe and that led a woman "to the experience of her own creativity and produce[d] a numinous impression on the man."[21] Circe, inasmuch as a Homeric character can be said to represent anything beyond his or her own being, represents, I believe, the power of this heritage, of this awe-provoking female ability to give shape to flesh and blood.

But clearly the tale we get in *Odyssey* 10 is of transformation gone awry, not creative or evolutionary but cruelly regressive. Circe gives shape, yes, but more importantly, she takes it away. Odysseus's men are imprisoned in the bodies of swine with their human consciousness intact and deprived of expression, lacking language and choice. Their predicament seems a nightmare precisely crafted to appall Homer's original audience. To Greeks just beginning to discover the vast range of the mind's power, its captivity within the unsubtle flesh of the sty must have seemed especially heinous.

Why does Circe do this? Homer does not say, but readers trying to understand the story have long found this question irresistible. Not out of sexual boredom, as allegorical commentators were later to imply; the sailors are not her cast-off lovers because they were never admitted to her bed in the first place. Homer's insistence on Circe's status as a goddess, as I will argue in chapter 2, provides good reason for connecting her with the goddess-centered religions powerful in earlier centuries that were severely weakened by the Olympian revolution. The nasty metamorphosis that Circe's drug brings about can thus be interpreted as the primordial feminine's acting according to its own nature and making manifest the comparative inferiority of *individual* male being. Because we all intimately know this primordial feminine, through the experience of being nourished and encompassed before we are born into the world, the sailors' suffering at the hands of Circe also takes on a psychological dimension.[22] It suggests the way in which ego consciousness can be easily ambushed and overwhelmed in those who do not take seriously the bodily and instinctual basis of their own natures.

Pigs were the animals most frequently associated with the old vegetation goddesses (see chapter 2). Odysseus retains his manly form because he has been graced by the Olympians, but also, perhaps, because he has already been pierced, symbolically innoculated, by the power of a pig. The long scar on his thigh that is intimately connected with his identity—the mark by which Eurycleia will later know him—was inflicted by a boar's tusk when he was hunting on Parnassos with his grandfather in his early adolescence. Unlike Osiris and Adonis, adored consorts of powerful female divinities, Odysseus is not castrated or gored to death by this animal that appeared in myth and ritual as a kind of totem of the feminine. Both the placement and the timing of the wound during puberty, however, signal it as an attack on his developing masculinity. Odysseus survives this early threat to his maleness to become in his maturity a new type of hero, one open to the feminine but not subordinate to it. He is fully receptive to Circe's power, unhesitatingly draining her cup. Yet he does not fall victim to her regressive pull.

Sword against stick, they confront each other in a ritual whose outcome, lovemaking, has already been dictated by Hermes. The most profound transformation that takes place in this myth is the turning of male-female hostility into union and trust. Circe's power becomes benevolent *after* it is challenged and fully met. It is as if she has been waiting all along for her "defeat" at the hands of Odysseus. What is actually defeated in their encounter, however, is the notion that one of them must have clear dominance over the other. Circe is in no way subject to Odysseus after he brandishes his sword, and he, for his part, continues to recognize her as a figure of mysterious authority and chooses to obey her instructions to make the dangerous passage to the Land of the Dead. From the moments when Circe swears her "great oath" and Odysseus enters her bed, the powers of both are shared, accepted, and on the whole unquestioned. Pleasure becomes their ground of trust.

Sex and death, the roots of our being: it is a more extensive knowledge of these mysteries that Circe stimulates in Odysseus. She offers him far more than the legendary sage Tiresias, whom she insists he call up from Hades. When he encounters Tiresias and the other bloodless shades, including his mother Anticleia, Odysseus stares at his own future, the deprivation that is death, and does not shy away. At Circe's instigation, he pushes his courage to the farthest human limit. In her he encounters and accepts the numinosity of the primordial feminine; he comes into necessary relation with it. Without knowing that he must be tied to the mast if he wishes to safely hear the Sirens' song, that he must not pause to fight with Scylla, that he must under no conditions touch the Oxen of the Sun, Odysseus would almost certainly die before reaching Ithaca. Circe makes possible his return to Penelope, who is for Odysseus the personal feminine and with whom he shares a great good that cannot flourish on Aiaia: love based upon human identity. These two female figures, the mysterious and the familiar, are the poles of his experience. It is his great good fortune that they are attuned.[23]

There is one remaining danger in the territory of the Unknown about whom Circe gives Odysseus no instruction whatsoever: the nymph Calypso. The position Calypso occupies in the *Odyssey* is midway between the archetypal and the personal, between Circe and Penelope. Homer himself seems unclear about her status, referring to her occasionally as "goddess" but usually as "nymph." Descriptions of her hair, her singing, her weaving, her silvery gown—even of the oath that Odysseus makes her swear—duplicate those found in the Circe episodes. But these similarities embellish a more important difference. Calypso is by far the most effective impediment Odysseus encounters on his journey home to Ithaca, holding him in a sensuous but tedious captivity for seven years, Lotusland revisited. Hermes intervenes to guide Odysseus *to* Circe, but to arrange his break *away* from Calypso.

Perennially young, perennially adoring, perennially lovely, Calypso would seem to be the image of what men, or at least many of them, fervently desire. It is one of the great subtleties of the *Odyssey* that she proves ultimately to be less kind to its hero than Circe, the dreaded shape-changer. Because Calypso is neither one thing nor the other, neither individual woman nor personified mystery, she cannot give Odysseus what he truly needs; he turns down her offer of shared immortality, preferring instead his human identity and human wife. Her greatest gift is actually the axe she hands him (at the instigation of Hermes) so that he can cut down trees with which to make a raft to leave her. The stasis of Odysseus's sojourn on Ogygia has a horror all its own; there are no challenges, no perils on this island—only a lush boredom that is less demanding and energizing than fear. The sole tension here is between Calypso's clinging possessiveness (reminiscent of the vines surrounding her cave) and Odysseus's longing for home. Finally the strength of this longing, the sight of her beloved hero weeping on a rock by the sea, motivates Athene to begin the arrangements for his escape.

Unlike Circe, Calypso conceives of Penelope as her rival and wants to detain Odysseus forever. Her poignancy is that she yearns toward the personal, the human. Appropriately, she dwells at the interface between the Unknown and the familiar. Odysseus goes directly from her shores to Nausicaa's civilized ones, where once again he lands in a condition of extreme vulnerability, having been battered by days of towering seas. In one of his most beautiful similes, Homer now compares Odysseus's fragile but tenacious life, as he burrows into a bed of olive leaves, to the glowing brand a shepherd banks with ashes so that it may be preserved for the next day's fire.

From this point on in the poem Athene, with her divine breath, will see that the spark of Odysseus's vitality remains strong. Now he is back in the realm of clarity and definiteness in which the virgin goddess, sprung from her father the skygod's forehead, prefers to move. As an Olympian, Athene derives from a later stage in the development of Greek religion than does the chthonic Circe; she presents an altogether less threatening image of divine female power, one in which the creative and capricious force of sexuality has been sacrificed in favor of a wisdom based on rationality. In the civilized (though disordered) world of the later books of the *Odyssey*, Athene replaces Circe as Odysseus's strategist and guide.

Athene and Circe offer opposing images of the feminine, yet they work in tandem to aid Odysseus in his return to Penelope; the fact that both shower him with favors and approval indicates the wholeness of this hero's appeal. He is truly, as James Joyce was later to remark, the "all-roundman,"[24] one who integrates the primordial and instinctual with more evolved and conscious aspects of human identity. Athene and Circe even address Odysseus with the same bantering but appreciative tone, both calling him "obstinate one" and admiring the firm will he bears within his breast (10.329, 12.21, 13.293, 330).

Their gifts, though generous, are not unearned. In spite of her fondness for the Ithacan, Athene abandons him after the destruction of her temple at Troy and does not smile upon him again until he has proved his courage and resourcefulness (virtues dear to her own militant intelligence) in facing the dangers of the Unknown. Only when he is back on his own rockbound island, waking up in the cave of the nymphs, does she appear to him directly. Then she describes the two of them as being "alike in cunning" (13.296–97) because of the suppleness with which they both assume new, disguised identities. Circe is not the only master of transformation in this poem; Athene and Odysseus also practice this art, though Odysseus, being human and male, restricts his efforts to himself and to the plasticity of words.

The wholeness of Odysseus is matched within the *Odyssey* by that of only one female presence: Penelope. She masquerades in the minds of many readers and throughout many of the poem's books as passive, patriarchal wife, but the depth and mettle of her character are amply revealed in books 19 and 23. Like Athene and Circe, Penelope *challenges* Odysseus. She invents the tests by which he proves himself as rightful king and husband: his stringing of the great bow and his knowledge, angrily revealed, that one post of their marriage bed has been carved from a living, rooted olive tree. Like Circe after Odysseus has proved himself equal to the challenge she has posed, Penelope is generous in her surrender. There is no more beautiful part of the *Odyssey* than the simile with which Homer describes their reunion. He is the shipwrecked swimmer and she the sunwarmed, longed-for earth that receives him— or is Penelope the swimmer and Odysseus the earth? (Homer's syntax in this passage [23.231–40] possesses its own transformative art.) Their joy triumphs over twenty years of mutual suffering, twenty years of persistence in the face of obstacles and doubt, and for this reason is truly satisfying, completing. It affirms Odysseus's identity as an individual man in a way in which his encounter with the numinous Circe, who exists in a realm of being unshadowed by doubt, cannot and does not do.

Penelope has been much and justly celebrated in the centuries following the *Odyssey*'s composition; Circe—as most of the following chapters will demonstrate—has been abhorred. Yet the poem as Homer tells it makes unmistakably clear Circe's role in leading Odysseus to Ithaca and Penelope. She embodies the power of the feminine in its primordial, highly ambivalent form. Because Odysseus does not shrink from this power but rather opens himself to it, Circe becomes beneficent and Odysseus becomes more whole. In effect, she gives him her blessing.

The understanding of the deep complementarity and essential equality of the sexes that is embedded, I believe, in Homer's version of the Circe-Odysseus myth became quite scarce in the work of later Greek poets and philosophers, many of whom assumed the inferiority of women and passed on this assumption to posterity. Homer's equable and untendentious vision may well have been influenced by his somewhat greater closeness to the era when great goddesses thought to control the ebb and flow of life itself were worshipped. Circe's connections with this tradition will be examined in chapter 2.

2

Where Did Circe Come From?

Long ago, when human existence was precarious and fertility therefore paramount, a Great Goddess, as the archaeological record now persuasively suggests, was venerated almost everywhere.[1] Our ancestors saw primal power as being feminine because it was obvious to them that life originated with and was immediately nourished by the female sex. Bulbous figurines of carved stone attest to this deity's presence in Europe during paleolithic times, more than fifteen thousand years ago. When we reflect that she was worshipped for a period at least three times as long as recorded history, it does not seem foolish to look for traces of her cult in Homeric times and within the *Odyssey* itself—or indeed, within our own deeply rooted psyches. Compared to her, Zeus was an upstart who originated as a storm god brought into the Greek peninsula around the beginning of the second millennium B.C.E. by invading Indo-European tribes.[2]

Who was she? Originally her attributes were all-encompassing. She was both nurturer and destroyer, controlling the mysteries of birth and death that were impenetrable to human intelligence. The essential perception behind Goddess symbolism, as it appears on the sculptures, wall paintings, pottery, and rock carvings left by her worshipers, is of the mysterious round of birth, death, and regeneration that governs not only human life, but all life on earth.[3] Her sexuality was thought to be connected with the fertility of animals and plants, her ebb and flow reflected in the rhythms of all living things. In later periods her different qualities were split off and incarnated in separate goddesses. By the classical era, for instance, Demeter had come to represent an abundant but rather asexual fertility, while Aphrodite embodied a robust sexuality divorced from childbirth and harvest. In spite of this splitting and the resulting proliferation of weaker goddesses, the consciousness persisted well into Roman times that the feminine divine was, in essence, one. In Apuleius's *Golden Ass,* when Isis appears in answer to Lucius's prayer, she announces herself as follows: "I am Nature, the universal Mother, mistress of all the elements, primordial child of time, sovereign of all things spiritual, queen of the dead, queen also of the immortals, the single manifestation of all gods and goddesses that are. . . . Though I am worshipped in many aspects, known by countless names, and propitiated with all manner of different rites, yet the whole round earth venerates me."[4] Isis, majestically aware of the centrality of her godhead, then proceeds to list some of the names by which she has been known in different parts of the Mediterranean world: Juno, Hecate, Proserpine, Cecroprian Artemis, the Paphian Aphrodite, the Eleusinian Mother of Corn. Certainly most modern students of ancient goddess worship, aware that these deities flow backward like rivers to the same spring, would agree that her point is well taken. A unity of identity does persist beneath a multiplicity of names.

What, if any, are Circe's connections with this extraordinarily fluid and vital religious tradition? In a general way, her character in Homer's myth possesses an abundance of both negative and positive powers, suggesting her affinity with both faces of the original life-giving, death-wielding Goddess of paleolithic and neolithic times. To answer this question more specifically, we need to follow several directions of investigation that Homer's portrayal of her suggests: her name; her association with both predatory animals and pigs; and last, her liaison with a mortal man.

An abundance of iconographic and some linguistic detail connects Circe with traditions of goddess worship in the eastern Mediterranean, particularly in Anatolia. These connections are richly suggestive, but they should not be construed as demonstrating incontestable links of influence. The archaeological record is full of gaps; neither the existence of Homer himself nor a firm date for the *Odyssey*'s composition can be proven. Thus to associate a Homeric character with iconography dating from many centuries before the poem's probable origin can only be speculation, no matter how thought-provoking or illuminating. But such speculation may sometimes serve as a foray into knowledge.

Hawk and Vulture Iconography

Let us begin with her name. Circe (*Kirke*) is the feminine form of *kirkos*, meaning falcon or hawk. *Kirkos* also has a secondary meaning—circle—perhaps originally suggested by the wheeling flight of hawks. Though the Neo-Platonic allegorists later based their interpretation of Circe's significance upon this secondary meaning of her name, there is no compelling reason to follow their lead. Homer normally uses the more common word for circle, *kuklos;* the one time *kirkos* appears in the epics with the meaning of circle it is in its alternate form, *krikos*. Besides, the more the association of hawks with Circe's character is investigated, the more convincing it becomes. The ornithological aspect of her name has a familial significance, since her brother Aietes's name derives from *aietos,* meaning eagle. The name of her island, Aiaia, may be based upon a West Semitic word for hawk, *ayya,* though we have no means of knowing for sure.[5] But there are better, more encompassing reasons for seeing the hawk in Circe.

Long before Homer imagined Circe, birds had been associated with the divine. According to Marija Gimbutas, birds appear in the prehistoric art of Europe and Asia Minor as the "main epiphany of the Goddess as Giver-of-all, including life and death, happiness, and wealth."[6] Coming from the sky, thought to represent not only the spirit of life but also the human soul, birds were considered by ancient worshipers of the Goddess "to be sacred above all other creatures."[7] In the *Iliad* and the *Odyssey* vestiges of this belief in avian epiphanies are apparent in the way diviners read bird flight for information about the future and in the frequency with which Athene takes on bird disguises. At the slaughter of the suitors, for instance, she flies through the hall as a swallow and disappears under the eaves (22.239). In Homer the deities rarely change themselves into any other animals but birds.[8]

The association of birds with divinities is a constant motif in ancient art from the eastern Mediterranean, whether from Mycenae, Crete, Egypt, or much older, neolithic settlements. Sometimes the avian and human elements in these images are well integrated, as in winged Artemises and winged Nikes dating from the centuries immediately following Homer, which look to the modern eye reassuringly like angels. The older images, however, tend to be more inscrutable. A stone sculpture of a large-breasted, long-necked, beak-faced figure, produced by the neolithic Proto-Sesklo culture in Thessaly, affords a glimpse of the Bird

Goddess in what was probably her primordial form (figure 2). She is elegant, ugly, and remote; compared to her, Homer's Circe seems ordinary and familiar.

Flesh-eating birds such as hawks and vultures possess a distinct but related tradition of iconography that was particularly strong in ancient Anatolia, along whose Aegean coast Homer probably spent most of his professional life. This tradition is particularly relevant to Circe. According to Gimbutas, birds of prey, when they appear in prehistoric art, "are omens of death and epiphanies of the Death Wielder."[9] The tradition of a Vulture/Hawk Goddess who was indigenous to Asia Minor appears to stretch from neolithic Çatal Hüyük (ca. 7250–6250 B.C.E.) to Hellenistic times; Circe, with her intimate knowledge of the Underworld and her raptorial name, may well be one of her later incarnations.

Çatal Hüyük has yielded more information about goddess-based religion than any other archaeological excavation. This neolithic city-settlement in south-central Anatolia, excavated by James Mellaart in the early 1960s, was inhabited continuously for over a thousand years, with no evidence of fortification. Undiverted by war, the energies and creative powers of this people were used to invent pottery, to develop a strain of bread-wheat, to construct and adorn numerous shrines. At one of the oldest levels of settlement (VII), Mellaart unearthed what he calls "Vulture Shrines," mudbrick rooms painted with murals depicting the great birds swooping down with their ominous, outspread wings upon headless human bodies (figure 3).[10] These murals pictured part of this people's death rites, for they exposed corpses to be picked clean before burying the bones beneath the floors of their houses. The human legs of one of the vultures suggest that it is more than just a bird, actually the Goddess herself in the form of a vulture. Gimbutas, following Mellaart's interpretation, calls her "She Who Takes Away Life, maleficent twin of She Who Gives Life."[11] The huge birds are painted not black but red, a color strongly associated with the blood of animal life and suggestive, therefore, of regeneration.

In a shrine at a higher level (VI) Mellaart's workers found a pair of heavy plaster breasts, with beaks in the place of nipples, protruding from a wall; they were found to be modeled over griffon vulture skulls.[12] What image could express more directly or intensely the two sides of the Goddess? More than eight thousand years after its creation, this symbolism still arrests and appalls.

The association of the Goddess with vultures, and with both birth

Figure 2. Bust of a bird-headed goddess, Thessaly, ca. 6000 B.C.E.

Figure 3. Vulture Shrine at Çatal Hüyük, Level VII. Courtesy of James Mellaart.

and death, is made less dramatically but more explicitly in wall paintings from a shrine on level V, dating from about 6500 B.C.E. (figure 4). Here multiple forms of a violin-shaped female figure, who encloses a child within herself, are flanked by intervening rows of stylized, huge-winged red and black birds that have the distinctive vulture head shape. The geometric design of this painting looks peculiarly modern, and motifs from it can in fact be found on kilims still being produced in central Turkey. This repetition of design is but one of several instances of sacred images from Çatal Hüyük wall paintings being used continuously, for over eight thousand years, in Anatolian folk art.[13]

In the millennia following Çatal Hüyük, raptors rather than vultures became the birds most often associated in Anatolia with the Goddess—perhaps because these newer cultures no longer exposed their dead. With its sharp, hooked beak adapted for flesh-eating, the hawk can easily be distinguished from other birds when it appears in ancient sculpture. It was used by the Neo-Hittites around 950 B.C.E., along with the buzzard, to represent their most important goddess, Kubaba, in hieroglyphs (figure 5). The Phrygians, a mysterious and highly artistic people who settled in west-central and southern Anatolia around 750 B.C.E., also associated the hawk with their primary goddess, whom they called Kybele. In reliefs unearthed at Gordion and at Baçelievler in Ankara, Kybele holds birds of raptorial profile in her left hand; whatever their exact meaning, the birds are clearly represented as one of her attributes.[14] The Lydians,

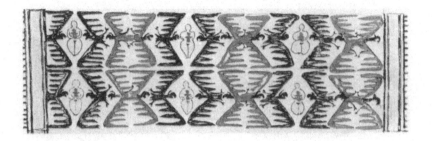

Figure 4. Wall painting from Çatal Hüyük, Level V. Courtesy of James Mellaart.

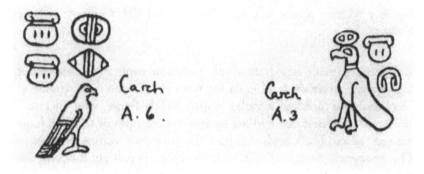

Figure 5. Neo-Hittite hieroglyphics representing the name of the goddess Kubaba, ca. 950 B.C.E.

who lived slightly west of the Phrygians, also valued the hawk as a symbolic animal, associating it with their Mermnadian dynasty of kings.[15] Gyges, who founded this dynasty, believed that his family had some special relationship with the Lydian Great Goddess, Kybebe.[16] Several centuries later, the Roman writer Aelian was quite familiar with this long-standing association between goddesses and birds of prey; he remarks that the buzzard is sacred to Artemis and the mermnus (a type of hawk) to the Mother of the Gods.[17] Kybele, often called the Mother of the Gods, was a sister goddess to the Ephesian Artemis, who was a familiar figure to the Ionian Greeks who were Homer's contemporaries.[18]

It is at the temple of Artemis at Ephesus—one of the seven wonders of the ancient world and also one of the places where Greek and Anatolian cultures most thoroughly merged—that we come closest to connecting Circe with the hawk goddess tradition. When its site at the mouth of the Cayster river was excavated by the British in 1906 and 1907, numerous small figurines of birds with hooked beaks were discovered, many of them in the foundation deposit of the lowest stratum. The leader of the expedition, D. G. Hogarth, concluded that the birds were "in most cases certainly, and in all cases probably Hawks" and that they were placed in the deposit intentionally "as offerings dedicated to the goddess, whose image would stand above them."[19] Also found at this depth was an ivory statuette of a *kore* or young priestess carrying a hawk atop a long pole on her head. She seems to be bearing the divine standard as part of a ritual procession (figures 6, 7). Hogarth mistakenly dated the foundation deposit to 700 B.C.E., which would have made it contemporary with the era generally thought to be Homer's. More recently, the deposit has been dated to the mid- or early seventh century because of the presence of coins found within it.[20] This later date indicates that the Ephesian Artemis was strongly associated with hawks *by* ca. 650 B.C.E.; she very likely also had been earlier, during Homer's time.

Since legend places Homer in Chios or Samos or Smyrna—all places along or immediately off the Aegean coast of Asia Minor, within easy traveling range of Ephesus—it seems credible that he would at least have heard of these votive offerings at Ephesus and been familiar with the tradition. He may also have known of the story, familiar to Pindar, Pausanias, Solinus, and other ancient writers, that Amazonian women were the original builders of the Ephesian shrine and that they were living in the park surrounding it when the Ionian Greeks arrived.[21] Here, perhaps, is the seed of book 10 of the *Odyssey:* a group of independent women in a green and pleasant place, spending their days absorbed in ritual, accosted by a company of adventurous strangers.

Though nothing in Homer other than her name connects Circe with flesh-eating birds, Apollonius Rhodius, several centuries later, tells of a strange cemetery in the "plain of Circe" that the Argonauts pass by on their way to Aietes' palace. Here male corpses are hung from willows, presumably to be picked clean.[22] This grisly detail recalls the shrines to the Vulture Goddess of Çatal Hüyük, that numinous Anatolian presence who was once thought to control the gates of death and rebirth—and who was transmuted rather than wholly rejected by succeeding cultures and tribes.

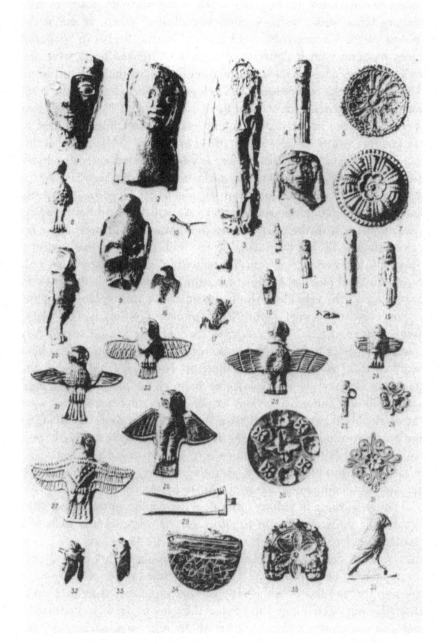

Figure 6. Gold and electrum hawks found in the Archaic Artemesion, Ephesus.

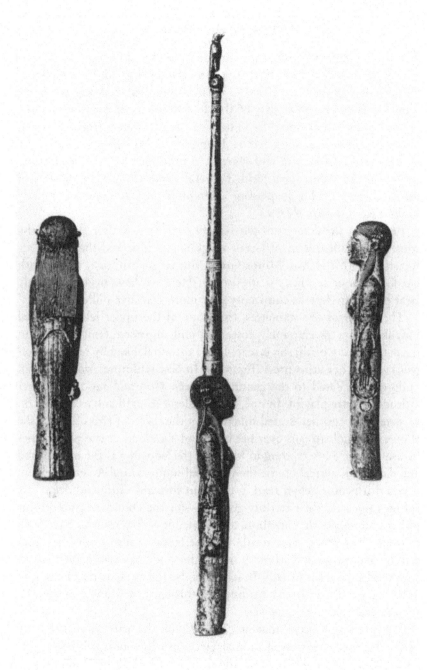

Figure 7. Ivory priestess statuette from the Archaic Artemesion, Ephesus.

Lady of the Beasts

The rearing, fawning wolves and mountain lions that seem so monstrous to Odysseus and his men when they enter the grove around Circe's house might have been quite natural to them in another context—on a seal ring, for instance, or as part of the accoutrement of a shrine. Tamed predatory animals, sometimes in heraldic stance, were a familiar part of religious symbolism long before Homeric or Mycenaean times. The mounds at Çatal Hüyük and Hacilar, another neolithic settlement excavated by Mellaart, have yielded several stone and clay sculptures of the Goddess with her leopard or catamount pets. Already she is Lady of the Beasts, *potnia theron.*

Regarding these very ancient female statuettes, Walter Burkert, the contemporary historian of Greek religion, has observed that their "association with the Asia Minor Great Mother of historical times, with her leopards or lions . . . is irresistible. Here we have overwhelmingly clear proof of religious continuity over more than five millennia."[23]

The oldest of the statuettes, from one of the upper levels of Çatal Hüyük, shows an extremely corpulent and impassive female figure in the act of giving birth; she is seated on a throne flanked by felines, upon whose backs her arms press (figure 8). In clay sculptures from Hacilar, radio-carbon dated to the century between 5500 and 5400 B.C.E., her attitude is more playful. In one, she fondles a leopard cub as she sits on its parent; in another, seated this time on the backs of two of them, she allows their tails to curl over her back and shoulders as she plumps her breasts (figure 9). According to Mellaart, the leopard was the most feared and dangerous animal on the then forested south-central Anatolian plain; it was this people's chief rival in the hunt for wild cattle and deer.[24] By subjugating it to their fertility goddess—for the abundant proportions of her body make that attribute unmistakable—they seem to have been affirming her power over death. Yet the leopards also probably represent the dangerous and arbitrary side of the Goddess's own nature, which she could unsheathe at will. In iconography the animals that belong to a deity generally represent attributes of this deity, defining its personality and exemplifying its power.

It appears significant that in Çatal Hüyük the artifacts of the Lady of the Beasts (or Mistress of Animals) were usually found at higher, more recent levels than those at which the shrines to the Vulture Goddess were unearthed; she is a less direct and more refined representation of the

Figure 8. Clay statuette of Mother Goddess, Çatal Hüyük.

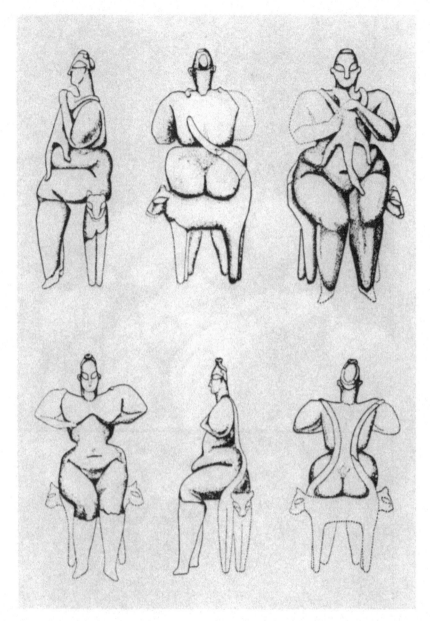

Figure 9. Clay figurines from Hacilar. Courtesy of James Mellaart.

affinity between fertility and death. Once the Lady of the Beasts became established in the religious imagination, there seems to have been less need for the Vulture Goddess, who could then subside into that less threatening, less loathsome creature, the hawk. In succeeding cultures and centuries, as the Mistress of Animals became slimmer and more attractive to the modern eye, her deadly aspect became elegant. She took on the grace of her feline companions.

Because the Mistress of Animals motif is so widespread in ancient cultures of the Mediterranean and Near East, it seems likely that it originated in other places besides south-central Anatolia. A striking image that brings to mind the spirit of Circe herself dates from about 2300 B.C.E. in Babylonia. She is the nude winged goddess on the terra-cotta Burney Plaque, who stands on the haunches of two reclining lions, flanked by owls that signify her deadly aspect (figure 10). Though she has talons for feet, she has nothing else in common with the grotesque, foreshortened Harpies that appear much later, in Hellenistic sculpture and in the *Aeneid.* Seductive and direct, everything about this mysterious goddess on the Burney Plaque is in proportion. Her beauty, like Circe's, is finely balanced against her ability to inspire terror. She was found in what appeared to be the shrine of a private house, and to this day no one knows for certain who she is.[25] Dating from close to the same era, a pre-Hittite tablet found in Cappadocia (which is now in central Turkey) shows a goddess flanked by two rearing goats with elaborate curved horns: one of the first instances of the heraldic posture.[26] A later Mycenaean carved ivory, found at their outpost at Ras Shamra on the coast of Syria and dating from about 1400 B.C.E., also shows a goddess with standing goats at either side.[27]

By far the most popular animal to rear and roar alongside the Goddess, however, was the lion. The Minoans and Mycenaeans were particularly fond of this beast, which was indigenous to their iconography if not their geographic territory. In the most famous of Cretan seals, a supremely confident bare-breasted goddess who has been titled Queen of the Mountain stands atop a stylized peak, her left arm extended as if in command, while a youth to the right pays her homage and paired lionesses raise themselves beneath her. To the left is a shrine structure with four pairs of sacral horns (figure 11). The image is celebratory, honoring a power seemingly beyond question or challenge. The same goddess may be on a seal found at the hilltop stronghold at Mycenae; again she is flanked by rearing lions, but this time

Figure 10. The Burney Plaque, Babylonia, ca. 2300 B.C.E.

Figure 11. Goddess with lions on seal from Crete.

Figure 12. Lentoid from Mycenae.

she has wavy lines above her curiously rendered head and above them the ritualistic double-axe (figure 12).

These images, it must be stressed, stand for many; the Goddess with her companion tamed beasts is an extremely persistent motif in ancient Mediterranean and Near Eastern religious iconography.

Within the Greek world, the *potnia theron* tradition leads inevitably to Artemis, who was for centuries the most popular female divinity and the most universally worshipped.[28] "Where has not Artemis danced?" asks an old saying. And indeed her shrines were everywhere—in Boeotia, Sparta, Crete, Ionia, Attica, Sicily—wherever there were forests and wild animals and local nature goddesses who could be assimilated with her tradition. This popular Artemis appears to have been an aboriginal heritage that the Greeks carried with them to the new places they settled. Although she was addressed as *parthenos,* the title was used in its original sense of "unmarried" rather than "virginal." Lewis Farnell, the eminent nineteenth-century scholar of Greek religion, speculates that "Artemis *Parthenos* may have been originally the goddess of a people who had not yet the advanced Hellenic institutions of settled marriage, who may have reckoned their descent through the female, and among whom women were proportionately powerful."[29]

Homer's chaste huntress, tallest and most beautiful among her nymphs, sister to Apollo, has only her independence and penchant for wildness in common with this ancestor. His portrait of Artemis represents not the first but a much later stage in the development of her na-

Figure 13. Detail of a cult statue of the Ephesian Artemis.

ture. The virginal huntress seems to have appeared in epic poetry *before*
she figured in the worship of the common people, who remained attached to the older, more sexual and fertile Artemis. Among the votive
gifts dated to 700–600 B.C.E. that were given to Artemis Orthia in Sparta,
animal types including lions, goats, and bulls were popular. Deer began
to appear during the following century, when Orthia apparently became
more identified with the Homeric type.[30] Gentle, elusive, swift, and wild:
these qualities of her new companion animal suggest that the Lady of
the Beasts herself became declawed. In this metamorphosis she lost much
of the sexuality she had once possessed as a goddess associated with human and animal fertility. Only by knowing her past can we understand

why Greeks of the classical era regarded Apollo's lovely sister as Eileithyia, the divine midwife who protected women in labor. The primitive, unvirginal Artemis may well have been more like Circe than like Nausicaa.

One feature of her temples at Ephesus and Laconia in Sparta particularly recalls book 10 of the *Odyssey.* Each was surrounded by a park that was a sanctuary for her sacred animals. The park at Ephesus was very old, for the one at Laconia, which Xenophon dedicated in the fourth century B.C.E., was modeled upon it.[31] Similar walled gardens where trees and wild animals could flourish—"paradises" in the etymological sense of the word—surrounded temples and palaces in the Semitic world.[32] In the second century A.C.E. the sanctuary of the great temple of Ishtar at Hierapolis, according to Lucian, contained lions and bears that were so tame they would not harm visitors.[33] One can imagine the awed accounts of pilgrims who traveled there—tales that would have been heightened as they were retold. Perhaps the sanctuary at Ephesus stimulated such legends in Homer's time. Though it is hard to believe that lions really sauntered and loped through the parks at Ephesus and Laconia, they certainly surround Artemis in reliefs and statuary found at these places; in a Hellenistic cult statue of the Ephesian Artemis, parts of her stone headdress are composed of deer, goat, cattle, and lions' heads (figure 13).

The tamed predators wandering through the grove around Circe's "sacred house" are akin to those inhabiting these temple parks. And she herself, as a goddess surrounded by these lethal but docile creatures, richly recalls an iconographic tradition that took root millennia before Homer's time, when it still continued to vigorously flourish.

The Ritual Significance of Pigs

In current popular opinion, pigs are greedy, undignified, and unclean: the lowest caste in the barnyard. The idea of using them for any spiritual or religious purpose seems ludicrous. Pigs, we have been conditioned to think, are *animals,* the very exemplars of carnality. When Circe turns the Greek sailors into swine, we see her as not only changing their smooth skin to bristled pelts, but also as stripping them of all dignity and control, visiting upon them the masculine equivalent of the fate worse than death. The imprisonment of their human consciousness within bodies not capable of expressing it seems a particularly vindictive twist.

The picture changes somewhat when we discover that pigs were for millennia the sacred animal of the Vegetation Goddess. True, the transformation still seems a crude display of power, but one accomplished for impersonal reasons—the act of a deity whose concerns are probably larger than merely reducing a particular group of human males to helplessness. There is an abundance of evidence connecting pigs with the vegetative cycle of sowing-harvesting-replanting (or birth-death-rebirth). It would be well to review these myths, rituals, and artifacts before deciding if and how they apply to the *Odyssey.*

Gimbutas speculates that, following the agricultural revolution, the paleolithic Pregnant Goddess, known to us from the stone "Venuses" of Willendorf and Lespogue, was transformed into an earth fertility deity who was often associated with the sow.[34] Early neolithic farmers seem to have regarded the fast-growing, rounded body of the pig as emblematic of seed and field fertility; perhaps they also saw the pig's large litters, a reproductive prodigality beyond that of any other domesticated animal, as harvests in themselves. In any case, artifacts connecting the sow with crops date back to the sixth millenium B.C.E.; fragments of pig figurines impressed with grain, radio-carbon dated to about 5500, have been unearthed in the valley of the Dniester near the Black Sea.[35] A considerable number of sow effigies and pig-shaped vases found in Romania and Northern Greece also suggest the importance of the sow in cult practice.

Of all the symbolic motifs connected with Circe, pigs are historically the most Greek. At Cnidos, Eleusis, Delphi, and throughout the Greek world, they were regarded as Demeter's own animal and occupied an important place in rites, such as the Thesmophoria and the Eleusinian Mysteries, which celebrated her power. The origins of these rites are shrouded in mystery, for they are far older than the written record. Yet their artifacts remain. On the slopes of Parnassos towering above Delphi, in the Corcyrian grotto, a great many small terra-cotta figurines of pigs and of women with headdresses have been found. Ancient and crudely modeled, they pre-date the worship of Apollo at the sanctuary. Of all the artifacts now in the museum at Delphi, only these and the navel-stone testify to an era when the earth's fertility was the most exalted human concern. The marble friezes and bronze statuary, the dazzling wealth of states and kings seeking to ratify their glory with the favor of the god, seem the work of another, more presumptuous species.

These figurines from the Corcyrian grotto may have been associated with the Thesmophoria, a festival honoring Demeter that occurred throughout the Greek world for many centuries at the sowing of new crops in October. Intended to promote the fertility of both plowed fields and female citizens, it was performed solely by women and lasted for three days and two nights. To the women participating, this festival afforded their one opportunity to leave home and family and to live apart from men.[36] They carried the rotting remains of suckling pigs (*delphakia*), which they had thrown to their deaths in caves or ravines several months before, to the altar to be mixed with seeds. This offering of something of the earth back to the earth was thought to ensure Demeter's blessing upon the crop.[37] Variants of this ancient, sympathetic fertility magic survived for a long time in many places in Europe. In southern Germany, near Meiningen, farmers in the nineteenth century mixed pork bones with their seeds before sowing.[38]

At Eleusis too the regenerative power of pigs was an integral part of the rites, linked there to a concept of rebirth that was spiritual rather than physical. The Mysteries enacted there each September were older by far than the Homeric poems; their Mycenaean origin seems assured, for the telesterion itself (the chamber from which the mysterious revelation occurred) was built upon the ruins of a Mycenaean building of the megaron type, thought to be the first temple of Demeter. On the third day of the annual ceremonies, after the priestesses and the Hierophant of Demeter had proceeded along the Sacred Way from Eleusis to Athens, the great mass of initiates—perhaps as many as 30,000—was called to go down to the sea. "With them they took young pigs, which they washed and then sacrificed, because they believed that the blood of this animal was the purest, and had the power to cleanse and rid the initiate's soul of hatred and evil. And because they believed that this was the finest gift that could be offered to the gods of the underworld, they buried the young pig after the sacrifice deep in the ground."[39]

After this cleansing and baptism, the initiates were considered ready to join the great procession to Eleusis, where on one of the last nights of the ceremonies they beheld the mystic vision that convinced them of the power of life over death, on the earth and within themselves. About this sight they were sworn to keep silent. Because this vow was kept, we can only guess what appeared to them. Some scholars say an ear of wheat; others, Kore herself returned from the dead, perhaps with a child. And still others believe the initiates saw an enactment of the sacred marriage of Zeus and Demeter, with the Hierophant and Chief Priestess taking the parts. Lasting over a thousand years and including among its initiates Aesclepios, Sophocles, and several emperors, the Mysteries at Eleusis must be considered a major religion, one that gave its believers an experience of spiritual union with the force of life itself. Purification with pig's blood was considered so essential to the preparation for this experience that the pig appeared on the small bronze coins issued by the Eleusinian city-state.[40]

Clearly, the Greeks of Homer's time and the centuries following would hardly concur with our view of the pig as an unclean animal. One surviving vase painting shows Apollo himself cleansing Orestes of the guilt of matricide, by holding over his head a pig dripping with blood.[41] In Apollonius Rhodius, also, the pig has purifying powers. When Jason and Medea go to Circe after they have murdered Absyrtus, she sacrifices a pig and uses its blood to ritually cleanse them.

To make fertile, to purify: these usages of the pig in the rituals of goddess-worship are indisputably positive. But the pig (or, more accurately, its wild cousin the boar) also had more sinister connections with the Great Goddess of the ancient imagination, particularly in the Near East. Over and over again, this ferocious and intelligent beast appears in myth as nemesis-antagonist of her young lover. Osiris, the twin and husband of the Egyptian queen-goddess Isis, is castrated and killed by his enemy Set disguised as a boar. The Babylonian shepherd-king Tammuz, beloved of the formidable Ishtar, is also gored to death by a wild pig. And Adonis, adored by golden Aphrodite and warned by her to stay out of the forest, is nevertheless lethally torn by the tusks of a boar he has pierced with an arrow. Where his blood has stained the earth, a crimson anemone springs up. In all these myths, the sacrifice of the male, though not overtly desired by the Goddess, serves to reaffirm her power, for she remains alive and intact to supervise the forces that will bring about the lover's regeneration. We might remember here that Odysseus, too, as a youth is attacked and severely wounded in the thigh by a boar, but he survives and grows up to prove himself Circe's equal. Homer gives this old, basically eastern mythic pattern a new direction and balance, one more reflective of the power of patriarchy, which had taken hold almost everywhere in the Mediterranean world by his time.

The pig or boar, then, functioned in radically different ways as a familiar of the Goddess. In its tame form it was the preferred sacrificial animal; in its wild, mythic form it was the instrument of sacrifice.[42] Of what relevance are these myths and rites to the transformation in book 10?

First of all, they probably explain why the sailors become pigs rather than sheep or goats, and why Circe accomplishes the metamorphosis with such methodical confidence. Their humanity is sacrificed to her power; the pig, by providing the form that imprisons them, once again proves the instrument of sacrifice. Yet this incident also contains seeds of regeneration. The French classicist Gabriel Germain, who investigated ritual and folkloric elements in the *Odyssey* more thoroughly than any other scholar, views the transformation as a ritual of initiation. He claims that Oysseus's men die to their old natures, take on some of the pig's powers of vitality by sliding into its skin, and are eventually reborn improved in every way, younger and more handsome than before.[43] He sees Circe as a priestess of the earth presiding over these rites.

Although this view must seem farfetched to a casual reader of the *Odyssey* or to one who believes the poem itself contains all the information necessary for its understanding, I believe Germain's interpretation contains some truth. Anyone who has investigated the connection of pigs with goddess worship and fertility rites must realize that the original audience for the Homeric poems, the crowds at the Pan-Ionian festivals or the nobility in their megarons, did not regard this animal as we do. Its stigmatization as unclean was the innovation of Judaism, an extremely father-oriented religion rigidly suppressive of older goddess worship, and it did not prevail in the Greece of Homer's time.[44]

Germain errs, however, in being too gracious to Circe. Only at Odysseus's request does she change his men to their heightened selves, and were she not intent on pleasing him, they would presumably stay swine forever. The metamorphosis seems intended as immolation, not initiation. Like Jehovah's sound-and-light show before the suffering Job, the act is a gratuitous display of power. It is as if Circe is saying "See. The Earth and its forces are mine; I can make you into my creature any time that I want." Only a divinity who felt her powers eroding and under attack, we might speculate, would be driven to act so unsubtly. The episode may well reflect a time of transition in cultural history: a time when patriarchy was replacing matricentral systems in myth, as it already had in social organization.

Goddesses and Mortal Men

What possible antecedents are there for Circe's liaison with Odysseus? He is a king, in rank and character stronger than his companions, and in Homer's story something indisputably positive issues from their union:

not a child, not fields ripe and heavy with grain, but directions for the future that enable Odysseus to return to his "fatherland" and wife, to a civilization that the values of the poem uphold. This configuration of goddess/mortal man/positive or sacred result is an ancient theme in mythology, one that was fundamental especially to Sumerian religious belief and ceremony.

At least by 2000 B.C.E. and perhaps as long as a millennium before that, the Sumerians celebrated an annual Sacred Marriage (*hieros gamos*) on New Year's Day between their chief goddess Inanna and the shepherd-king Dumuzi. The participants seem to have been the High Priestess and reigning King of Uruk, who consummated their union upon a bed of cedar and rushes within the royal palace or temple.[45] No rite was more important to the Sumerians, for Inanna was believed to control productivity of the land and fruitfulness of the womb for both humans and beasts. The King's most important duty was her satisfaction. And since Sumer's teeming and wealthy urban centers could only be sustained by a prosperous agricultural and pastoral economy, the stakes were very high.

The Sacred Marriage rite seems to have developed at a time of relative balance between the sexes—after the male role in procreation was known, but before females were subordinated in myth. The sexual act in this ceremony was a homecoming to the Goddess, a holy act performed in her service, enabling her to fulfill her powers. Inanna herself was not shy about expressing her desire or appreciation, and her voice in the sacred poetry is as alive and full of wonder now as it was four or five thousand years ago:

> He has brought me into it, he has brought me into it.
> My brother has brought me into the garden.
> Dumuzi has brought me into the garden,
> I strolled with him among the standing trees.
> I stood with him by its lying trees,
> By an apple tree I kneeled as is proper. . . .
> I poured out plants from my womb,
> I placed plants before him, I poured out plants before him,
> I placed grain before him, I poured out grain before him.[46]

Inanna's bountifulness, her dignity and directness, all recall Circe's behavior once Odysseus has blunted her danger with his sword and his moly.

Dumuzi, however, has no way of blunting Inanna's danger, no "great oaths" to make her swear. To the Sumerians, she represented great impersonal forces that deigned only temporarily to enter into relationship with a mortal man. The king looked upon the Goddess's nakedness at his own peril, as she herself makes clear:

> My brother, I have brought about an evil fate for you, my brother of
>   fairest face.
> Your right hand you have placed on my vulva,
> Your left, stroked my head,
> You have touched your mouth to mine,
> You have pressed my lips to your head,
> That is why you have been decreed an evil fate . . .[47]

The doom that befalls Dumuzi is to spend half of his remaining life in the Underworld. He is sent there by Inanna as precious ransom for her own freedom from Ereshkigal, the Sumerian goddess of the dead who has temporarily captured her, and he remains until his adoring sister Geshtianna offers to substitute for him. Inanna then decides that she will accept Geshtianna's offer for half of every year; Dumuzi resurrects every spring, along with the vegetation his own seed has enabled to grow.

There is one other echo from the Sumerian world concerning the dangers of a mortal man's acquiring carnal knowledge of a goddess—an echo that has convincing relevance to the *Odyssey*. In the *Epic of Gilgamesh*, which originated in the middle of the third millennium B.C.E., the hero flouts Inanna's offers of love, for he is well acquainted with her fickleness:

> Which of your lovers [he asks her] did you ever love forever? What shepherd of yours has pleased you for all time? Listen to me while I tell the tale of your lovers. There was Tammuz, the lover of your youth, for him you decreed wailing year after year. . . . You have loved the shepherd of the flock; he made meal-cake for you day after day, he killed kids for your sake. You struck and turned him into a wolf; now his own herd-boys chase him away, his own hounds worry his flanks. . . . And if you and I should be lovers, should not I be served in the same fashion as all these others whom you loved once?[48]

As could be expected, these words provoke Inanna's bitter wrath, and in revenge she sends the Bull of Heaven to destroy Enkidu, Gilgamesh's beloved friend. Perhaps something similar would have happened to Odysseus had he ignored Hermes' counsel and spurned Circe, but the tone of Homer's episode is altogether more harmonious and less charged with sexual enmity than is *Gilgamesh.*

Homer may well have been familiar with *Gilgamesh,* for the epic was widely known in the ancient Near East. Tablets containing the poem have been found at the capital of the Hittites, and knowledge of it may well have survived among the Neo-Hittites and Lydians, with whom the Ionian Greeks were in close contact.[49] Inanna's transformations of men to animals are thus a possible source for Circe's,[50] though Homer never states directly that Circe's animals are her erstwhile lovers. There is a crucial difference of tone, however, between the two stories. The Goddess's sexual desire is not entangled with her will to power in Homer, who shows Circe to be capricious, but also capable of trust and relationship. Compared to Inanna or Ishtar, she is an appealingly human goddess, one who gives without demanding a life for her pleasure.

The Sacred Marriage ceremony did not, apparently, become strongly established within the world of Greek religion, and consequently we must search hard to find instances of the goddess/mortal man/positive or sacred result configuration in Greek myth. As Martin P. Nilsson remarks, "it is too little observed that Greek goddesses do not associate themselves with mortal men."[51] Although Nilsson here seems to overlook Homer's unambiguous declaration of Circe's divine status, his point is otherwise well taken. Aphrodite's liaison with Anchises upon Mount Ida is one of the few exceptions that springs to mind—and for that the boastful Anchises was rewarded with a permanent limp. Only to the much later Virgil, who eulogizes their child Aeneas as the founder of Rome, are the results of this liaison indisputably positive. Nor does Demeter's celebrated lovemaking in a thrice-ploughed field with the Cretan Iasion, and the subsequent birth of their munificent son Plutus, bear out the goddess/mortal man/positive or sacred result pattern—for Iasion was a descendant of the Titans and thus not a bona fide mortal.[52] The liaison between Circe and Odysseus may well have stronger claim to being a *hieros gamos* than any other in Greek legend.

As a female divinity who fancies mortal men, Circe has strong affinities with the mythic world of the great Near Eastern goddesses. Like them, she mingles the sexual, the bountiful, and the lethal, but to this potent mixture Homer has added a capacity for trust.

Whether Circe existed in a lost myth that Homer reshaped, or whether he was the first to imagine her, her kinship with ancient religious traditions is very strong. She is a composite figure, in whom elements of Near Eastern and Greek goddess worship are blended and unified. The force of her character is not Indo-European but reminiscent of the potent, often terrifying female deities of Asia Minor. If Homer really existed as an Ionian Greek, living on or near the Aegean coast of Anatolia, he would very likely have known about this religious tradition.

Within the *Odyssey*, the conjunction of Homer's hawk goddess and his hero can be interpreted as a fertile encounter between East and West or, more accurately, between an ancient order that hung on more persistently in the East and the "new," thoroughly patriarchal order exemplified by the Mycenaeans.[53] Circe seduces or penetrates her way into Homer's treasured store of Mycenaean legends, but once she is there he shapes her to the needs of the poem, giving to her character a tinge of humanity, a capacity for relationship not to be found in her frightening predecessors. Can we imagine Inanna voluntarily curbing her capricious behavior toward Dumuzi or—even more preposterous and unlikely— the original Vulture Goddess of Çatal Hüyük bothering to speak in a human tongue? Creating a Great Goddess figure who relates on terms of intimate trust with a mortal man is truly a Homeric innovation.

The male-female hostility with which the Circe myth begins can be found, of course, in several other Greek myths as well. The sexual enmity that permeates these myths reflects, I believe, the social tension that prevailed when the power of women began to be repressed by emerging patriarchies.[54] Consider the Amazons, the militant and fiercely independent women who supposedly dwelt by the Thermodon river, near the southern shore of the Black Sea.[55] To the post-Homeric Greek imagination, Amazons existed to be warred against and defeated, and so they are—thoroughly but tastefully—in the marble friezes at Delphi and on the Parthenon. In actuality, the Amazon wars were fought only *within* Athenian culture; they symbolize the assault upon women's freedom and the establishment of male social and political supremacy.

In Homer, artistry never becomes tendentiousness. With deliberative spirit, he acknowledges this bitterness between the sexes and relegates it to the background (mainly to the oft-quoted story of Agamemnon and Clytemnestra), where it cannot disturb his plot. In the foreground is Aiaia, the province of a goddess far removed from civilization who is visited by the most supple and resourceful of Mycenaean heroes. With the help of an herb, a touch of grace, he appears as her equal and she recognizes him as such. She is not declassed or overthrown, but rather survives with her powers undiminished. When he wishes to leave, she gives him her blessing, the benediction of the old order upon the new. And he has the wisdom to take what she offers, to recognize her knowledge as essential to his own course. Homer's myth thus can be read as an exquisite parable of an achieved balance and harmony between the sexes—a balance that has, in many lives and societies, yet to be lived out.

Certainly the following era failed to do so. In it, Circe's career as a witch began.

3

From Myth to Allegory

Between Homer's time and Plato's, a revolution in thought took place. This change was so encompassing, influencing the development of the Greek language itself and therefore, in all probability, patterns of perception that language partially controls, that it is difficult to know how to begin to describe it. As any student of Homer—accustomed to thumbing through lexicons to find the meaning of yet another of his names for one of the ten thousand shining things of this world—knows all too well, the linguistic resources the poet drew upon were vast. Homer uses an abundance of concrete nouns and a multiplicity of verbs to express discrete objects and shades of action. Fifth- and fourth-century writers may puzzle their modern readers' minds with intricate grammatical constructions, but they do not tire those readers' thumbs as much as Homer, for they are more likely to gather phenomena within an abstract or general, and correspondingly smaller, vocabulary. The vocabulary of abstraction, which seems with few exceptions not to have been available to Homer, expresses experience that has been processed and classified by mind: experience at one remove from the senses. Bruno Snell, a German classicist who has traced shifts in the use of words between Homer's time and Plato's, has dramatically labeled this development toward abstraction and classification as "the discovery of the mind."[1] The phrase is apt, for it suggests that for the first time human consciousness was perceived as an entity in itself, standing apart from nature as well as within it.

If we focus on one important example, the word *logos*, we can better see the implications of this shift. In Homer, *logos* merely means "the spoken word" directly as it comes from tongue and lips, whether in conversation or narration; it derives from the verb meaning "to speak" (*lego*) and is virtually interchangeable with *mythos,* also meaning "the spoken word." But gradually *logos* came to denote inward thought itself, rather than (or in addition to) the word(s) by which inward thought was expressed.[2] To Plato and the Stoics *logos* meant reason, the specific ordering principle of thought; to the much later writers of the New Testament, *logos* signified the divine Word and cosmic principle of order, far removed from humble human lips and error.

Mythos continued to denote that which is spoken, but gradually came to mean the word in its most ancient aspect, as in the legendary tales of gods and heroes told by Homer and Hesiod. Only after the cleavage between *logos* and *mythos* was accomplished could allegorical commentary develop, for it consists of the operations of *logos* upon *mythos,* with *mythos,* so to speak, as the patient spread out on the table. Sometimes these operations amounted to amputations. Early allegorists lopped off the last half of the Circe-Odysseus myth, for instance, because it did not fit the underlying pattern of meaning that they perceived as the story's raison d'être, and consequently Circe's role as Odysseus's teacher and guide was ignored or undervalued, as we shall see, for well over two thousand years.

Allegorical commentary upon myth is dualistic in nature, for it seeks to locate and follow a lode of meaning running beneath the literal surface of a text. Ancient allegorical interpretation, which begins in the late sixth century B.C.E. with commentary upon the Homeric poems, depends upon a belief in the penetrating power of mind and assumes the right of that mind to impose its logic upon a text. The intention of the allegorical commentator, to penetrate to and reveal the truth, is thus far more aggressive (though not necessarily more ambitious) than Homer's original intention, to render the song of the muse.[3] Homer was notably tolerant of ripely sexual non-Olympian goddesses, but this tolerance was not shared by later commentators, who tended to strip Circe of her divinity and to see in her a personification of passion and vice. That this should have happened is not surprising, considering the social and intellectual assumptions of the classical and Hellenistic eras. What is surprising is the tight, persistent hold that allegorical views of Circe have had on later poets drawn to her myth.

How and why did this allegorical tradition develop? Once developed, why was it invested with such authority, particularly considering all the riches of myth that it could not account for? Searching for answers to these questions requires looking beyond literature itself: first, at the development of philosophical ideas about the primacy of the soul or mind over the body; and second, at the change in the concept of divinity from an immanent force to a transcendent one. The tendency of post-Homeric Greek thinkers to consider the elevated as the good created a climate of thought that sanctioned the assumption upon which allegory depends: that meaning is superior to the text (or experience) from which it derives.

This tendency to consider the elevated as the good also affected attitudes toward women, who were valued for their reproductive capacity and seen as inextricably connected with sexuality and childbirth, but hardly as suitable companions for the strenuous and comradely flights of thought that Plato describes. Once this over-under kind of dualistic thinking had developed, therefore, females were the natural occupants of the lower category of the dualism. An ideology of misogyny, which finds much expression in post-Homeric literature, gradually developed. Before discussing the early allegorical commentary on Circe, I will briefly review these attitudes, so that the commentary can be seen within its proper context.

Development of the Concept of Soul

The Homeric epics are innocent of dualism. Homer's view of human nature is essentially organic and unitary; his characters are not divided against themselves, nor swept by conflicting emotions. Achilles could never proclaim with Faust that "two warring souls dwell within my breast." When this great soldier sulks in his tent, he is pure in his anger, untormented by feelings of guilt about his absence from the battlefield. Nor is there any separation or opposition between the corporeal and mental life of Homer's heroes; appropriately, their organs of consciousness are located right in their torsos. These include the *thymos*, which is the generator of motion and emotion and which is sometimes heard as an inner voice;[4] the *nóos*, the cause of ideas and images; and the *phrenes*, which promoted careful understanding and discretion and which were located somewhere near the kidneys. All mental phenomena were distributed so as to fall within the sphere of one of these organs. Thus, when Circe wishes to express her amazement at Odysseus's ability to drink her potion and yet retain his manly form, she exclaims "some steady will is in your breast" (10.329). *Psyche*, the word that later Greeks use for "soul," has no connection with thinking or feeling in Homer. He uses the word in a more primitive sense; for him, *psyche* is the life-force dwelling within every human being. Homer seems to take the presence of *psyche* for granted in the living man and thus has little to say about it. Only at the moment of death does the *psyche* take on a separate existence and become notable. Then it is breathed forth to fly off to Hades, leaving usually through the mouth but sometimes through open wounds. The corpse that it leaves behind Homer calls the *soma,* the term that later Greeks generally used for "body." But, as Aristarchus, the great Alexandrine editor of Homer was the first to notice, Homer never uses this word in reference to a living person. When he wishes to refer to someone's physical being, he uses one of two words meaning "limbs," avoiding the more general or abstract term.[5]

This linguistic analysis strongly suggests that the Greeks of Homer's time did not even conceive of a human being's having a mental or spiritual life not expressed directly through the body. In the epics, the whole person is exposed and present in his words and actions. Only rarely—as when Odysseus debates whether to use honeyed words to persuade Nausicaa to help him, or whether immediately to seize her knees—do we sense a reserve of consciousness within. Because the Homeric character is exposed, he is vulnerable to the forces of emotion and danger pressing upon him from within and without, and he shares this vulnerability with all other human beings, including servants and women. With the possible exception of Odysseus, whose mental agility looks forward to that of heroes to come, he does not know how to retreat into the refuge of his own consciousness or how to put distance between himself and the moment. In Homer's poems, human consciousness is not yet protected by the hard shell of the skull.

Only when the unity of a Homeric character is undone at death, does his *psyche* come into its own. Yet what a paltry existence it comes into. Deprived of their powers of physical expression, the shades or *psyches* in Hades are pitiable, pale, and vapid—so insubstantial that, like Anticleia within Odysseus's disappointed embrace, they can be compressed into thin air. They represent a state to which no sane Homeric Greek would conceivably aspire. Since salvation, or any afterlife other than fame (*kleos*), is not a motivating factor in Homer, his characters live richly, sensuously in the present. This focus results in an abundantly rich particularity of vocabulary, as has already been mentioned. Homer uses no less than nine different verbs to denote the operation of sight, many of them connoting certain expressions in the eyes; by the classical age this choice of verbs had shrunk to two.[6] Clearly, the Greeks lost as well as gained as their thought moved from concrete and primitive modes to more abstract and sophisticated ones.

In the era between Homer and Plato, the discovery of mind went hand in hand with the discovery of soul. Whether the word *logos* or *psyche* predominates in the work of an individual writer seems to depend on his intellectual or spiritual bent. Both words are used to connote the inner life, the power of consciousness.[7] The first writer to call the soul of a living man *psyche* was Heraclitus of Ephesus (ca. 500 B.C.E.); in his opinion the soul was endowed with qualities that differed greatly from those of the body and physical organs.[8] Heraclitus, however, did not invent the soul-body distinction; it was already current in the Orphic sect, whose original doctrinal literature has not survived, though we know of its existence through other ancient sources.[9]

The mid-sixth century B.C.E. was a time of considerable activity in the Orphic sect, a mystery-religion believed to have been revealed to mankind by Orpheus, a legendary priest and musician of prehistoric Thrace. "Mankind" is here probably the accurate generic term, for Orpheus, according to at least one later writer, would not allow women to participate in the group's rites or to enter the sacred precincts.[10] He preached a radically new ethical doctrine, stressing vegetarianism, asceticism, and individual responsibility for moral choice. These practices were thought to purify the soul, whose earthly existence was regarded as a temporary punishment, part of a cycle of reincarnations that might eventually end in permanent liberation from the body and a blissful existence in the highest heaven. Meanwhile, however, the impure soul was doomed to lengthy periods of residence in the house of Hades in between earthly incarnations. Obviously, the Orphics held a dualistic view of human nature; they believed it had a spiritual or divine portion, deriving from the god Dionysos, and an inferior, physical one, deriving from the earthbound Titans who had consumed Dionysos.

Because many Orphic concepts are familiar to us from Christianity and Buddhism, it is difficult to see them in perspective, to appreciate fully the originality of the sect. For the first time in history, it would appear, a religious group was preaching the possibility of transcending the earthly cycle of life and death—the cycle that had long been held to be holy in itself by believers in the goddess religions.[11] To the Orphics the soul or *psyche* within the living person was immortal, *athanatos*. That they described it with the epithet that Homer had used to characterize the gods in distinction from human beings was truly a revolution.[12] The immortal soul, of course, was later to become enshrined in Plato's dialogues and, through St. Paul, in Christian doctrine—making the Orphics' revolution so successful that we forget it ever took place. One of the tremors resulting from this turnaround in thought, this belief that each immortal soul is encased in a mortal and mutable body, was a fissure in our sense of our own human nature.

In spite of its long-term influence and consequences, Orphism itself remained a religion of the few. Its promise of an escape from death may have had universal human appeal, but its insistence on an ascetic way of life did not. The puritanism of the Orphics, their revulsion against the body and the life of the senses, was quite new in Greece and did not take wide hold.[13] Yet certain portions of its doctrine influenced some of the culture's greatest minds, including Pythagoras and Plato.

Pythagoras, in fact, may have been the author of some of the lost Orphic literature.[14] Born in Samos in 549 B.C.E., he was renowned in his own time as a spiritual leader and philosopher as well as a mathematician. He and his followers founded several spiritual communities where many of the Orphic precepts, including vegetarianism and bloodless sacrifice, became part of daily life. The best known of these was at Croton in southern Italy. Though they worshipped Apollo instead of the Orphics' Dionysos, the Pythagoreans too practiced asceticism and purification, holding their goods in common and shunning material wealth and unnecessary physical pleasures. The saying *"soma* equals *sema"* (or "body equals tomb"), which echoes so clearly in certain Platonic dialogues, particularly the *Phaedo,* could have originated among either the Orphics or the Pythagoreans. Philolaos, a Pythagorean contemporary of Socrates, wrote that "ancient theologians and priests testify that the soul is conjoined to the body through a certain punishment, and that it is buried in this body as in a sepulchre."[15]

Although this bias against the flesh has, historically, often been generalized to include a bias against women as producers and enticers of the flesh, the Pythagoreans were scrupulous about not doing so. Women were full participating members in their communities, which must have been among the few places in the ancient Mediterranean world where a sexual double standard was not tolerated.[16] Pythagoras was interested in the human as well as the mathematical and celestial aspects of harmony. He believed that its presence in a marriage depended upon mutual fidelity.[17]

The Orphic and Pythagorean tradition was almost certainly of great influence on Plato, nourishing the transcendental and metaphysical elements in his thought. In 390 B.C.E. he visited a Pythagorean community in West Greece, and he maintained a lifelong friendship with one of their sect.[18] The Socrates of the *Phaedo,* imprisoned and awaiting the hemlock on the day of his death, is a noble and courageous spokesman for this metaphysical tradition. Explaining to his friends why he views death as liberation rather than as loss or tragedy, and why he has no fear of it, he says "Death is, that the body separates from the soul, and remains by itself apart from the soul, and the soul, separated from the body, exists by itself apart from the body. Is death anything but that?"[19] He is convinced this separation will make genuine gratification possible, for "so long as we have the body with us in our enquiry, and our soul is mixed up with so great an evil (*toioutou kakou*), we shall never attain sufficiently what we desire, and that, we say, is the truth" (83D). Employing a metaphor both powerful and disturbing, he sees the soul as crucified in its physical existence: "each pleasure and pain seems to have a nail (*helon*), and nails the soul to the body and pins it on and makes it bodily, and so it thinks the same things are true which the body says are true" (ibid.). Here Plato emphasizes the concept of nailing by using two different verbs to describe it. The only adequate palliative for this kind of exquisite spiritual torture is, Socrates believes, *philosophia,* or the love of wisdom. "Those who love wisdom are practising dying, and death to them is the least terrible thing in the world" (67E). In the *Phaedo* the judgment of earthly, physical life as a *sentence,* as an unwelcome and forced distraction from the real life elsewhere, of truth, stands unappealed.

Perhaps nowhere else in Plato's writing is the soul-body distinction stated so bluntly and unambiguously. Elsewhere, in the *Gorgias,* the *Phaedrus,* and the *Republic,* the operative distinction becomes more subtle, being no longer between body and soul but among the soul's rational, spirited, and appetitive parts. Yet the dynamics of the tug-of-war remain the same, with the "lower" appetitive part, the body's advocate, constantly trying to grab the control that properly belongs to the soul's "higher" rational and spirited parts. It is on the terrain of *eros* that this tug-of-war is waged most fiercely, and therefore I want briefly to examine the *Phaedrus* and the *Symposium,* Plato's inquiries into the nature of love. How does he present the relationship between sexuality and spirituality? through what metaphors? And what part, if any, do women have in his presentation?

In the *Phaedrus,* as Socrates and his friend leisurely stroll outside the city walls, he is at first a passive listener, taking a long time to come to his own point. When he gets there, in the dialogue's great middle section, he praises erotic desire as a heaven-sent madness that can grip the lover's soul and stimulate it to grow the wings on which it will ascend toward a clearer apprehension of that pure being that was its birthright, but that it now only dimly recollects. Erotic desire thus leads, ideally, to the soul's gratification. This gratification Plato expresses metaphorically as nourishment, using the homely language of the body's needs to express the soul's rapture: "Now even as the mind of a god is nourished by reason and knowledge, so also is it with every soul that has a care to receive her proper food; wherefore when at last she has beheld being she is well content, and contemplating truth she is nourished and prospers."[20] In a passage of ecstatic vision (250B–C) Plato makes clear that beauty is the earthly sign by which the soul is enabled to recognize its proper sustenance.

He then contrasts the reaction of two different kinds of lovers to the sight of the beautiful beloved. The first—whose "purity has been sullied," "whose vision of the mystery is long past"—rather than growing wings surrenders to his body's craving for satisfaction and pursues his beloved "after the fashion of a four-footed beast." If his object is female, he begets offspring of the flesh; if male, he consorts "with wantonness" and runs after "unnatural pleasures" (250E). The implication is plain that sexual gratification nullifies any opportunity for spiritual gratification, for it dissipates the soul's ascendant energies.

The second lover comes "fresh from the mystery" and is thus able to discern the face of beauty itself beyond the features of a comely youth. (Ensconsed in this passage's diction is the assumption that this youth can only be male . . . a *paidos kallos.*) Such a lover suffers a kind of spiritual tumescence: "by reason of the stream of beauty entering in through his eyes there comes a warmth, whereby his soul's plumage is fostered . . . the stump of the wing swells and hastens to grow from the root over the whole substance of the soul, for aforetime the whole soul was furnished with wings" (251B). With his one wing erect, with the power of the appetitive portion of his soul aroused but under control, this lover approaches not only his fair youth but also the wonder of being itself. In this long and remarkable passage, Plato again and again draws his metaphors from the physiology of desire, thus giving pause to anyone inclined to think of "Platonic love" as unlibidinous or serene or easy.

In a slightly later passage (253D–254E) he hints at just how violent and extreme the process of self-mastery that spiritual ascent necessitates may be. Here Plato compares the lover's soul to a chariot with a driver and two steeds, an obedient white horse and an unruly dark one, who wants only to plunge nearer to the beloved. After repeatedly having its tongue and jaws bloodied by the driver's strong jerks on the bit, the dark horse of appetite at last becomes broken and consents to the driver's command. So fond is Plato of this horse and chariot metaphor, that he shortly picks it up again (255E–256B), this time to describe what may transpire when two lovers lie together. Unless the charioteers hold in subjection "that which causes evil in the soul," their dark horses, they are doomed to an undistinguished existence. Once again the relationship between sexual gratification and spiritual health is antithetical. The idea that physical pleasure can be a source of learning, of surrender of boundaries and enlargement of being, is never considered. Though he was a prodigious myth-spinner, it is nearly impossible to imagine Plato being captivated by a story like that of Circe and Odysseus, where trust and direction seem to evolve naturally as a result of their experience together in bed.

The puritanical strain in Plato, his disposition to write as a "psychophiliac somatophobe,"[21] is not misogynistic in itself but certainly appears so *if* we consider it in relation to the status of women in fifth- and fourth-century Athens, where citizen wives were rigidly excluded from public and intellectual life and expected to remain sequestered within their households.[22] Under Solon's legal code, adopted when democracy was founded in the early sixth century, women were lifelong legal minors who had no political rights and practically no financial ones. Their voices were considered most pleasing when modest or silent, and therefore they have not come down to us.[23] Under the social and political structure of the city-state, women were recognized as aspects of men's existence rather than as beings in their own right.[24] The most important part of their role as handmaids was to receive and incubate their husbands' seed, to provide legitimate heirs for the household and citizens for the state. Valued primarily for their reproductive capacity, for the abundance of their bodies, these contemporary Athenian women were thus disqualified in Plato's terms for the life of true *eros* and self-mastery. He thought them altogether too likely to be dominated by the baser portion of their souls, by the "mob of motley appetites and pleasure and pains one would find chiefly in children and women and slaves" (*Republic* 431C). Though in the *Meno* and in book 5 of the *Republic* Plato does state that men have no monopoly on virtue or natural ability, which he sees as belonging to both sexes alike, the sincerity of this farsighted and idealistic belief in the basic equality of the sexes deserves to be questioned every time he uses women as exemplars of the unenlightened life of appetite. Insofar as Plato represents women's lives as quintessentially body-directed, he consigns them to the lower category of his dualism.

No matter how disrespectful of women's full humanity Athenians were during Plato's time, they could hardly afford to sneer at the female ability to bring forth life. In the *Symposium,* the second of Plato's writings about the nature of love, this ability contributes his basic metaphor—a concept as central to his thought here as is the notion of winging and ascent in the *Phaedrus.* It is probably no accident that the metaphor originates with Diotima, the highly unusual, "Mantinean" priestess whom Socrates quotes as his mentor concerning *philosophia* and *eros.* According to Socrates and Diotima, "to love is to bring forth upon the beautiful, both in body and soul" (206B).[25] "Those whose procreancy is of the body turn to woman as the object of their love and raise a family . . . but those [creative artists and philosophers] whose procreancy is of the spirit rather than of the flesh . . . conceive and bear the things of the spirit" (208E–209A). Implicit in this reproductive metaphor is a kind of organic, dialectical logic: the sense of two differing energies or forces coming together to create a third. Obviously, the metaphor is well suited to illuminate Diotima's theory of love as a participation in creation— or, for that matter, to describe the ability of *eros* to gather together the forces of the whole person, body *and* soul.

Yet Plato is not willing to let the synthesis-promoting nature of this metaphor imperil his basic and hierarchical dualism; Socrates, once more quoting Diotima, hastens to remind us that "the beauties of the body are as nothing to the beauties of the soul" (210B). He therefore insists that the philosophical conceptions of male lovers should be regarded as superior to the flesh-and-blood progeny brought forth by women: "he and his friend will help each other rear the issue of their friendship— and so the bond between them will be more binding, and their communion even more complete, than that which comes of bringing children up, because they have created something lovelier and less mortal than human seed" (209C). In the *Theatetus,* also, the physical labor and fruitfulness of women are denigrated when compared to the creative processes of male philosophers. Again using the reproductive metaphor, Socrates describes himself as a midwife who is the son of a midwife (149A).[26] But unlike those of his mother, Phaenarete, *his* patients are male: intellectual and spiritual seekers who are in the throes of doubt and travail as they struggle to bring forth more soul: "those who seek my company have the same experience as a woman with child; they suffer the pains of labor and, by night and day, are full of distress far greater than a woman's, and my art has power to bring on these pangs or to allay them" (151A–B). Usually disarmingly quick to proclaim his own ignorance, Socrates utterly fails to recognize it here. And so he passes judgment on other people's pain without ever questioning the measure by which he calibrates it.

As Page duBois persuasively argues in *Sowing the Body,* Plato, by using the reproductive metaphor, appropriates the part of female experience that his culture most valued and uses it to empower the male philosopher in his transcendent, body-scorning pursuits.[27] Like Zeus bringing forth Athene, the participants in Socratic discourse attempt to give birth through their heads.

From Immanence to Transcendence

Just as the Greek philosophers came to value a person's soul or reasonable consciousness as the essential, superior part of his nature, so the Greek people gradually came to reverence those gods who lived on the lofty, clear heights of Olympos, far removed from the older generation of Titans whose bodies had been molded from earth and from their mother Gaia, the ancient Earth Goddess herself. By the time Homer wrote, this revolution had already taken place in oral poetry, although it seems to have had little popular impact because all over Greece local nature and fertility deities were still being worshipped at country shrines.[28] In the following century Hesiod extolled the Olympian revolution in his *Theogony,* a long poem that makes clear that the struggle between sky gods and earth gods was often a struggle between male and female deities. As Marylin Arthur states, "Hesiod makes a polar tension between male and female a primary fact of his cosmology."[29] At issue in this struggle was not only sovereignty, but also control of reproduction.

As Hesiod tells it, the two original powers—both feminine beings capable of reproducing through parthenogenesis—were Chaos, the mother of Night and all things formless, and Gaia "the broad-breasted," the divinely substantial matriarch from whom the Olympians ultimately traced their descent. Though sufficient unto herself, Gaia seems to have preferred involvement with males; she mates with her son Ouranos, the Sky, to produce the generation of Titans. Immediately following their birth, Ouranos tries to cram his children back into their mother's womb. Gaia sides with her offspring and eventually hands the sickle for castrating Ouranos to Cronos, their youngest child. This pattern of father-son and male-female enmity is repeated in the next generation when Cronos devours most of his children and Zeus, with his mother Rhea's connivance, tricks him into disgorging them. We can only wonder what the pattern means, for the *Theogony* in itself is pristine, uninterpretive. But certainly male jealousy of female reproductive power and of the bond between mother and child seems to be presented here as one of the primal facts of the cosmos.

In the latter half of the poem there is no occasion for any such jealousy. Zeus the sky god and grandson of Gaia assumes supremacy over all the other divine powers with her blessing. He defeats first the Titans and then Typhon, the multiple-headed reptilean monster whom the *Theogony* presents as Gaia's youngest child but who appears in the Homeric Hymn to the Delphian Apollo as Hera's parthenogenetically produced son. He celebrates his victory by marrying Metis, whose name means "resourcefulness" or "wisdom" and whom Hesiod describes as "wiser than all gods and mortal men" (l. 887).[30] Threatened by her superior qualities of mind and by the prophecy that she is destined to bear a son who will overthrow him, Zeus uses his father's method to suppress her. At Gaia's suggestion he swallows Metis whole while she is pregnant with Athene, who is then left to push herself out through her father's forehead. No myth could speak more clearly about male assimilation of formerly female powers. Athene's birth sets up an alliance between father and child and signifies the suppression of the old parthenogenetic female powers, who have legitimized Zeus's patriarchal cannabalism by smiling upon it. Now, having safely incorporated Metis's wisdom, he is free to marry a much less dangerous wife, Themis, whose name means "established custom" and who bears him "Lawfulness and Justice and blooming Peace" (l. 902). With the cosmos now in order and the evolution from supreme matriarch to supreme patriarch completed, the *Theogony,* one of the primary cultural documents of ancient Greece, approaches its end.

An important sequel to the story of Athene's birth is told in the Homeric Hymn to the Delphian Apollo. In this Hymn Apollo crosses the sea to Delphi and fights a she-dragon (*drakaina*) to take possession of the shrine. We are told that this dragon—later called Python—has been the nurse to Typhon, the monstrous child whom Hera brought forth to spite Zeus after Athene's birth. Because of the similarity of their names, it is reasonable to suppose that Python and Typhon are the same creature.[31] Later versions of the myth add the detail that Python guarded the shrine for the goddess Ge (or Gaia), who herself spoke the oracles.[32] When Apollo, the most radiant and perfect of the sons of Zeus, slays the dragon and takes possession of the sacred space, his victory puts the seal on those his father has already won. These myths also make the incidental point that the children Zeus fathers without Hera's help (Athene, Apollo) are vastly superior to the ill-shapen ones she brings forth without his aid. Even at the quintessentially female business of reproduction, Hera is outclassed.

That Apollo was an intruder at Delphi is borne out by archaeological evidence as well as myth. The French excavators of the site have concluded that a female deity appeared at Delphi sometime after the Neolithic and think that she was the Earth Goddess herself.[33] They have found numerous terra-cotta statuettes of nude female figures and animals, including some from the Corcyrian grotto high up on Parnassos, which may have been the location of the oldest oracle. The rich, complicated history of Delphi is that of the mainstream of ancient Greek religion: the story of the overthrow of a female deity, immanent in nature and embodying fertility, by the most transcendent and removed of the male Olympians, the god associated above all others with light, form, and the clarity of reason. The only female deity worshipped at the site after 700 B.C.E. was the cerebral and virginal Athene, Apollo's closest female counterpart because she is untainted by the wildness that clings to his sister Artemis. The terraces around the lovely lower sanctuary of Athene Pronaia at Delphi have, ironically, proved to be especially rich in yielding objects from the older goddess cult.[34]

At least one other cultural document focuses intensely on the transmission of power from old, female earth deities to younger, male sky gods: the *Eumenides,* the concluding play of Aeschylus's Oresteian trilogy, which was first performed in 458 B.C.E. The *Eumenides* also makes clear that as the gods go, so does human society: if Zeus is king on Olympos, then the father rightly reigns in his house. In ending the *Oresteia* in this manner, Aeschylus thus provides powerful mythic justification for the sociopolitical arrangements of the Athenian state.

At the play's opening, Orestes takes refuge in the sanctuary of Apollo at Delphi; he seeks to be cleansed of blood-guilt for murdering his mother, Clytemnestra, in order to avenge her slaughter of his father, Agamemnon. Apollo, who admits the murder was done at his instigation, purifies Orestes but nevertheless sends him on to Athens to stand trial. The Furies (*Erinyes*)—dark and mysterious beings who are the granddaughters of Chaos and the guardians of mother-right—hound his steps. Aeschylus presents them as female foulness incarnate, in rhetoric that foreshadows that of the sixteenth-century witch-hunters:

> . . . black and utterly
> repulsive . . . they snore with breath that drives one back.
> From their eyes drips the foul ooze . . .
>
> (ll. 52–54)[35]

Though Aeschylus's sympathies hardly attend them, he does give them full opportunity to have their say. They are enraged not only by Orestes' matricide, but also by the way the younger gods "hold / by unconditional force, beyond all right, a throne / that runs reeking blood" (ll. 162–64). To them this crime within an aristocratic family duplicates the violation of primeval bonds that has already taken place in the cosmos.

When the Furies plead their case before a jury of Athenian citizens on the hill of Ares, they are countered by Apollo, who contends that Orestes' murder of his mother was both fully justified and, compared to Clytemnestra's crime, unimportant. To Apollo, "The mother is no parent of that which is called / her child, but only nurse of the new-planted seed / that grows. The parent is he who mounts" (ll. 658–60). He then points to Athene as living proof that "there can be a father without any mother." (Though Aeschylus must have known about Metis, any mention of her here would subvert his argument.) Apollo's ideological genetics convince only half of the jury, so Athene is left to cast the deciding vote—for Orestes, of course. As she does she declares herself "always for the male / with all my heart, and strongly on my father's side" (ll. 737–38).

The propaganda for patriarchy here is so strong and demands so much of an abeyance of common human experience and sense that the reader is led to wonder what Aeschylus is really arguing *against*. Some goddess-worshipping, pre-Cecropsian matrilineal social order that he feared might come again if men let down their guard? In any case, the *Eumenides* strongly links the victory of sky god over earth deities with that of father over mother and of legally established justice over the claims of common blood.

The play ends, however, not with bitterness, but with appeasement and co-option. Athene finally persuades the Furies to become benevolent deities-in-residence beneath the Acropolis, promising them generous libations poured out by her citizens and control over plant, animal, and human fertility. And so the *Erinyes* metamorphose into the *Eumenides,* the Gracious Ones. In the play's last lines, these ancient female powers go back underground, where Aeschuylus presumably thinks they belong. Their way down is lit by torches held by the lovely and seemly women of Athens. Like the Circe-Odysseus myth, the *Eumenides* ends with the blessing of representatives of the old, female-centered order upon the new, patriarchal one. In Aeschylus this blessing is grudgingly given, as the result of a hard bargain driven by the male-sympathizing Athene. In Homer it is free, unasked for and unstinting.

The *Eumenides,* the *Theogony,* and the mythology concerning Delphi are, then, mutually corroborative, all emphasizing the suppression of immanent, earth-connected deities by transcendent sky gods. And yet to leave the impression that this mainstream development in Greek religion was the *only* development would be to misrepresent the culture. The continuity of worship of earth-related goddesses at Eleusis from Mycenaean to Roman times is proof enough that the old deities could remain powerful even after the newer ones had triumphed. The democratic cast to the worship at Eleusis, where slaves and foreigners (providing they spoke Greek) were permitted to become initiates differed greatly from the emphasis that the priests of Apollo at Delphi placed upon the sumptuous gifts of kings and city-states. The survival of the rites at Eleusis, even as the concept of deity was becoming elevated above nature, is testimony to the tremendous vitality and intellectual tolerance of ancient Greek culture. Generalizations about the ascendancy of male over female and of mind over matter in Greek philosophy and religion, no matter how carefully arrived at, cannot do complete justice to the culture's complexity.

Toward Misogyny

What about attitudes toward women expressed in Greek literature? Did they change substantially between Homer's time and the time in which allegorical commentary began to flourish?

The answer to this second question must be an unambiguous "yes." Social organization in the *Iliad* and the *Odyssey* is thoroughly patriarchal, and except for Circe and Calypso, island goddesses exempt from human institutions, we see no instance of a female's living independently or holding property in her own right. Yet nowhere in the Homeric poems is the role of women denigrated or disparaged; nor do we find the expressions of misogyny that became quite common in later Greek literature.[36]

Homer emphasizes women's inclusion in the aristocratic society he portrays, rather than their exclusion.[37] In his portrait of Arete making decisions of state on Phaiacia, and in Odysseus's elaborate comparison of Penelope's character to that of a just king reigning over a fertile land, we sense that the poet fully believes women to be capable of noble decision and action. They take part in feasts in the great halls as assuredly as in domestic work in their own quarters. And in the magnificent scenes between Odysseus and Penelope in books 19 and 23, Homer shows their marriage to be based upon mutual affection and respect: a union of two human beings who, no matter what the customs of their time may have prescribed, regard each other as equals. Nowhere is this essential equality expressed more beautifully than in the great simile describing their reunion, wherein both are shipwrecked mariners who finally come to shore in the other's arms. As readers, we enter this simile on Odysseus's side and come out, unexpectedly and mysteriously, on Penelope's.

Homer's respect for women and lack of misogyny are part of the very structure of his verse. Whether these attitudes reflect his own enlightenment more than his culture's, we cannot know for certain. It is likely, however, that the Greek cities in Ionia were affected by the freer attitudes toward women current in Anatolia. Since oral poetry is a communal enterprise and Homer probably the most gifted of shapers rather than originator, it is reasonable to suppose that the regard for women expressed in the epics was consistent with his society's. Within a century and a half of Homer's time, his poems were known throughout the Greek mainland, standardized in text, and used as a basis for education.[38] They may have helped to temper the negative attitudes toward women becoming dominant in Attica.

Hesiod, in the seventh century B.C.E., can fairly be regarded as the father of Greek misogyny. His account of the creation and deeds of the first woman, Pandora, in *Works and Days* rivals the *Genesis* account of Eve and the Fall in its scapegoating of the female sex. Pandora is a "beautiful evil," a *kalon kakon,* whom Zeus bestows upon mankind in retaliation for Prometheus's theft of fire. Though golden Aphrodite has shed grace on her head, Zeus commands Hermes "to put in her a bitch's mind and a thieving heart."[39] All the plagues that blight humanity can be blamed on her, for she has deliberately freed them from the jar in which they were confined. Hesiod regards Pandora and her sex as a "steep trap from which there is no escape." One feels that he would counsel universal celibacy if only it would not result in suicide of the species. Since marriage and the propagation of children are necessary, he advises the prospective groom to assure himself of the upper hand by choosing a much younger wife: "You are at the right age to bring a wife to your house when you are not much less than thirty, and not much more. . . . Your wife should be four years past puberty and be married to you in the fifth. Marry a virgin so you can teach her good habits" (ll. 695–99).

Hesiod's hostility was echoed by the poet-philosopher Semonides and, in the next century, by Phocylides, both of whom compare women to species of lifestock.[40] His opinion that mature men should choose teenage brides seems to have become accepted social custom and finds expression later in Xenophon's *Oeconomicus,* an early fourth-century dialogue about household management. When Socrates, in the *Oeconomicus,* asks Ischomachus whether his wife came to him as a good household manager or was educated to become one, he receives this reply: "How, Socrates . . . could she have known anything when I took her, since she came to me when she was not yet fifteen, and had lived under diligent supervision in order that she might see and hear as little as possible and ask the fewest possible questions?"[41] Any reservations that Ischomachus might have had about the rightness of his domestic arrangements are laid to rest by his beliefs. Since women have "fearful souls," he tells Socrates, "the god directly prepared the women's nature for indoor works and indoor concerns" (7.25, 22).

The *Oeconomicus* is both evidence and apology for the privatization of Athenian women. The same social system that excluded these citizen women from public life depended upon them, however, to replenish the state with citizens. This paradox, of power residing in the bodies of the powerless, helps to explain why Athenian dramatists viewed the female sex with great fascination and unease.

On stage the contradictions and vulnerabilities of the social system were exposed. Aristophanes often chose the ideological gulf between the sexes as his comic terrain. Within this gulf, deception and misinformation seem to have flourished. In the *Thesmophoriazusae* (ll. 502–3) he satirizes in passing the false childbirths of his time. Apparently some men knew their wives so slenderly that it was possible for these women to feign pregnancy and labor in order to produce the purchased "heirs" who would save them from being divorced for barrenness. And in the *Lysistrata* he brilliantly exposes, through the device of the sex strike, the fundamental dependence of the Athenian state on its politically ignored women.

It was in tragedy, however, that unease about the position of women found its most penetrating and disturbing expression. Greek tragedy is filled with female characters whose strength of presence has rarely been equaled on stage.[42] In their remorselessness, their willful eloquence, their insistence on public exercise of their own personal power, Aescyhlus's Clytemnestra and Euripides' Medea are the dark shadow of the radically privatized Athenian woman. Clytemnestra, by claiming the right to rule and the right to choose a lover, violates the bonds upon which most patriarchal societies have been based; Medea, by murdering her own children, violates the primary connection upon which all societies rest. And yet Medea, as Euripides presents her, is not an outcast beyond the reach of the audience's sympathies. He permits her to speak for all of her sex:

> Of all things which are living and can form a judgment
> We women are the most unfortunate creatures.
> Firstly, with an excess of wealth it is required
> For us to buy a husband and take for our bodies
> A master; for not to take one is even worse . . .
> And if we work out all this well and carefully,
> And the husband lives with us and lightly bears his yoke,
> Then life is enviable. If not, I'd rather die.
> A man, when he's tired of the company in his home,
> Goes out of the house and puts an end to his boredom
> And turns to a friend or companion of his own age.
> But we are forced to keep our eyes on one alone.[43]

Medea's words here seem to be an unexaggerated assessment of the lives of citizen women. Furthermore, they accomplish her objective of persuading the chorus of Corinthian women to support her. The chorus vows not to tell their king that Medea, a foreigner, is planning a revenge upon Jason in which he too will be harmed. Euripides, with brilliant iconoclasm, imagines a situation in which the compliant silence of women is turned against the state. Understandably, his play did not win the state-sponsored festival competition in the year (431 B.C.E.) it was presented.

Drama is the most subversive of literary genres because it depends upon conflict for plot and because it grants even "evil" characters a full personal voice. In its reverberant, torchlit space the world can be turned upside down. Athenian drama remains the best evidence of the far-reaching commitment to freedom by the society that produced it. Yet because this prized freedom was not made available to women—who were then ill-respected because they did not possess it—Athenian society undermined its own ideal of human worth.

Development of Allegory

The attitudes whose evolution I have traced—the inclination to take pride in newly discovered powers of mind and to view them as only tenuously connected with the body, the tendency to conceive of the divine as transcendent rather than earth-connected and immanent, and the inclination to regard women with increased disrespect—are all part of the climate of thought in which allegory was invented. Seeking for causal connections among currents of thought within this climate is hazardous. To argue that the development of allegorical thinking depended upon a prior tradition of misogynistic thought would be patently absurd. Yet there is some connection, I believe, between the two. Both of these phenomena are indicative of the general trend in Greek culture to view the elevated as the good, and of the wish to use reason to impose meaningful order on the random or uncontrolled. Once this over-under kind of dualistic thinking had developed, women tended to be seen as the natural occupants of the lower category of the dualism because of their intimate connection with the mysterious and hard-to-control processes of pregnancy, childbirth, and menstruation.[44] Erections notwithstanding, anatomy apparently made it easier for men than for women to convince themselves that they were preeminently creatures of mind.

Once invented, allegorical commentary lent itself very easily to the expression of negative attitudes current toward women, as the commentary on Circe makes plain.

The first reader who professed to see an underlying symbolic sense in Homer was Theagenes of Rhegium, a rhapsode who lived in the later part of the sixth century and may have been a Pythagorean. His commentary on the battle of the gods in *Iliad* 20 was preserved by Porphyry, almost eight hundred years later. According to Theagenes, the strife beween divinities does not really represent deity at war with itself, but rather the strife between different elements of nature—Apollo representing fire, Poseidon water, and so on—or between different faculties of the soul.[45] Theagenes may have been defending Homer from charges by Xenophanes of Colophon that his gods were immoral, or he may have been merely exercising a taste for symbolic thinking. So little evidence survives from the sixth century that it is impossible to know whether the original impetus for allegorical thinking was defensive or positive.

Jean Pépin, who has studied the subject more thoroughly than anyone else, surmises that the Pythagoreans, holding Homer in high esteem, developed their own symbolic exegesis of his work and used it in their purifications.[46] If so, it has been lost. Pépin's theory makes good sense, however, for the Pythagoreans were known to communicate symbolically with each other, especially in the presence of noninitiated strangers. Accustomed as they were to look for the soul within the person, they must also have been inclined to look for the soul, or underlying meaning, within a text.

This underlying meaning was known as the *hyponoia,* literally the "undersense"; the first surviving use of the term comes from the fourth century B.C.E., though it must have been current before then.[47] The term *allegoria,* meaning literally "saying something else," may have been used by Stoic philosophers in the third century B.C.E., but the first sure attestation occurs in rhetorical contexts of the first century B.C.E. Only slightly later, Philo of Alexandria, applying the tradition of philosophical interpretation of texts to the Pentateuch, uses both terms in his commentary. Subsequently both terms are used by Neo-Platonists and Christian writers.

Plato's attack on Homer and other poets in *The Republic* gave urgency to the development of allegorical interpretation, for now it became necessary to prove that the stories in the epics were not blasphemous or merely frivolous. What, specifically, are Plato's charges against Homer? First, that he lies about the gods, attributing to them crimes of parricide, deception, and adultery not reconcilable with the idea of a divinity wholly good and immutable (2.377–80). Second, that Homer presents death as a terrible misfortune, to be lamented by the living, when in reality death is not a state to be feared (3.386–88). In book 10 Plato develops the more general charge that provides the philosophical basis for the others: that poetry is inherently false because, as an imitation of earthly life that is itself but an imperfect representation of the Ideal, poetry is at least two removes from truth and thus must appeal to an inferior part of the soul in its listeners (10.597–605). For all these reasons, Plato would ban poets from his republic and prevent them from corrupting the minds of youth. Even if Homer's objectionable tales have an underlying moral meaning, he says, they are not to be read or sung in his state, for young people cannot distinguish between the allegorical and the literal (2.379). Plato's awareness that Homer's poems were claimed to have underlying moral meaning shows that the tradition of allegory had begun to develop during or before his time.

The wish to defend Homer from Plato's charges was a primary motive among early allegorical commentators; they believed they could do so most effectively by stealing their opponents' fire, by finding philosophy *within* the epics. No writer of the time seems to have thought of defending mythic poetry on its own grounds against the virulence of this attack. This sort of defense would not occur until the time of the German Romantics, until sufficient centuries had elapsed for thinkers to gain perspective upon reason itself. Instead, early supporters of Homer tended to share Plato's assumptions even as they argued against him.

As might be expected, they read the *Odyssey* as a parable of the reasonable, temperate soul who stays on course in spite of an alluring assortment of carnal temptations. The complexity and balance of Homer's version of the Circe-Odysseus myth, which defy shaping to any clear and simple moral pattern, are ignored by the allegorical writers. Instead, they focus on the moment of Odysseus's drinking Circe's potion and on his meeting with Hermes immediately before it. If we had to divine the story through allusions in non-Homeric classical and Renaissance sources, we would have great difficulty discovering that Odysseus consented to become Circe's lover or that she gave him directions to find his way home. These commentators shear the whole last half of the myth away. Their work shows how readily bias can be established as truth and, once established as such, how tenaciously it can flourish.

The ancients distinguished between two types of allegory, physical and moral. Physical allegory, to which historical exegesis was closely allied, attempted to relate Homer's poems to the familiar material world, to point out, for instance, the precise geographic locations of his fabled isles. According to one writer of this persuasion, Circe was merely a highly skilled *hetaira*, like the educated courtesans who flourished in the refined establishments of Periclean Athens.[48] Moral allegory, which was far more ambitious, attempted to uncover the psychological or spiritual meaning of Homer's work. All the interpretations that I will discuss belong to this second category.

Two of Plato's contemporaries were the forgers of the Odysseus-as-Reasonable-Soul interpretation. Antisthenes (455–360 B.C.E.), who founded the Cynics and influenced the doctrines of the later Stoics, wrote many allegorical tracts on Homer, of which only fragments remain. According to him, it is Odysseus's temperance that permits him to escape the enchantments of Circe, just as it is the gluttony of his companions that puts them at her mercy.[49] Perhaps this point of view derives ultimately from Socrates, the teacher of Antisthenes. In Xenophon's *Memorabilia* (1.3, 7) Socrates remarks that the counsel of Hermes, whom he thinks represents Odysseus's own temperance and repugnance for taking food beyond the point of satiety, saves him from becoming a pig.[50] Diogenes of Sinope (400–325 B.C.E.), a pupil of Antisthenes, put forth an interpretation that has more psychological subtlety and force. He views sensual pleasure, not merely gluttony, as the antithesis of reason. Circe he regards as the personification of such pleasure, "more dangerous than all other enemies, because it attacks treacherously, like a magical drug, and makes a siege against each of the senses."[51]

Behind Diogenes' words lies a distrust of the body. His imagination focuses on the lives of Odysseus's men in the sty and on the animals in Circe's yard. They are "brutes without reason," "the image of the soul become the pitiable slave of pleasure, immobilised by the easy life and incapable of reaction which would free them." "They serve her without ceasing, remain by her gate, without any desire but for the voluptuousness which enslaves them, enduring a thousand other sufferings."[52] What did Diogenes make of Hermes' advice to Odysseus not to spurn Circe's offer of the pleasures of her bed, of Odysseus's own consent to this union and his year-long stay in her palace? No fragments that survive address such matters.

The next extant allegorical interpretation of Circe's role in the *Odyssey* dates from several centuries later, though it shows no discernible differences in perspective or conviction. The *Homeric Allegories* of Heraclitus[53] is usually dated to the age of Augustus on the basis of internal evidence; it is a collection of commentaries on selected passages of Homer, arranged according to the order in which they appear in the epics. These commentaries show no trace of the mystical exegesis favored by the slightly later Neo-Platonists. Because the value they uphold is, above all, reason itself, they seem firmly within the Stoic tradition. Odysseus, to Heraclitus, represents wisdom, the crown of all the virtues; he is imbued with the Stoic sense of the divine as "the right reason which penetrates all things."[54]

Heraclitus introduces his work by taking cognizance of Plato's attack and saying "everything [in Homer] is profane, if nothing is allegorical."[55] Positive, of course, that everything *is* allegorical, he regards Homer's verse as milk fit for suckling the young (1.5). Like other ancient interpreters, Heraclitus does not distinguish between what he sees in Homer and what Homer intended. He firmly believes that Homer himself is the allegorizer; whenever he uses the verb "to allegorize," Homer is its grammatical subject.

The greater part of Heraclitus's discussion of the Odysseus-Circe encounter concentrates on its prelude, Odysseus's meeting with Hermes. This most unpredictable and mercurial of gods represents, to Heraclitus, "reason of one's own," *ho emphron logos* (72.4). His wings symbolize the rapidity of the spoken word, his epithets his propensity to beam forth clarity. When Odysseus speaks with this god he is actually conversing, according to Heraclitus, with the better part of himself (73.9). The gift of moly, the plant of dark, tenacious root and milky flower, actually represents the coming of wisdom, a virtue difficult to acquire but luminous when possessed (73.10–12). Its presence is sufficient to overcome the powers of Circe, who symbolizes—what else?—sensual pleasure. Circe herself is not a major character in Heraclitus's exegesis, nor does he touch upon what transpires after Odysseus puts down her cup. Combining a sophistication that recognizes the divine as present in human intelligence with a sophistry that ignores the inconvenient, Heraclitus's interpretation of the episode has proved remarkably long-lasting. It is occasionally expressed as the author's point of view even in twentieth-century Homeric commentary.[56]

Pseudo-Plutarch, the unknown writer of a strange, second-century A.C.E. work called *The Life and Poetry of Homer,* embraces a variety of Stoic, Pythagorean, and Platonic influences in his interpretation. His grand, inflated plan in the *Life,* which was once attributed to Plutarch, is to show that Homer is the source of all philosophy, and of rhetoric and several other human skills as well. He often states that Homer "hints at" (*ainittetai*) various ideas of later thinkers, and he clearly regards the epics as a vast storehouse of knowledge with a somewhat obscure structure of meaning.[57] One of Ps.-Plutarch's concerns is to demonstrate that the Platonic-

Pythagorean concept of the soul as immortal but temporarily imprisoned in the body derives from Homer. Accordingly, he views Circe as the doyenne of metempsychosis, presiding over the transit of souls from body to body, form to form: "The changing of the companions of Odysseus into pigs and that sort of creature, suggests that the souls of foolish men take on the form of beastly animals, rushing into the turning circuit of all things, which is called Circe by name and placed under the direction of the seemly child of Helios, living on the island of Aiaia. And he [Homer] has called it that because men from the dead wail and lament there. The sensible man, Odysseus himself, does not suffer that kind of transformation because Hermes, who is reason, keeps him unharmed."[58] Several points here are worthy of notice. First, Ps.-Plutarch is adapting and attributing to Homer a doctrine Socrates expounds in the *Phaedo* (81E–82B), that the souls of the foolish (or cruel) are likely to be reborn into animals whose natures match their own. Second, he does not see Circe as representing bodily pleasure, as allegorists had been regarding her for several centuries, but as far more cosmic in her powers, since she is the turner of the wheel of incarnation. In this respect, he looks ahead to Porphyry and the Neo-Platonists, who believed that the significance of her name derived from its secondary meaning, "circle." Ps.-Plutarch's Odysseus remains in his usual role as Reasonable Soul, as capable of triumphing over rebirth as he is over pleasure. Once again the interpretation ends not at the Homeric episode's ending, but at the point of convenience to the interpreter. Did Odysseus's men suddenly gain wisdom in the sty, thus meriting their change back into men taller, younger, more beautiful than before? If Ps.-Plutarch knows what Homer is hinting at in this second transformation, he prefers not to say.

The most philosophical and detailed of all the ancient allegorical commentaries on the episode is that of Porphyry (232–305 A.C.E.), a student of Plotinus and the translator of his work from Greek to Latin. Excerpted from an unknown work and preserved in the anthology of Stobaeus, it differs from the other interpretations discussed so far in that it uses the transformation of the sailors as the occasion for a fully developed exposition of the fate of the soul after death. The emphasis is clearly on Porphyry's own abstract, Neo-Platonic ideas, only incidentally on the details of Homer's plot; thus the interpretation very nearly stands in its own right. Porphyry does, however, see Circe as a personification, and his notion of what she personifies is connected with the secondary meaning of her name: "Homer, for his part, calls the cyclical progress and rotation of metemsomatosis 'Circe,' making her a child of the sun, which is constantly linking destruction with birth and birth back again with destruction and stringing them together."[59] He expands upon the interpretation offered a century or so earlier by Ps.-Plutarch:

> Clearly, this myth is a riddle concealing what Pythagoras and Plato have said about the soul: that it is indestructible by nature and eternal, but not immune to experience and change, and that it undergoes change and transfer into other types of bodies when it goes through what we call "destruction" or "death." . . . The urge for pleasure makes them [the souls] long for their accustomed way of life in and through the flesh, and so they fall back into the witch's brew of *genesis,* which truly mixes and brews together the immortal and the mortal, the rational and the emotional, the Olympian and the terrestrial. The souls are bewitched and softened by the pleasures that lead them back again into *genesis,* and at this point they have special need of great good fortune and self-restraint lest they follow and give in to their worst parts and emotions and take on an accursed and beastly life.[60]

Porphyry's view of Circe, strangely, partakes of the ancient regard with which devotees beheld the Great Goddess. She, they believed, both gave life and took it away, "constantly linking destruction with birth and birth back again with destruction." But wonder and fear are absent in Porphyry's account, replaced by a calmer note of understanding, by the perspective that sees the entire wheel of incarnations as a temporary, sublunary phenomenon from which the lucid soul yearns to be liberated. In Porphyry's philosophy of transcendence, Circe is Great Goddess of this world of *genesis*—but *this* world is, finally, not the one that counts. His powers of intellectualized belief have put her in a lesser place.

The great good fortune and self-restraint that Porphyry thinks will preserve souls from incarnation as beasts are, once again, personified as Hermes, "in reality, reason [*logos*]."[61] The chief difference between the ways in which these Stoic and Neo-Platonic commentators regard reason is that while the former view it as an end in itself, Porphyry sees it as a quality pointing the way to the transcendent good. If we can judge adequately from the passages discussed, both schools of philosophers have a pronounced and equal distrust of pleasure and sexuality.

By throwing away the last half of Homer's story, these allegorists, in effect, wrote a new myth, one that celebrates the Triumph of Reason.

What a long, convoluted path has been traveled since Homer shaped his tale of a mortal hero's liaison with a dangerous divinity and of the trust and direction that evolved from it. In the dualistic and often simplistic writings of these early allegorical commentators, the sexual and the spiritual are thoroughly at war with each other—as, for the most part, they are in Plato's dialogues (though Plato sees potential for the soul's development in erotic desire, if not in erotic satisfaction). In the writings of Greek intelligentsia from the fourth century B.C.E. onward, the impulses toward pleasure and transcendence are usually presented as incompatible by nature. Homer's view of human nature as unitary, at one with itself and open to the gods, seems to have dropped out of culture during the eras following his poems' composition. As the Greek language developed from abundant particularity toward abstraction, as the gods moved from earth to the airy heights of Olympos, as the seat of human consciousness moved upward, from the torso to the head, our at-homeness in this world and in our bodies was proportionately diminished. Women—always the sex that most obviously possessed the awesome and very messy physical ability to bring forth life—were the losers in this shifting of the cultural ideology toward transcendence.

It may be that "the maturing of human consciousness is reflected in the great step from *mythos* to *logos*."[62] If so, we need to define this maturing also as a splitting, as a separation of consciousness from currents of life flowing both within and without the person. The characters in allegorical commentary go by the names of Homer's original heroes and deities, but they move in a diminished, less radiant world. As C. S. Lewis so eloquently put it, "the gods died into allegory."[63]

The ancient commentaries on Homer we have looked at are not, it might well be argued, very important in themselves. Yet if we regard them as among the few extant passages and texts from a once thriving and influential tradition, they take on undeniable consequence. These early allegorical Circes mothered later poetic ones.

4

The Legacy of Allegory

How was Circe seen during the period from Hellenistic times to late antiquity? To follow her traces through these centuries is to become aware of a complicated interplay between the poetic imagination and allegorical thinking. The Circes of Apollonius Rhodius, Virgil, and Ovid are all so different from Homer's that they strongly suggest non-Homeric influences upon them. Almost certainly, these poets were familiar with some of the moralistic interpretations of Homer's goddess discussed in the previous chapter, and this familiarity entered into their reshapings of her. If we compare their Circes with a tantalizing, two-line fragment from Alcman, writing in the seventh century B.C.E. before the allegorical tradition developed, the older poet's freedom to emphasize the positive in her character is at once noticeable. Alcman shows Circe acting as a protector, applying wax with her own hands to the ears of Odysseus's men, so they might be saved from the Sirens' songs.[1]

Four hundred years later, in the *Argonautica* of Apollonius Rhodius, this benevolence is gone and only her sinister strangeness remains. "Sinister" is too mild a word for the Circes of the two Roman poets, who see her as a profoundly dangerous natural force. Not surprisingly, Ovid's imaginative portrait of her was later to draw the attention of Christian allegorists, who perceived her as a kind of Eve raised to a higher power, a demonic figure personifying the linkage between the feminine, the natural, and the deadly. Stripped of its positive side, the figure of Circe fit in remarkably well with Christian doctrines concerning the nature of women and sexuality that the early church fathers promulgated during this period and passed on to the Middle Ages.

The Circe of Apollonius Rhodius, the first major poet since Homer to work with her character, is relatively innocuous. In this Hellenistic epic, the enchantress dwells by herself near the head of the Adriatic and is visited in book 4 by Jason and Medea, who have escaped from Colchis via the Danube and the Rhone.[2] Medea comes to her aunt to be purified of the murder and dismemberment of her brother Absyrtus. Though Circe obliges the pair, drenching them with the blood of a suckling pig, offering prayers to Zeus on their behalf, and listening to Medea's partial confession, she is not eager to have them linger and demands soon afterward that they leave her house. She functions more as a priestess than as a goddess, and Apollonius never uses the word *thea* in reference to her. All in all, she is a minor character in the *Argonautica*, barely figuring in its plot but providing a stroke of the bizarre.

Through the bizarre details of his portrait of her, Apollonius consistently associates Circe with the ancient and the elemental. We first see her surrounded by a flock of shambling monsters, neither men nor beasts, who accompany her to her daily bath in the sea (4.662–84). These hobbling, ill-shaped creatures, we are told, are like those formed when the earth was still primeval ooze. They correspond to the fawning wolves and mountain lions in Homer, but also attest to Circe's connection with an epoch when life had not yet settled into its familiar forms, when anything could happen. Her eyes, too, reveal her elemental nature. They flash with intense rays of golden light, making her immediately recognizable to her niece Medea—and indeed to anyone—as a daughter of the Sun (4.728–30). Sea, blood, and fire—all agencies of transformation—are the stuff of everyday life and work to Apollonius's Circe. She seems to have little taste for the differentiated and human and, since she lives in isolation, little impact on society.

The Circes of the two Roman poets are more negative than that of Apollonius and even further removed from the deep reservoir of ancient Mediterranean and Near Eastern myth, accessible to Homer, in which the feminine represented the source of both life and death and carried a full range of positive and negative meanings. The goddess-splitting and weakening phenomenon noticeable in the development of Mediterranean religions occurs within poetry, too. Of the three roles Circe plays in the *Odyssey*—sinister mistress of animals, lover of the hero, director of his journey to the Underworld—she is allotted only the first by Virgil in the *Aeneid*. The second is capably and tragically filled by Dido in book 4 and the third by the Cumaean Sybil in book 6. Significantly, the Sybil is a chaste priestess of Apollo, and her visionary powers derive from her devotion to this god. Presenting a sexual, nature-based female divinity as guide to the hero is a Homeric example that Virgil chooses not to follow.

Virgil's Circe, though a very minor character in her own right, is symptomatic of his treatment of the feminine throughout his epic. She makes a brief, haunting appearance at the beginning of book 7, when Aeneas and his men are about to land on Italian shores. Although she never again enters the narrative, the glimpse Virgil gives us of the intense hostility between the sexes acted out on her isle brings into sharp focus a tension latent and troubling throughout much of the rest of the *Aeneid.* Circe appears right at the poem's center, at the transitional point between Aeneas's Odyssean wanderings of the first six books and his Iliadic battles of the second six. Her presence reveals the grave underlying disturbance between masculine and feminine that mars this otherwise very balanced, structured poem.

Virgil's description of Aeneas's ship as it brushes by the coast of Circe's howling isle retains several of Homer's details: her song, her loom, her fires of cedar. The terrible sounds, however, are original with Virgil, perhaps inspired by a knowledge of Aiaia as meaning "wailing":

> They passed
> The isle of Circe close inshore: that isle
> Where, in the grove men shun, the Sun's rich daughter
> Sings the hours away. She lights her hall
> By night with fires of fragrant cedar wood,
> Making her shuttle hum across the warp.
> Out of this island now they could hear lions
> Growling low in anger at their chains,
> Then roaring in the deep night; bristling boars
> And fenced-in bears, foaming in rage, and shapes
> Of huge wolves howling. Men they once had been,
> But with her magic herbs the cruel goddess
> Dressed them in the form and pelt of brutes.
> That night, to spare good Trojans foul enchantment—
> Should they put in, or near the dangerous beach—
> Neptune puffed out their sails with wind astern,
> Giving clear passage, carrying them onward
> Past the boiling surf.[3]

In Homer, whether or not the animals in Circe's park were once men is left ambiguous. The cowardly Eurylochos is convinced that they were, but Odysseus pays no attention to his theory. In Virgil, this prior transformation is fact. Nothing argues against his striking auditory image of enraged male energies kept chained by a female divinity. *Dea saeva,* "wrathful goddess," he calls her, and he attributes to her the ability to evoke *furor* in all creatures that come under her spell. Any Homeric details that do not fit his picture of Circe presiding over a rustic and enraged domain Virgil is careful to suppress. There are no tokens of civilized refinement, no golden bowls, silver ewers, or ivory-inlaid chairs.[4] And certainly no flawless beds. Virgil's Circe is a clear caveat, like the figures in Renaissance emblem books. "Beware of the feminine: its disorderly passions are contagious" would be an appropriate motto to accompany this portrait.

Perhaps the most telling touch in Virgil's passage on Circe is the strong wind that Neptune gives to the Trojans, enabling them to quickly pass her by. She is altogether too close to the mouth of the Tiber, to the future Rome, for Aeneas, were he ever to engage with her, to leave her conveniently behind—as he has already left, inadvertently, his wife Creusa and, deliberately, his lover Dido. And why should he want to engage? Virgil has made her purely negative, a witch stripped of charm. There is no hint that Aeneas has anything to learn from her, as Odysseus learns from Circe. Circe in the *Aeneid* represents the archetypal feminine projected as evil and then evaded, safely skirted by. When we come to the end of book 12, however, with its nightmare vision of men turned to raging beasts on the battlefield and of trust torn and dishonored, we might well ask whether the atmosphere of Circe's island has, after all, been left behind. Like a repression returning to wreak havoc in the life of the person who could not bear its truth, the power that Virgil attributes to Circe refuses to be ignored. Aeneas's own war-chariot is pulled by a team of fire-breathing horses that she has bred.

To bear out the contention that Virgil's treatment of Circe is symptomatic of his treatment of the feminine throughout the epic it is necessary to look at other episodes and passages in some detail. But before doing so I wish to make a central if obvious point. The whole motion of the *Aeneid* is away from home, away from the Troy Aeneas has known, from his wife and childhood, from his emotional center. He is impelled toward an abstract, glorious future (imperial Rome) by the persuasive hand of Fate: a power that is expressed primarily through the will of

Jupiter and secondarily through Venus, Mercury, and, most compellingly, by his father Anchises. Virgil loosely based the wanderings of Aeneas in the first half of his poem upon the wanderings of Odysseus, but the directions of the two heroes are diametrically opposed. Odysseus, yearning to return to wife and home, where he perceives his deepest identity to lie, must necessarily remain on good terms with the feminine. It represents both his completion and his origins. His search is marked by his acceptance of positive female values: "Odysseus' quest for identity is in fact inextricably bound up with the feminine. In seeking the wholeness of his being, he passes through intimate experience with various embodiments of archetypal woman, each reflecting some aspect of what he as masculine hero lacks."[5] And so Odysseus does not hesitate to accept the dangerous knowledge of Circe or the fresh and very practical adoration of Nausicaa, for he senses that what they offer is integral to his quest. Aeneas, seeking a future not yet grounded in reality, seemingly has less need of the feminine. Because territory is the first imperative of that future, the labor to bring it to birth requires, above all, the masculine arts of war.

Empire and home are two different poles of the imagination, the one implying dominance and control, the other nourishment, safety, and surrender. Traditionally and stereotypically, male energies have been associated with the one, female energies with the other. Seen in this light, the *Aeneid,* which celebrates the birth of Rome, is an almost exclusively masculine poem. It is a great poem, however, because Virgil shows the human *cost* of this imbalance, of this emphasis on the arts of war.

At many places in his epic Virgil makes clear that the *furor,* or violent, disruptive passion that threatens Aeneas's controlled obedience to Fate, is predominantly the work of females. Some of them are divine, others human. Juno is foremost among these hostile figures, as the first passage of the poem makes plain. Still smarting from her failure to be awarded the golden apple by Paris, she retaliates by throwing storms and obstacles in the way of his countryman Aeneas. Virgil trivializes the cause of her anger, but he shows its strength to be ferocious. Through her messenger Iris, Juno incites the Trojan women in book 5 to burn their own ships while the men are off participating in Anchises' anniversary games. The women are "wrought to a frenzy" (5.659), raging out of control like the flames consuming masts and thwarts. A second outbreak of communal female madness, also indirectly fanned by Juno, occurs in book 7, after the Trojans have landed in Latium. The Fury Allecto, charged by the Queen of Heaven with the mission of stirring up hatred between Trojan and Latin, plucks a snake from her writhing tresses and tosses it at Amata, wife of King Latinus. The results are drastic:

> in her viscera
> The serpent's evil madness circulated,
> Suffusing her; the poor queen, now enflamed
> By prodigies of hell, went wild indeed
> And with insane abandon roamed the city.
>
> (7.374–77)

Amata in turn incites the other Latin women, who become "fired by sudden madness" to roam the forests like Bacchantes and who listen to her sing marriage hymns for Turnus and Lavinia. In both these scenes women's natural feeling (the Trojan women's weariness with sea travel, Amata's fond wish to see Turnus as her son-in-law) is roused to an insane pitch. Like the Stoic allegorists, Virgil distrusts female nature, viewing it as a reservoir of potentially roiling passions that, if liberated, can also infect men and threaten male achievement and control.

The most compelling impediment to Aeneas's fathering of the future Rome is, of course, Dido, the queen of Carthage. She provides the clearest instance in the poem of a woman's natural feeling suddenly heightened to destructive fury. Virgil has imagined her as a kind of alter-Aeneas, like him noble, bereaved, and dedicated to the great work of founding a city; thus her willingness to let her life and work be consumed by passion illustrates a tragedy possible for Aeneas too. But it is this very willingness to love fully and intensely that has caused readers to sympathize with Dido, to be moved by her arias of grief and rage when she is abandoned by Aeneas. In this incident—perhaps the finest and most memorable of the poem—Virgil has "deliberately presented Dido as a heroine and Aeneas as an inglorious deserter."[6] Why, if not to make plain to readers the terrible cost, which is nothing less than suppressing the imperatives of his heart, which Aeneas's allegiance to his destiny demands? Like the much later knights of Spenser's *Faerie Queene*, Aeneas cannot simultaneously satisfy himself and satisfy his mission. Both Virgil's and Spenser's poems resonate with the tension between the private and the public.

It takes the intervention of a god, the sudden descent of Mercury, to separate Aeneas from Dido. Yet once Mercury reminds him of his mission, Aeneas's decision to leave Carthage is instantaneous:

By what his eyes had seen, Aeneas felt
His hackles rise, his voice choke in his throat.
As the sharp admonition and command
From heaven had shaken him awake, he now
Burned only to be gone, to leave that land
Of the sweet life behind.

(4.278–82)

Compare this scene with its closest Homeric parallel, Hermes' intercep-
tion of Odysseus on his way to Circe's house. There the divine advice is
not to abandon but to engage with the feminine. Odysseus's relationship with Circe eventually helps him toward his goal; there is no conflict
in him between the personal and the strategic or political. In Aeneas,
however, "the personal and the political are experienced as mutually exclusive."[7] Once he resolves to go, no feminine pleas can change his mind.
He weeps, yes, but his tears are empty because they do not affect his
will. *Lacrimae inanes* Virgil calls them.

Again, in book 6, which recounts Aeneas's visit to the Underworld,
Virgil seems subtly to question the Augustan values that his poem overtly
espouses. When Aeneas sees Dido there she glares at him with magnificent dignity, unresponsive to his pleas to speak, to relate. In this, their
final encounter, she is clearly the victor, the one who demonstrates superior force of character.

Aeneas's most abiding and influential encounter in the Underworld,
however, is with his father Anchises. Together they stand on a ridge overlooking the Elysian Fields and admire the host of martial, virtuous souls
mustered to be reborn as Romans. This vision of the glory to come is a
moment of grace for Aeneas, the closest Virgil allows him to come to
seeing his mission fulfilled. Yet after this moment of enlightenment,
Aeneas returns to the upper world through the Gate of Ivory, through
which false dreams pass. For centuries lovers of Virgil have wondered
why he did not permit his hero to return through the reliable Gate of
Horn. The most popular answer has been that since Aeneas is a living
man, not a true shade, he is not eligible for passage there. Could the
substance of his vision also have helped to determine which gate he passes through? Women are strikingly absent from this illustrious lineup of
future Romans. Virgil may be suggesting an incompleteness, and hence
a falsity, in this vision of a martial civilization that ignores half of its
members.

The subversive, questioning subtext of the *Aeneid* becomes dominant at the poem's ending. In the poem's final lines, the usually controlled Aeneas gives in to a lust for revenge and kills an at last humbled Turnus. This murder of a suppliant comes as an emotional shock that Virgil does nothing to mute. No glimpse of dazzling and destined cities, no scene of enemies united by their common grief for the dead (as they are in the *Iliad*'s last book) mitigates the pure destruction of this ending. It is as if Virgil has realized the human inadequacy of his ideology of empire and decided to dramatize it in this stark, brutal image of dominance and submission. *Aeneid* 12 offers a terrible contrast to the compassion and grandeur of *Iliad* 24, in which Achilles yields to Priam's request for Hector's body and shares the old man's sorrow. When we consider these two final books side by side, Brooks Otis's contention that "we can partially describe the *Aeneid* as the creation of Roman civilization out of Homeric barbarism"[8] becomes untenable. Michael Putnam's observation that in the *Aeneid*'s final scene Aeneas becomes identified with or parallel to Juno, whose *furor* is unremittingly negative, is a more discerning assessment of its moral quality.[9] Putnam sees Aeneas as yielding, finally, to the very *furor* against which he has struggled throughout the poem.

This final emergence of destructive passion from within Aeneas is linked to the overall imbalance between masculine and feminine in the epic. What Virgil has repressed in Aeneas and projected onto an unruly host of mortal and divine females finally comes back to demand expression. The ending of the poem is profoundly truthful because it reveals the terrible cost of attempting to sacrifice passion—stereotyped as feminine—to duty and control, rather than integrating these forces. From this perspective, it is not so strange that Virgil chose, whether intuitively or deliberately, to end his national epic with an atmosphere more suggestive of Circe's island than of the *pax Romana*. If he had lived to revise the poem to his satisfaction it might have concluded differently.[10] As it is, the ending subverts the poem's overall Augustan ideology in favor of a more timeless truth.

Virgil's younger contemporary Ovid appears never to have been comfortable with the grandiloquence of Augustan ideology. Very early in his writings, in the first poem of the second book of the *Amores*, he explains how he was once working on "an inflated epic about War in Heaven," but dropped it when his mistress locked him out of her chamber.[11] Deprived of her favors, he came to realize that "her shut door ran to larger bolts" than any Jupiter wielded. And so he went back to "verses and compliments, my natural weapons," depending on the magic of elegiac poetry to soften and transform her will. This witty story, with its unceremonious relegation of Jove to the limbo of lost drafts, seems to tell the truth about Ovid's deliberate rejection of heroic poetry, about his decision not to compete with Virgil. Its cavalier treatment of the cosmic *paterfamilias* has anti-Augustan overtones. So unsympathetic was Ovid to the new official ideology of empire and moral correctness that Augustus perceived his presence in Rome as a threat and banished him to the west shore of the Black Sea in 8 A.C.E. Ovid's libertine attitudes in *The Art of Love* were cited as one of the reasons for his exile.

In his erotic poetry, Ovid views love as a consummate game in which women and men are equal players, both sexes being manipulative and both vulnerable. This sophisticated attitude mirrors the social milieu that had prevailed in late republican Rome, in which women had very much been active participants, not at all the excluded stay-at-homes that their Athenian counterparts had been. In the poetry of the late republican period "both sexuality in general and the sexual relations between men and women are evaluated positively."[12] But under Augustus, whose program of moral rearmament promoted chastity and the growth of the nuclear family, this free social atmosphere changed. Ovid, who persisted in celebrating the charms of the boudoir over those of the marriage bed, was part of the old guard.

There is a mystery connected with Ovid's portrayal of Circe in the *Metamorphoses*. Why should this poet, so sensuous and undoctrinaire, aware beyond most others of the power of passion to transform personality, treat the mythic figure most clearly associated with metamorphosis in so heavy-handed a fashion? He gives Circe star billing in the fourteenth book of the *Metamorphoses,* and the role she plays can fairly be described as Queen of Lust. To Ovid, Circe personifies a female passion so extreme that it destroys all who impede its satisfaction. He tells three tales about her, concerning her desire for Glaucus, Odysseus, and Picus. In each she is like an exaggeration of Diogenes of Sinope's allegorical figure, an abstract idea given new, voluptuous flesh and body. To say that she is unsubtle is vastly to understate the case. If her libido is not gratified, she is capable of changing a man who spurns her into an angry bird, of girding a rival's body with the heads of barking dogs, of making the air itself writhe with unnatural forms. Since Ovid is obviously not disapproving of sexual passion per se, why does he present Circe as such an unattractive caricature of it?

There are two related answers to this question. First, a stereotype, partially provided by the Homeric allegorists' view of Circe, intervened. Although Ovid would not have been moved by the allegorists' philosophy, the image they provided might well have mingled in his mind with another current one, that of the bawd-sorceress who counsels her beautiful young mistress not to waste her charms on poets but to go after someone rich. In *Amores* 1.8 Ovid denounces a witch like this, a hag named Dipsas who "mutters magical cantrips, can make rivers / Run uphill, knows the best aphrodisiacs." Dipsas may have been modeled after a similar figure in Propertius 4.5 and is a familiar type in Roman elegy.[13] Ovid's disdain for witchcraft is expressed many times in the *Amores, The Art of Love* and *Cures for Love.* Perhaps he found the sorceresses of his time easy to disparage because they often were servants, but there is a deeper reason also for his negative attitude toward them and toward Circe.

He believed in poetry itself as a magical art. Repeatedly in his early work, Ovid plays with the multiple meanings of *carmen,* which can signify "poem" or "magical incantation" or "spell."[14] In *Amores* 2.1, the same poem in which he discards his ambitions as an epic poet so that he can press his affair with Corinna, Ovid proclaims:

> There's magic in poetry, its power
> Can pull down the bloody moon,
> Turn back the sun, make serpents burst asunder
> Or rivers flow upstream.
> Doors are no match for such spellbinding, the toughest
> Locks can be open-sesamed by its charms.
>
> (ll. 23–28)

Behind the outrageous bravado of these claims lies the justified pride of someone who has himself experienced the process of creation, who has played with forms and transformed. For Ovid, making poetry was a means of generating and transmitting the currents of life. His confidence in his own subtle art made him look down upon Circe's. In the *Remedia* (ll. 263–88) he mentions her only to dismiss her as pitiable and inconsequential, since her command of drugs and magic cannot soothe her own swollen passion for Odysseus. "She could subject men to a thousand metamorphoses," Ovid remarks, but "the laws of her own heart she could never change." Like Calypso, like Dido, this Circe wants only to cling to her restless man. If she had placed her trust in Apollo's gift of "holy song" rather than in her own pharmacopia, Ovid implies, she would have been better off.

The Circe of the *Metamorphoses* is aggressive and vengeful but every bit as powerless to control her own heart as the lovelorn *maga* of the *Remedia*. In the first of her three tales, about Glaucus, Ovid introduces us to her "more than ladylike desires" and explains the origins of the monster Scylla. Spurned by Glaucus because he is already in love with Scylla (who was originally a fair young maiden), Circe steals to the girl's bathing cove and poisons the water with magical herbs that distort her shapely body. Circe's behavior with Picus in the third tale follows a similar pattern. Having met him by chance in the woods, she lures him away from his hunting party, offers her love and, when he refuses because of his passion for the lyrical Canens, changes him into a bird. In both cases, the transformations are clearly motivated by personal revenge—unlike those in Homer, which seem the result of an earth goddess's determination to show off her divine powers. Ovid's Circe, for all her menace and flash, has no fundamental mystery or remoteness. She is an ordinary woman scorned, raised to an exponential power.

Ovid's imagination, like that of Apollonius, is impressed by Circe's affinities with the elements. Twice (14.382, 438) he calls her "Titaness," as if he were aware of her connection with the ancient Earth Goddess, Ge. He shows Circe herself taking pride in her primeval pedigree, for twice she advertises herself to potential lovers as a daughter of the Sun. Her power can shake the elemental framework of nature. When Picus's subjects come searching and ask her the whereabouts of their king (now become woodpecker), Circe throws restraint to the winds and puts on what must be the most impressive magic show in the *Metamorphoses:*

> she, too quick for them, thrust like a veil
> Of raining mist her magic at their heads,
> The distillation of a million herbs,
> And called the ancient gods of night to help her,
> Gods from Erebus, ever-falling Chaos,
> And Hecate who heard her winding cries.
> Then (strange to say) the forest seemed to float;
> The earth groaned under it and trees, white-haired,
> Were like an arbour turned to frost in winter,

And where her raining mist touched plants and grasses
Blood stained the ground and stones began to bark,
And through that midnight crawled snakes, horny lizards,
And souls of those long dead weaved through the air.
The young who witnessed horror in her magic
Shook with their fears and as she touched their faces
They changed from men to beasts who roamed the darkness.[15]

Such effects, though pleasurable as melodrama, are impossible to take seriously. Ovid may have tired by this time of showing nymphs gracefully flowing into rivers and women branching into trees. In order to top his previous effects, he strains toward surreal excess and Circe's pharmaceutical skills easily lend themselves to such exploitation. The profusion and exaggeration of this passage, at the end of her appearance in the *Metamorphoses,* sate the reader and prepare the way, by contrast, for the calm entrance of the philosopher, Pythagoras, in the poem's next and last book.

Ovid's treatment of the Circe-Odysseus episode, which follows Homer quite closely in detail though it is much condensed, has a different, more muted tone. It is narrated by Macareus, a deserter from Odysseus's crew. The chief advantage of this point of view is that it offers a firsthand description of how it feels to change from man to pig to man. Macareus stresses his thirst, his eagerness to take Circe's cup, the lightness of her touch. In his case the transformation is deft; he slips into it as into an ordinary drunken moment: "The floor beneath me slipped and there I was / With pigskin growing on me, tough and hairy" (14.279–81). The retransformation bears more resemblance to a dancing bear's delicate, deliberate defiance of gravity than to the poignancy of the scene in the *Odyssey:* "We raised our heads, then seemed to stand almost / On our hind legs, and as her songs went on, / We found our feet, our shoulders grew, our arms / reached out to wind themselves around Ulysses" (14.302–6). Circe's musical incantations here take the place of the heartrending groans of the men in Homer. While this description is quite artful, it cannot compare to the intensity of the parallel moment in the *Odyssey,* when the whole spectrum of creation—goddess, man, and beast—is joined together in pain and pity.

Surprisingly, Ovid does not dwell on the sexual connection between Circe and Odysseus. While it is clear that they are lovers, their dalliance takes place well offstage. He also de-emphasizes the sailing direc-

tions that Circe gives, condensing them to two lines. Yet this is the first
time since Alcman that they appear in the tale at all! On the whole, Ovid
is not untrue to Homer's Circe; he just seems not much interested in
her, much preferring his own casting of the goddess as spurned, revenge-
ful Queen of Lust.

Ovid received from the allegorical tradition, I believe, a distorted, one-
sided Circe, and for reasons of his own he chose to give this distortion
flesh and blood, a new poetic existence. Because she lacks complexity,
she has not much power to stir feeling in modern readers; yet Ovid's
Circe has proved, from his time until the beginning of this century, more
influential than Homer's. She was witch of choice to the Renaissance.

The Homeric allegorists' vision of a voluptuous Circe beckoning the
rational, temperate Odysseus to drink from her poisoned cup possesses
obvious similarities to the figure of Eve holding out the fruit of the Tree
of Knowledge to a still-innocent Adam in Genesis 3. True, their status
differs in an important respect: Eve is merely a mortal woman; the strict
monotheism of the Hebrews and orthodox Christians left no room for
female divinities. But she is the protagonist of the most important bib-
lical myth concerning women and sexuality, and the biases the early
church fathers brought to its interpretation are essentially the same biases that the allegorists brought to bear upon Circe.

Any full and unbiased discussion of the myth of the Fall in Genesis
should address the fact that this myth had already been retold and rein-
terpreted before it became part of the Bible. The Hebraic narrative in
Genesis is a changed version of a much earlier Sumerian-Canaanite myth
in which the Goddess, associated with her serpent familiar and with the
central world-tree, holds out the fruit of life to a visiting male.[16] According to Joseph Campbell, "there is a historical rejection of the Mother
Goddess implied in the story of the Garden of Eden."[17] Campbell believes that the Hebrews, by identifying the woman and the serpent with
sin, gave the myth a twist "that amounts to a refusal to affirm life." What
the Hebrews did to the older, positive myth parallels what the allegorists did to Homer's Circe. The import of the Hebraic retelling, however, was far greater. Because the myth of the Fall became part of sacred
canon, it took on a prescriptive function and was used as justification
for women's subjection. If loss of paradise and separation from God were
the consequences attendant upon Eve's following her unbridled will, then
clearly—so many of the church fathers reasoned—her sisters and de-

scendants must be restrained to prevent them from causing further rents in the order ordained by God. The writer of an epistle attributed to St. Paul provides a sample of this argument:

> But I suffer not a woman to teach, nor to usurp authority over the man, but to be in silence.
> For Adam was first formed, then Eve.
> And Adam was not deceived, but the woman being deceived was in transgression.
>
> (1 Tim. 2:12–15)

In another pseudo-Pauline letter the writer uses the metaphor of the body's proper subordination to the head to clarify the relationship of wife to husband:

> Wives, subject yourself to your own husbands as to the Lord.
> For the husband is head [*kephale*] of the wife, as also Christ is Head [*kephale*] of the church: and he is the saviour of the body [*tou somatos*].
> Therefore as the church is subject unto Christ, so let the wives be to their own husbands in everything.
>
> (Eph. 5:22–24)

This particular passage echoes and elaborates upon Paul's words in 1 Corinthians 11:3: "the head of every man is Christ; and the head of a woman is the man; and the head of Christ is God." Paul, like the writers of the inauthentic epistles, ratifies the structures of conventional patriarchal marriage. Of far greater concern to him than the institution of marriage, however, was the spiritual purity of his followers. He saw the married state as an expedient meant only for those incapable of soul-enhancing celibacy. Like Plato, he favored sexual asceticism because he viewed the passions of the flesh as distractions to the spirit in its quest for God. In Romans 7:18, he laments that "in me (that is, in my flesh,) dwelleth no good thing." And he goes on to remark, several verses later, "I see another law in my members, warring against the law of my mind, and bringing me into captivity to the law of sin which is in my members."

The spirit-flesh dichotomy that Paul impressed upon Christian doctrine has a distinctively Greek cast. Prejudice against women was so often associated with this dichotomy that it went unremarked in Greek culture, for it was part of the mental climate in which Greek writers lived and moved after the sixth century B.C.E. Here is Aristotle on what he perceived as the basic division in human nature: "It is clear that the rule of the soul over the body, and of the mind and the rational element over the passionate is natural and expedient; whereas the equality of the two or the rule of the inferior is always hurtful . . . the male is by nature superior, and the female inferior, and the one rules, and the other is ruled: this principle of necessity extends to all mankind."[18] Aristotle's linkage of male superiority with the superiority of the soul to the passions needs only to be expressed with more urbanity and grace to become that of Plutarch several centuries later: "And control ought to be exercised by the man over the woman, not as the owner has control of a piece of property, but, as the soul controls the body, by entering into her feelings and being knit to her through goodwill . . . so it is possible to govern a wife, and at the same time to delight and gratify her."[19] Plutarch's understanding tone, very much that of the temperate, accomplished man of the world, cannot obscure the vastness of his assumption, that one sex has the ontological right to control the other. Yet we do not have Plutarch to thank or blame for the fact that the ideas he expresses here are so familiar to us. That honor belongs to Paul and his followers, who made the spirit-body dualism and its correspondence to the sexes part of Christian scripture and thus enabled it to influence Western culture for centuries. They were better evangelists than they could have imagined.

Paul, in some of his authentic epistles, does express ideas about men and women without rancor and with the tempering advice that they love one another. This equanimity cannot be found in the tone of Tertullian, a skilled rhetor who became bishop of Carthage during the early part of the third century, whose writings did much to promote an aversion to sex and distrust of female nature in later Christian doctrine. In a passage from "On the Apparel of Women," which was later to be quoted during the Renaissance, Tertullian addresses his female fellow Christians: "*You* are the devil's gateway . . . *you* are the first deserter of the divine law; *you* are she who persuaded him whom the devil was not valiant enough to attack. *You* destroyed so easily God's image, man. On account of *your* desert—that is, death—even the Son of God had to die."[20] The vindictiveness of this point of view must have been hard to reconcile with Jesus' own emphasis on the spiritual imperatives of love and forgiveness.

Tertullian's view of Eve as the destroyer of the more virtuous sex has something in common with Clement of Alexandria's attitude toward

Circe. Of the early church fathers, Clement, who wrote around the turn of the third century, was the one most steeped in Platonism and Greek culture. His familiarity with Homer, whom he considered the most gifted and authoritative of the pagan poets, was extensive. In his collection of miscellanies entitled *Stromateis,* Clement alludes to Circe to illustrate a point when describing the journey and choices to be made by the Christian soul. Eventually, he says, such a person will come to a point of crisis when he must choose between the *Logos* (Christ) and love of the things of this world. He compares the position of the Christian at such a time to that of Odysseus on the path toward Circe's house: "As if . . . one were to become a beast instead of a man, like those who were changed by Circe's drugs, so is it with him who has spurned the tradition of the Church and has suddenly taken up with the fancies of human sects; he has lost the character of a man of God, and of enduring trust in the Lord. But he who has returned from this deceit, after hearing the Scriptures, and has turned his life to the truth, such an one becomes in the end as it were a god instead of a man."[21] There is no great difference between the way Clement uses Circe here and the way the pagan Neo-Platonists were about to; both see her as the goddess of this world, whose pleasures deflect the spiritual wayfarer from the *Logos,* or transcendent truth, which is represented to Clement exclusively by Christ. To Clement, Circe's powers are limited, for men hardly need aid in turning themselves into beasts. The truly wondrous transformations are those wrought by Christian revelation.

St. Augustine, writing almost two centuries later, also alludes to Circe and also sees her powers as limited. This allusion is unusual for Augustine, for he rarely refers to Homer and had only a minimal knowledge of Greek.[22] But in the eighteenth book of *The City of God* he devotes three sections to tales of men changed into animals and can hardly avoid mentioning Circe. *Maga famosissima* he calls her, "most famous sorceress."[23] His identification of her as a demon is all but explicit, for he devotes the entire next section (18) to explaining how these transformations are more apparent than real, since they are wrought not by the hand of God but by demons with limited, secondary powers. Augustine's writings were enormously influential during the Latin Middle Ages and his near-typology of Circe as demon was later to have echoes of its own.

Of much greater import than this isolated reference to Circe, however, is Augustine's overall attitude toward sexuality. He did not, like

Tertullian, scapegoat the female sex; the biographical evidence shows him to have been a warm and passionate man. For fifteen years during his twenties and thirties he lived, apparently harmoniously, with a woman with whom he had a son, and he remained extremely close to his devoutly Christian mother until her death. Yet he came to scapegoat sexuality itself, or rather to view it as the element in human nature that most intractably threatened spiritual development.[24] In the *Confessions* Augustine quotes the Pauline text that finally converted him: "Put ye on the Lord Jesus Christ, and make not provision for the flesh, in concupiscence" (Rom. 13:13ff.). For him personally, the acceptance of Christ involved abandoning sexual life.

Not until his old age, however, when his polemics against the Pelagians brought out the rigid, intransigent side of his nature, did he prescribe this abandonment for others. In his writings against the Pelagians, who denied the reality of Original Sin, Augustine isolates sexual intercourse as an element of evil within every marriage.[25] He finally came to view sexual desire itself as the mark of the Fall—as a brand that seared each new baby at the passionate moment of its conception. The hereditary transmission of Original Sin has been the official doctrine of the Catholic church since Augustine's time. Far more than Paul, who viewed sexual experience as soul-distracting but not as inherently evil, Augustine is responsible for transmitting negative and pessimistic views of sexuality to the Christian West.

Boethius is the last Christian thinker of antiquity to refer to Circe in his writings. She appears in a poem in the fourth book of *The Consolation of Philosophy*, written ca. 523, when he was in prison and under sentence of death. Boethius's extensive knowledge of Greek literature and philosophy was rare for his time. He bases his view of the extent of Circe's powers on two lines from the *Odyssey*, 10.239–40, which state that though the heads and voices and skins of Odysseus's men became those of hogs, their minds remained unchanged. To him this is evidence of the feebleness of her brew:

> Her herbs were powerless;
> They changed the body's limbs
> But could not change the heart;
> Safe in a secret fastness
> The strength of man lies hid.
> Those poisons, though, are stronger,

> Which creeping deep within,
> Dethrone a man's true self:
> They do not harm the body,
> But cruelly wound the mind.[26]

Boethius's view of Circe here is highly idiosyncratic: not only does he ignore her positive side, he sees her negative side too as negligible. Evil, to him, resulted from the heart's desire to turn away from one's human nature and consequently to sink to the level of an animal. Right before the poem in which Circe appears, he remarks that "a man wallowing in foul and impure lusts is occupied by the filthy pleasures of a sow." Alone among all the commentators who have seen moral meanings in Homer's tale, Boethius insists that pigdom is caused by a man's free will and not by his victimization by any witch or goddess. Boethius seems relatively unaffected by the misogynist current that joined with Christian doctrine not long after the death of Christ.

Well over a century before Boethius's time, during the reign of Theodosius from 378–95, Christianity had been proclaimed as the official state religion of the Roman empire. Theodosius essentially declared open season on paganism. Temples of divinities of both sexes were sacked and destroyed by roving bands of monks, including the temple of Demeter at Eleusis and the Artemision at Ephesus, which had once been considered foremost of the world's seven wonders. Most of the huge marble blocks used to construct the temple at Ephesus were reused as building materials for the new church of St. John Theologos, situated on a hill overlooking the ruins of Artemis's age-old sanctuary on the plain by the Cayster river. This high vantage point seems appropriate for the church of a saint who thought that creation began with something as immaterial as "the Word." The world of ancient goddess religions, of those who believed that creation began within a female divinity's womb, now lay in ruins all around the Mediterranean.

The destructive energy turned against pagan temples still survives in many tracts written "Against the Heathen" by Christian polemicists. The tracts of Arnobius and Athanasius, both writing in the fourth century, show how far away the religious thinking of the time had moved from the veneration of anthropomorphic, nature-based divinities. Arnobius attacks the Greek and Roman penchant for adorning temples with marble effigies of unmistakably male or female deities. "Have the gods, then, sexes?" he asks, "and are they disfigured by those parts, the very mention of whose names by modest lips is disgraceful?"[27] His revulsion against divine sexuality extends to every step of the reproductive process. He denounces the notion of "goddesses pregnant, goddesses with child . . . faltering in their steps, through the irksomeness of the burden they bear with them . . . shrieking as they are attacked by keen pangs and grievous pains." One can imagine Arnobius's spirited disbelief were he to be told that, at one point in human history, gravid goddesses were deemed the most awesome and potent force in the universe.

Arnobius's contemporary Athanasius lacks his tone of inspired prudery, but he objects to goddess worship on grounds that are more firmly based in the social realities of his time. He is particularly irked by the pagans' assumption that females are worthy of worship. "Would that their idolatrous madness had stopped short at males," he exclaims, "and that they had not brought down the title of deity to females. For even women, whom it is not safe to admit to deliberation about public affairs, they worship and serve with the honour due to God."[28]

The views of Arnobius and Athanasius and their fellow believers prevailed; in the late empire paganism was as vigorously suppressed as Christianity had been. Goddess worship was finished in Europe. Not until the yearning to complement the masculine divine with the feminine prompted the cult of Mary in the twelfth century did a version of it reappear.

During the period from the sixth to the fifteenth centuries, the texts of the Homeric poems were lost to the West, and his writing existed there only as fragments embedded in the literature of rhetoric and philosophy. During this period the Homeric tales themselves, burdened by now with centuries of moralizing, became thoroughly dissociated from the poetry that had been their medium and largely reverted to the oral tradition. As a glance at popular Renaissance mythographies will show, it was Circe as *maga famosissima* who flourished in this tradition, not Circe as *dia theon*.

Undoubtedly, Ovid's portrait of Circe in the *Metamorphoses*—which continued to be read, since the knowledge of Latin was never lost—contributed to her reputation as foremost among sorceresses. Numerous allegorical commentaries were written on the *Metamorphoses* during the twelfth century that still repose, unpublished, on library shelves.[29] In the *Ovide Moralisé,* an anonymous Old French commentary on the poem dating from the beginning of the fourteenth century, she figures as a type for "la vile venismes" of this world, from which "Jhesucris" will save us.[30] Ovid's brief alternative portrait of an extravagantly lovelorn Circe in the *Remedia* also inspired medieval descendants; in Benoît de Sainte-Maure's *Roman de Troie,* which appeared in 1160, she mourns for Ulysses inconsolably after he leaves her. Within a century vernacular translations of Benoît's poem, which emphasizes story rather than moralizing, were produced all over Europe. John Lydgate's *Troy Book,* which appeared in England in 1420, ultimately derives from Benoît.

As for Virgil's contribution to Circe's legend during the Middle Ages, he himself cannot be blamed for it. That distinction belongs to Servius, author of the most widely read ancient commentary on the *Aeneid,* written around the turn of the fifth century. In his notes on the Circe passage in book 7, Servius describes her as *clarissima meretrix,* a "most radiant prostitute."[31] The prostitute label stuck, for Servius was regarded as an important authority and was read for centuries; it was to become part of the Renaissance mythographers' stereotypical view of the enchantress. Because Servius was writing after the time when Christianity was accepted as the religion of the empire, it is likely that his labeling of Circe as a prostitute was influenced by negative Christian attitudes toward sexuality.

For intellectuals who preferred commentary to epic narrative, the complex goddess had already been eclipsed by the witch as far back as Plato's time. Even the first of her allegorical interpreters had seen Circe as purely negative, and this one-sided attitude remains remarkably consistent from Stoic to Neo-Platonist to Christian. Gathered in a hypothetical room, these commentators might quibble among themselves about why she was dangerous or evil, but only Boethius, who considers her worthy of only brief notice, might argue with the justice of that description. She would find no real champions.

Hence Circe, who survived as a remnant of the ancient Goddess within the Mycenaean setting of Homer's epic, could not survive with plenitude and divinity intact in the Christian West.

5

Renaissance Circes

Legend has it that pages of Homer's poems reentered Italy as a packing material buffering bottles of wine imported by a merchant in the fourteenth century. Perhaps the legend is true, for certainly Petrarch and his circle knew and valued some of Homer's work by the latter part of the Trecento. Widespread appreciation of the *Iliad* and the *Odyssey* in western Europe did not develop, however, until over a hundred years later, until after Constantinople had fallen to the Turks and some of the Byzantine Homeric scholars centered there had emigrated to Florence with their texts.[1] The first printed edition of Homer appeared in Florence in 1488, shortly to be translated into Latin and thereafter accessible to the European learned community.[2] Now the malevolent-beneficent goddess of the *Odyssey* could take her place beside Virgil's and particularly Ovid's later versions of her character and could be shaped against prevailing Christian and patristic notions of women's nature. The resultant stereotype of the seductive, dangerous, controlling woman was a dark muse for many European poets of the sixteenth and seventeenth centuries. Ariosto, Tasso, Grandi, Trissino, Spenser, Calderón, Milton: all were drawn to this figure and recreated her in some form. Never before or after has Circe had such a hold on the Western imagination.

Why—besides the obvious reasons that she was rediscovered in Homer and that classical mythology had become modish among the literate—did Circe exert such a powerful fascination during and right after the Renaissance? Nothing attracts like the forbidden, which Circe voluptuously embodied. Her surge in popularity was in large part due to

Augustine, whose harsh view that sexuality is the brand of sin upon human nature had been promulgated by the church for centuries. Circe—
particularly Ovid's caricature of her—exemplified and flaunted passions
that believers were taught to view not merely as spiritually distracting
but as *shameful,* passions that they therefore needed to deny in themselves and project onto proxies. What better proxy than the ready-made,
already distorted image of a lusty female powerful enough to make males
her groveling, innocent thralls? The stereotypical Circe thus answered a
pressing psychological need, and she received much exposure in Renaissance mythographies and emblem books.

She also acted as a magnet for some of the anxieties of the age. More
clearly than any other mythic figure, Circe embodied the unsettling power of woman *over* man: a power that ran counter to the established man-
over-woman sexual hierarchy that was one of the few secure anchors in
this era of tumultuous economic, political, and religious change. The
magical or supernatural quality of her powers was also disturbing, for
what was to differentiate it from the influence of demons, or her deeds
from witchcraft? She was the mythic "witch" most familiar to this period still sufficiently medieval to believe in the power of witches and
sufficiently disturbed to see these powers almost everywhere.

In this chapter I explore the stereotypical Renaissance Circe, as well
as a few departures from the stereotype. Her reincarnations by sixteenth-
and seventeenth-century poets will be left for succeeding chapters.

In 1531 the prototype of a characteristic Renaissance genre, the emblem book, first appeared. This was the *Emblemata* of Andreas Alciati,
which used visual images to communicate moralistic messages made explicit in coordinated mottoes and poems. Alciati's book was vastly popular, probably because it offered crisp and accessible interpretations of
classical learning in messages bold and unambiguous as the lines of its
woodcuts. The *Emblemata* went through many editions, including some
with alternative woodcuts and some with additional commentary. It may
have been translated from Latin into English in 1551, though, if so, no
copies of that edition have survived.[3] In 1586 Geffrey Whitney borrowed
some of the woodcuts from the 1581 Dutch edition of Alciati, adding
some from other sources as well and then publishing the collection as
A Choice of Emblemes accompanied by English verses. Whitney or Alciati were part of the libraries of several Elizabethan poets; certainly
Spenser was well acquainted with the emblem form by the time he wrote

The Shepheardes Calender. In their premise that a surface image can teach moral meanings, emblem books are typical of medieval as well as Renaissance allegorical thinking. They draw, however, on many other sources of classical mythology besides Ovid's *Metamorphoses,* the only collection accessible to the Middle Ages.

Comparison of the Circe emblems from the 1551 Leiden edition of Alciati, the 1621 Padua edition (figure 14), and the 1586 Whitney volume (figure 15) reveals an important similarity. In each the female figure, holding some token of power, towers over her hapless victims, who kneel or cower before her. The unmediated visual message is "beware of the woman who stands over you." These woodcuts accord well with the woman-on-top *topos* that sported with—but did not seriously challenge—the prevailing sexual order of the times. In popular art of the sixteenth century, the spectacle of an aggressive woman dominating a henpecked man was not at all unusual.[4] An engraving by Martin Treu, from about 1540 or shortly thereafter, shows a determined wife, curls flying, in the process of beating a husband bent before her (figure 16). In it she is the one wearing the pants. Much better known was Hans Baldung Grien's 1513 image of Phyllis riding Aristotle (figure 17), based on the legend that Alexander's beautiful favorite got revenge on his woman-scorning tutor by persuading the old sage to get down on all fours and carry her naked through the garden as a prelude to enjoying her sexual favors. In the Grien woodcut youth triumphs over age, passion over reason, and the female over the male. It represents the kind of reversal of hierarchies that the hierarchical societies of the Renaissance loved to contemplate and act out in festivals, as long as the acting out could be safely contained.

The emblem book images of Circe with her rod or bowl can be interpreted as high-toned examples of this popular woman-on-top *topos.* Myth—perhaps because it seemed safely removed from daily life—was combed for examples of what might be expected if females were allowed to assume a dominant position in society and in relationship. Among the literati, who were newly familiar with Herodotos's exotic tales, references to Amazons proliferated.[5] These mythical Amazons and the stereotypical Circe evoked a mixture of fascination and horror because they touched a nerve in the culture. Confronted with daily evidence of women's competence and strength,[6] but clinging to an ideology that held that women were created inferior, many people in early modern Europe were willing to entertain the notion that women could be dominant or su-

Cauendum à meretricibus.

EMBLEMA LXXVI.

SOLE fatæ Circes tam magna potentia fertur ,
    Verterit vt multos in noua monstra viros .
Testis equum domitor Picus , tum Scylla biformis ,
    Atque Ithaci postquàm vina bibere sues .
Indicat illustri meretricem nomine Circe ;
    Et rationem animi perdere , quisquis amat .

Figure 14. Circe in Alciati's *Emblemata,* Padua, 1621.

82   *Homines voluptatibus transformantur.*

Virgil.Aeneid.7.
Ouid. Metam.
lib. 14.

SEE here VLISSES men, transformed ftraunge to heare:
Some had the fhape of Goates, and Hogges, fome Apes, and
Affes weare.
Who, when they might haue had their former fhape againe,
They did refufe, and rather wifh'd, ftill brutifhe to remaine.
Which fhowes thofe foolifhe forte, whome wicked loue dothe thrall,
Like brutifhe beaftes do paffe theire time, and haue no fence at all.
And thoughe that wifedome woulde, they fhoulde againe retire,
Yet, they had rather CIRCES ferue, and burne in theire defire.
Then, loue the onelie croffe, that clogges the worlde with care,
Oh ftoppe your eares, and fhutte your eies, of CIRCES cuppes beware.

Horat.1. Epiſt.1.

Sirenum voces, & Circes pocula noſti:
Quæ ſi cum ſociis ſtultus, cupiduſq; bibiſſet,
Sub domina meretrice fuiſſet turpis, & excors,
Vixiſſet canis immundus, vel amica luto ſus.

Figure 15. Circe in Whitney's *A Choice of Emblemes*, 1586.

Figure 16. Husband-dominator in engraving by Martin Treu, ca. 1540-43.

Figure 17. "Aristotle and Phyllis," woodcut by Hans Grien, 1513.

perior as long as that notion did not intrude on their actual social or economic arrangements. Almost no one, however, questioned the idea of hierarchy itself; dominance-submission patterns might be flipped in the imagination, but they were not resolved there into equality.[7]

Several of the details of Alciati's woodcuts indicate that Homer's Circe was not the one he had in mind. In the Leiden illustration, curs and baboons—creatures not indigenous to Aiaia—cluster round her feet. In the Padua one, Circe holds out her brew while two of Ulysses' sailors drink it from smaller bowls as they kneel in a small open boat. Their posture is that of communicants, hers that of a priestess serving a Black Mass. Both images are accompanied by the motto *Cavendum a meretricibus* ("Beware of Prostitutes")—showing that Alciati, like Servius, casts her as a whore. In the six-line verse that accompanies each image he refers to Picus and Scylla as well as "the men of Ithaca," revealing Ovid to be his primary source. The last line, "and whoever loves her has lost his mind's reason," makes clear that Alciati agrees with the long line of commentators who saw Circe's transformations of men as metaphorical and therefore able to be suffered again and again by any male who, in the grip of the sexual obsession she inspired, sacrificed his will to pursue other goals. She, as the whore, as the unclean female, is the one blamed for sexual feelings and their consequences.

The motto accompanying Whitney's borrowed woodcut of Circe is, in fact, "Men are transformed by pleasure" (*Homines voluptatibus transformantur*).[8] In this image the vile deed has already been accomplished, and Circe strokes the back of a hog with her wand while an ass, a goat, and a dog docilely look on. Whitney cites Virgil and Ovid as sources for his verse, but his main source must have been a little-known dialogue by Plutarch, "Whether Beasts Have Reason," in which one recalcitrant victim of Circe eloquently expounds his reasons for preferring life as a hog and for refusing retransformation.[9] According to Whitney, *all* of Ulysses' men refused this offer "and rather wish'd, still brutishe to remaine." He concludes his verse with a quaint but wholesale condemnation of sexual love itself: "love the onelie crosse, that clogges the world with care, / Oh stoppe your eares, and shutte your eies, of Circe's cup beware." A similar admonition to remain sealed from desire, lest the self be polluted by it, can be found in Whitney's verse accompanying the Sirens emblem. These enterprising Sirens flop out into the surf with horns and lyres, but wise Ulysses discerns their mermaid shapes beneath the waves and remains cold to their charms. "The face, he lik'de: the nether parte, did loathe" is the way Whitney puts it.[10] The line recalls Lear's rant that "down from the waist" women are centaurs. It also brings to mind Spenser's Errour and Duessa, the one attractive in her upper body and the other attractive on the surface, but both loathsome in their private parts.

A distrust of and revulsion against female sexuality was endemic in early modern Europe, having been fostered by centuries of patristic influence upon Christian doctrine. The conviction of two Dominican inquisitors who were the authors of a well-known witch-hunting manual published in 1486, the *Malleus Maleficarum,* that "all witchcraft comes from carnal lust, which is in women insatiable" was merely commonly held opinion given an exaggerated twist.[11] In his popular *Anatomy of Melancholy,* which appeared in 1621, Robert Burton wrote that lust was "worse . . . in women than in men"; he cited examples of caterwauling old widows who "must have a stallion, a champion" and of fourteen-year-old girls who "offer themselves and plainly rage."[12] This ferociously strong female libido, thought to be an attribute of all women during the Middle Ages and Renaissance but only of "bad" ones by the time of Victoria, becomes comprehensible only when we reflect that it included the exteriorized and projected sexual feelings of men. Made to bear the carnality of both sexes, women were then endowed by men with correspondingly capacious libidos. Alciati's and Whitney's woodcuts merely reflect these psychodynamics.

Whatever their shortcomings in complexity, these emblem books have the virtue of making graphic the root of the fear evoked by the Circe myth: the fear of surrender to, of engulfment by, sexual feelings. Most of the entries for her in Renaissance dictionaries are just as tiresomely negative, but the information they present does not cohere around any central point. Thomas Cooper, in his 1548 augmented edition of Thomas Elyot's Latin-English dictionary, mentions that Circe was once married to the king of the Scythians, whom she poisoned so that she could become a tyrant in her own right. She was then expelled by her rebellious subjects, according to Cooper, and later fled to a deserted island. He gives no source for this obscure twist to her myth, which also appears in Natalis Comes' 1551 compendium of mythology. Comes attributes this legend to Dionysiodorus and uses it to explain Circe's emigration from the region of the Black Sea to the coast of Italy.[13] The Elyot-Cooper dictionary does show, unmistakably, that its editor has read the *Odyssey,* for he ends his Circe entry with a fact about her that had been suppressed in Homeric commentary for roughly twenty centuries: that she caused Odysseus's men to become younger and more beautiful than they were before!

Cooper's 1573 *Thesaurus Linguae Romanae et Brittanica* and John Florio's *A World of Words,* an Italian-English dictionary published in 1598, do not contain entries for Circe per se, but both mention an herb that bore a variation of her name. "Circea" or "Circaeium" was also known as mandrake, the plant whose forked, man-shaped root was used to make a potent but dangerous narcotic syrup. Perhaps Pliny, the ancient authority Cooper cites for this identification, imagined the herb as the *pharmakon kakon* Circe mixed with her barley, cheese, and Pramnian wine.

The last of the Renaissance dictionaries at which I have glanced, Ambrogio Calepino's eight-language lexicon published in 1609, contains in its entry for Circe a wealth of information drawn from various sources. She murdered her husband, the king of the Sarmatians;[14] she mothered Telegonos; she ruled cruelly and poorly; she loved inordinately. Readers basing their knowledge solely on what Calepino and his fellow lexicographers said about the enchantress would have come away with treasures of odd information, but no narrative consistency or sense.

To remedy that deficiency, they could have turned to Natalis Comes' *Mythologiae,* the most famous and influential of the Renaissance mythographies and, like Alciati's *Emblemata,* a likely volume to be found in the libraries of Renaissance poets. It was first published in 1551 and was later issued in various editions. Comes' organizational strategy was thorough; he begins each entry by citing and briefly quoting from an abundance of classical sources, then he ambitiously presumes to tell his readers what they all mean. In his explication of names at the back of his work, Comes—with complete originality—derives Circe's name from the Greek *kirnasthai,* the passive or middle form of *kirnao,* meaning "to mix wine with water." After reading his commentary, one realizes that Comes has put aside the literal meaning of this verb and instead uses it in a most imaginative way. He correlates it with the Latin verb *miscendo,* which has definite sexual connotations.

Comes sees Circe herself as a mixture of two elements, heat and water, because of her derivation from Perse, daughter of Oceanos, and Helios, god of the sun. This pedigree, Comes believed, aptly qualified her to be the power supervising sex and births, for "lust is made in animals out of moisture and heat." Therefore, "the conception and begin-

ning of those things which are generated by the body belong to the powers of Circe, as she was said to be the daughter of the sun and the daughter of the ocean."[15] He sees her as personifying Nature itself, as a daughter of the elements who supervises their mingling and brings forth new
forms. Comes, however, sees nothing sublime in this process and never
refers to her as *dea*. To him the natural and the divine are antithetical.
And so she represents "the worthless force of nature," which is unable
to corrupt the "divine affable reason" and "immortal soul" of Odysseus.[16]
Comes is essentially reviving Porphyry's interpretation of the incident,
though he avoids Neo-Platonic terminology and uses a slightly Chris-
tianized vocabulary. What else could the moly represent to Comes but
grace—the "divine mercy" that is manifested in "the gift of Mercury"?
The logical next step for Comes would have been to condemn nature
as a corruption wrought by Satan and to label Circe as his handmaid
and witch, but something—perhaps his fundamental respect for mythology—prevents him from doing so.

Arthur Golding, whose 1567 English translation of the *Metamorpho-*
ses was used by Shakespeare, had fewer scruples about labeling. In his
"Epistle" prefacing Ovid's poem, Golding instructs both his readers and
his patron, the Earl of Leicester, concerning the proper allegorical interpretations of the tales. "What else are Circe's witchcrafts and en-
chauntments," he asks us, "than the vyle / And filthy pleasures of the
flesh which doo our soules defyle?"[17] His translation of book 14 twice
renders *maga* as "witch," though he also occasionally refers to Circe as
a "goddess" and does not suppress Ovid's usages of *dea*. Fortunately,
Golding does not often allow his ideological disdain of sexual pleasure
to intrude directly upon Ovid's fables of passion. His labeling of Circe
as "witch" is entirely understandable, given Ovid's original caricature of
her and given the fact that his translation was published at a time when
witch hysteria in England was intensifying.[18]

Golding does not seem to have known Comes' *Mythologiae*. But in
1626, when George Sandys, the second English translator of the *Meta-*
morphoses, published his version of the poem "Englished, Mythologized,
and Represented in Figures," he included unattributed translations from
Comes as part of his commentary on book 14. "Circe is so called of mix-
ing," Comes-Sandys says, "because the mixture of the elements is necessary in generation which cannot bee performed but by the motion of
the Sun: Persis, or moisture supplying the place of the female, and the
Sun of the male, which gives forme to the matter: wherefore that com-

mixtion in generation is properly Circe, the issue of these parents."[19] Sandys also told his readers that Ulysses' "immortal soul" was not in danger of being polluted by the *maga's* inferior powers. The influence of Comes on this later English version of Ovid is hardly surprising, given the prestige of his *Mythology* and the age-old persistence of the view of Circe he adopts.

The modern reader, prompted by both common sense and analytical psychology to view sexuality as an integral, essential part of human nature, can only marvel at Comes' assumptions in his commentary on Circe. Why is he so *comfortable* in condemning nature? Why does he fail to see that to reject nature is to reject human life, since we indisputably dwell on this earth and in our bodies? Comes' thinking merely echoes Augustine's and offers good evidence for the grip of Augustine's ideas on centuries of Christian culture. Interpreting mortality and sexual generation as the consequences of Adam and Eve's sin, as processes that did not exist before the bite into forbidden fruit, Augustine thus denied the existence of nature as we know it apart from this sin.[20] Earth felt the suppurating wound then and ever after, or so anyone caught within this cultural conditioning believed.

Every era possesses a leavening of individuals whose clarity of mind and spirit is not obscured by cultural conditioning. Such a person was Giovanni Battista Gelli, born in 1498 in a small town a few kilometers along the Arno from Florence. In his maturity Gelli was a respected member of the circle of Neo-Platonic thinkers at the Florentine Academy and a valued acquaintance of Cosimo de Medici. He insisted, however, on practicing his shoemaker's trade until the end of his life and refused invitations to become a man of letters solely dependent on patronage. The measure of independence the self-educated Gelli preserved for himself is evident in his thought on almost every page of his *Circe*, a collection of dialogues between Ulysses, Circe, and the animals she has transformed that was first published in 1549. Though Gelli is now only an obscure footnote to cultural history, he was well known in his time; his *Circe* ran to five Italian editions before the end of the century, was translated into Latin and most modern languages, and could have been read by Spenser in the 1557 English translation of Henry Iden.

Gelli's *Circe* is a fresh, surprisingly modern, even subversive work enclosed within a seemingly conventional framework. It begins with an obsequious letter of dedication to Cosimo de Medici and ends with the standard denunciation of Circe as a "deceitful and subtle woman" by the one transformed animal (an elephant) who chooses to come back to human shape. In between, Gelli gently and wittily exposes the sexism of his own and prior times—including that expressed in Aristotle's philosophy—and shows himself to be cognizant of the limits of language itself. On almost every page the animating sentiment is that it is difficult to be human, that consciousness is a painful burden. Not the least among Gelli's subversions is recreating the character of Homer's Circe and endowing her with a lively, intelligent voice.

The scheme of the work is borrowed from Plutarch's "Whether Beasts Have Reason." Ulysses, finally restless on Circe's island, tells her that he wishes to go back to Ithaca and to take with him any of her menagerie who were originally Greeks. Circe—dignified, aware of her excellence, in all respects akin to the lover Homer's Odysseus addresses as *potnia*, Lady—replies that he is free to go himself, but may take with him only those countrymen whom he can persuade to become human again. To aid his persuasions, she promises to bestow the ability to speak upon any animal with whom he wishes to converse. Ulysses then tries out his oratorical powers on a variety of creatures from the lower half of the Great Chain of Being: an oyster, a mole, a hare (who describes metamorphosis as "an experience which I can compare to nothing so aptly as to falling into a delicious and pleasant sleep"),[21] a deer, a dog, a horse, an elephant, and others. The horse, whom Gelli presents as an exemplar of temperance, speaks for practically all of them when he says "while I was a man, I liked my condition well enough, and had a very low opinion of beasts; but now I have tried their way of living, I am resolved to live and die like a horse" (113). Against such contentment, Ulysses' eloquence grows blunt. He comes away rather shaken in his own sense of identity, which depends heavily on verbal resourcefulness. Most of the dialogues are exercises in mutual incomprehension; only the two I will examine in more detail end in agreement.

The deer is the only one of the animals who is female and the only one who wins Ulysses over to her point of view. He starts off as an egregious sexist, ready to walk away when he discovers the deer's femaleness, for he is convinced that "you women merely confound yourselves when you consider too long, for your mental capacities are but very shallow" (84). Nevertheless, he pauses to listen to her arguments. The doe, like the Wife of Bath, shows off her classical learning, refuting Aristotle's ideas about sexual reproduction with a heavy dose of common sense:

"We are so scorned that some of your wise men have asserted that we are not of the same species; others have asserted that a female is only a spoiled male or that nature has somehow been deficient in producing them. Now this is obviously directly contrary to the law of nature, for we are as necessary for the generation of men as man himself is" (ibid.).[22] She also blames men for women's lack of achievement in historical times, for "you confine them within the walls of your house to such sordid business as is fit only for slaves, saying that only she is praiseworthy whose actions exceed not the limits of her own house" (85). Here the doe sounds like a refugee from Periclean Athens, disgusted with its mores. Lastly and even more daringly, she rails against the sexual double standard itself: "Why isn't a family tainted by your unbridled appetites as you pretend it would be by ours?" she asks Ulysses (90).

The best evidence that Gelli's Ulysses has preserved his Homeric suppleness of mind and sympathetic understanding of the feminine is his gracious capitulation to the doe's arguments. He comes to realize that "being a deer, she enjoys liberty, the most desirable thing in the world, whereas, should she be a woman again, she must become a servant, than which nothing is more irksome to a real human being" (96).

Gelli's quite remarkable feminism here is not muted by its playful context. No other Renaissance thinker except Agrippa sees so acutely that the inferior social and political position of women results from cultural bias and not from nature.[23] At a time when Aristotle's *Politics* and *On the Generation of Animals* had added a powerful ancient authority to the chorus of Christian fathers and clergy who denounced women as inferior by nature, and when even humanists who advocated education for women did not assume their full equality, Gelli stands almost alone in implying that women are as deserving of liberty and self-determination as men. He expresses his feminism through humor and indirection, but he does so much more ably than most of the Renaissance "defenders" of women did in their formal polemics.[24]

The other dialogue in Gelli's *Circe* that has a clear winner is the last and most complex of the volume. Ulysses succeeds in convincing an elephant that humans, because of their spiritual cravings and dim intimations of a more perfect form of existence, are superior to beasts. Here Ulysses draws heavily on the Neo-Platonic philosophy of Marsilio Ficino, which Gelli knew well. And so the elephant chooses to become a man again. A hunger for the divine awakens in him as his limbs shrink and smooth to human shape. His first impulse after re-metamorphosis is to give thanks to God. His second is to denounce Circe as a "perni-cious enchantress" who robs her pets of their reason. (He quickly for-gets that he is human again only by her dispensation.) Ulysses does not join the elephant in insulting Circe, with whom he remains on courtly terms. He freely admits, however, that he desires nothing more than leav-ing her isle (179).

What is Gelli's own point of view in this ending? Does he agree with the elephant's ingratitude, as he seems to agree with his affinity for Neo-Platonic thought? Since we know relatively little about Gelli, there is no way of answering these questions with certainty. His book leaves the overall impression of being a good-natured, gently ironic exposé of hu-man arrogance. There is a fair possibility that Gelli's irony extends to its last pages as well and that, through this portrait of the elephant-in-grate, he is commenting tongue-in-cheek on the human propensity to devalue the natural as soon as our consciousness of the transcendent awakens. Gelli as philosopher-shoemaker was uniquely equipped to rec-ognize this propensity, and, in describing the elephant's tandem impulses to pray and to denounce immediately upon regaining human form, he may well be satirizing the way the loftiest of thinkers often turn out to be biased or prudish regarding the natural world. Gelli's seeming agree-ment with the orthodox allegorical view of Circe in this last dialogue could be camouflage—and camouflage that is part of his irony. His over-all portrait of the queen of metamorphoses is complex and original, very different in spirit from the brief, negative comments about her in writ-ings by other members of the Florentine Platonic Academy.[25]

At least one other Renaissance Italian approached Circe from a com-pletely fresh point of view: Giordano Bruno, the Neopolitan philoso-pher and scientific thinker whose challenges to traditional earth-centered cosmology caused him to be put to death by the Inquisition in 1600. An intellectual maverick far ahead of his time, Bruno saw nature as con-stantly evolving through a dialectical process in which contraries strug-gle, subsume, and give rise to each other. The hierarchical conception of the universe common to both Christianity and Neo-Platonism had no place in Bruno's thought. To him, the spiritual and the corporeal were contraries to be brought into harmony, the infinite was to be found in the finite. William Blake's later dictum that "Eternity is in love with the productions of Time" captures much of the gist of Bruno's thinking.

Bruno regarded Circe as a symbolic figure, the doyenne of Time's pro-ductions, and was much intrigued by her role. She appears in two of his works, the early *Cantus Circaeus* (or "Incantation of Circe") and the later and more important *De gli eroici furori* ("The Heroic Frenzies"), published in London in 1585. This latter work, a compendium of sonnets, emblems, and philosophical dialogues, quaint in form but not in ideas, features Circe in its concluding dialogue. As the turner of the wheel of incarnation, the goddess who, Bruno says, allegorically represents "the generative matter of all things,"[26] this Circe bears an uncanny resemblance to Porphyry's Neo-Platonic one. Bruno's conception of her, however, is much larger; he endows her with a vision of the soul's pilgrimage and with a knowledge of what incarnation means to that pilgrimage. He thus restores to her her long-lost competence as moral guide.

In the story he tells, nine men, all rejected by the same beautiful but reluctant lady, happen upon Circe and her gorgeous palace. They recognize her as a goddess and fall on their knees before her, entreating her to give them some pharmaceutical potion that will change the lady's mind. Instead, she strikes them blind and gives them a sealed vessel containing waters that she tells them can be poured out only when "lofty wisdom and noble chastity and beauty together apply their hands to it."[27] Even as she blinds them she makes them into seekers. Like Oedipus or Odysseus, they wander lost and miserable, ending up ten years later in England by the banks of the Thames, whose nymphs take mercy on them. Diana, the foremost nymph, opens the vessel with ease and sprinkles them with its waters. Suddenly they *see*—not only the light they lost long ago, but also "the image of the supreme good on earth," who is Diana herself. The dialogue ends with them joyously singing praise to Circe, to rocks and twigs and thorns and all things of the earth, to the wheel of Creation itself.

Allegorically, Bruno's tale is a fable about learning to recognize the infinite and eternal within the forms of the finite. It affirms earthly experience in a way that Christianity did not, though it stops short of praising sexuality. Diana's hands are chaste—like those of Elizabeth, whose favor Bruno was courting with this work. To a modern reader, *De gli eroici furori* seems a period piece in which the writer's imagination remains partially confined within the forms of his time. His vision of a Circe with vision, however, harkens back to Homer. Beside this Circe, as beside Gelli's, those of the Renaissance mythographers reveal themselves as figments of a stale, programmed imagination shaped by unexamined prejudices acquired secondhand.

Figure 18. "Circe," painting by Dosso Dossi, ca. 1518.

The mystery and power of Circe also attracted sixteenth-century Italian painters. Several works in which she is the primary figure, or in which she shares the focus with Ulysses, survive; they are canvases and frescoes by Dosso Dossi, Pellegrino Tibaldi, and Annibale Carracci. Taken as a whole, these painters' images of the enchantress are more exploratory and less bound by conventional morality than those of the poets and mythographers of their time. Perhaps because they worked with materials more sensuous and immediate than words, these painters seem relatively free of stale preconceptions.

Dosso Dossi, an artist at the court of the d'Estes in Ferrara, was a friend and contemporary of Ariosto, whose *Orlando Furioso* was being read and celebrated all over Europe. In a large painting now in the National Gallery of Art in Washington and dating from early in his career, probably before 1520, Dosso shows a luminous, nude Circe teaching mysteries from her tablets to a small group of animals and birds gathered about her (figure 18). Perhaps she is appealing to their still-human consciousness, which Homer insists Odysseus's men retained in their bestial form. Impassioned and abstracted, gazing diagonally across the canvas and out of its frame, she holds court like a Moses wandered into the Peaceable Kingdom. The painting is one of the best examples of "Dossi's personal style of symbolism—eliptical, arbitrary and elusive."[28] Why the tablets? Why do none of the creatures look at her or each other as she speaks? The immediate visual impression, aided by Dossi's predominantly dark palette, is of mystery, of currents of life arrested mid-breath. Only a stork who dips his bill into the shallow waters of a pond at her feet seems unaffected by this atmosphere of imposed and static peace.

Dosso, as Bernard Berenson speculates, was temperamentally a lover of high romance, able to create it with "a touch of magic" and drawn irresistibly to portraying legendary enchantresses.[29] A *maga* holding tablets presumably full of arcane knowledge is depicted by Dosso not only in this "Circe" but also in his "Sybil" and in a mysterious third painting variously identified as "Circe" or "Melissa." Berenson errs, however, in accepting the traditional identification of the enchantress in this third painting, which has been in the Borghese collection in Rome for centuries, as Circe (figure 19). There is evidence within the painting that its subject derives from Ariosto. To the upper left, miniscule figures of men are either merging into or emerging from the twin trunks of a tree, while at the tree's foot the artist has placed part of an empty suit of armor. These details seem to be a clear visual reference to the episode in canto 6 of the *Orlando Furioso* in which the knight Astolpho, who is imprisoned within a myrtle tree, tells what has happened to him and to other chivalric lovers of the enchantress Alcina.

Since Homer's Circe restricted her transformative efforts to fauna, having nothing to do with trees, it is exceedingly doubtful that Dossi had her in mind when he painted this sumptuous *maga*. Dossi's woman is seated within a magic circle rimmed with cabalistic inscriptions, arrayed in a turban and a gown of richly articulated crimsons and greens. Much of the detailing of the painting suggests an Oriental locale, which would accord with Ariosto's location of Alcina's isle as somewhere between the East Indies and Europe (6.34). The walls and citadel in the right and central background also agree with descriptions of her domain.

But is this enchantress the evil Alcina, who entraps the males she seduces within rocks, trees, and animals, or the good Melissa, who liberates the former's victims? The current expert on the Dossis, Felton Gibbons, identifies her as Melissa, citing her "benign . . . relaxed and calm"

Figure 19. Painting by Dosso Dossi variously identified as Circe, Melissa, or Alcina, ca. 1520.

manner.[30] No doubt Alcina appeared so to the men she drew within her magnetic field; the one indisputable message Ariosto gives us about her is that her pleasant, serene appearance masks a sinister reality. Gibbons argues that "were the magician the evil Alcina . . . presumably the knights in the middle distance would not sit so easily but would have the sense to try to make their escape." This point ignores the evidence of the poem, which describes Alcina's island as filled with enraptured, lolling courtiers. Only after Melissa has released Alcina's cast-off lovers from their plant and animal forms do they depart "with all the hast[e] they might."[31] Since the *maga*'s rod and tablet are Dossi's inventions, nowhere

Figure 20. Fresco of Circe and Ulysses by Pellegrino Tibaldi, ca. 1554. Palazzo Poggi, Bologna.

mentioned in the poem, an identification cannot be based on them. The direction of her gaze, however, provides a clue. If we focus on the upper left of this otherwise richly sensuous painting, looking to the spot where the enchantress herself is gazing—at the homunculi fastened to bark—the impression received is overwhelmingly sinister and grotesque. As if to corroborate this grotesquerie, the dog with whom she shares the foreground stares with uncanny directness at the empty suit of armor, left at the base of the tree like a locust shell. These oddities suggest convincingly that she is Alcina, sister in spirit to Dossi's Circe, whose appearance is also quite lovely.

Pellegrino Tibaldi's fresco of Circe and Ulysses, executed around 1554 and one of a series of dramatic images based on the *Odyssey* in the Room of Ulysses at the Palazzo Poggi in Bologna, is altogether less mysterious (figure 20). Like the fresco of the blinding of Polyphemos found in the same room, it is a celebration of masculine force. In its right center an impossibly muscular Ulysses—naked except for loincloth, cape, and plumed helmet—is arrested mid-reach as he draws his sword. In reaction, Circe and the partially transformed creatures at her feet throw up their arms to protect themselves. Though Circe herself looks athletic and though her high status is indicated by her temple-like palace, Tibaldi

Figure 21. Fresco of Ulysses and Circe by Annibale Carracci, ca. 1595. Palazzo Farnese, Rome.

leaves no doubt about who is going to win this contest. Even Mercury seems to flee in fear from Ulysses' superior power. This fresco, like most of the others in the room, offers straightforward, unallegorical homage to its hyper-masculine hero.

Far more subtle and graceful, and more ambiguous in effect, is Annibale Carracci's fresco of the goddess and hero in the Camerino of the Palazzo Farnese in Rome, "the most impressive of all Renaissance palaces"[32] (figure 21). As a Bolognese, Carracci certainly knew and was influenced by Tibaldi's work; the figure of a man with the head of a swine in the right foreground of his painting, created between 1595 and 1597, has the same posture and placement as one in Tibaldi's. The Ulysses-Circe fresco in the Camerino is one element in an overall ceiling design that allegorically illustrates the theme of Virtue. Specifically, the virtue that this painting is intended to picture is Chastity, for in the oval space right above it appears the figure of a young woman holding a turtledove (this bird was used as the emblem of marital fidelity because when it loses its mate it never seeks another).[33] As a painter, Carracci himself would most likely not have been entrusted to choose the overall scheme for the room; that privilege probably belonged to Fulvio Orsini, a humanist in the service of the Farneses.[34] This circumstance probably explains why the visual impact of the painting does not accord harmoniously with its allegorical intention.

Carracci chose not to follow Tibaldi in emphasizing the hostility in the myth. Instead, he bases his composition on that pregnant moment when Circe holds out the charmed drink and Ulysses accepts it from her. Beneath the shallow bowl, their fingers—like those of Michelangelo's Adam and God—almost touch. Their mutual, yearning gaze (though it is wary yearning on Ulysses' part) also echoes that of the figures in the great painting of the Sistine Chapel ceiling. And Circe's reclining, inclining posture is similar to Adam's. Michelangelo's compositional influence on this fresco seems far more subtle and pervasive than Tibaldi's; it has the effect of emphasizing the cord of attraction between Circe and Ulysses and thus calling into question Ulysses' supposed chastity. From behind the hero's back, Mercury reaches forth surreptitiously to place his moly in the bowl, so the viewer knows that this Ulysses will not surrender to bestiality. But will he surrender to his own, and to her, sexuality? The gravity of the painting and the queenly demeanor of its partially disrobed Circe suggest that he will. Carracci, whether or not he read the *Odyssey*, has captured the spirit of this moment as Homer describes it.

A fresh recreation of the enchantress is also to be found, rather surprisingly, in George Chapman's English translation of the *Odyssey*, published in two parts in 1614–15. I say "surprisingly" because Chapman's cast of mind was nothing if not allegorical. In a note explaining a distinction he has interpolated in line 97 of book 1, concerning the opposing pulls of Odysseus's "judgment" and "affections" as he languishes during his seventh year on Calypso's island, Chapman reveals his conception of the poem as a whole: "This is thus translated the rather to express and approve the Allegorie driven through the whole Odysses, deciphering the intangling of the Wisest in his affections and the torments that breede in every pious minde: to be thereby hindred to arrive so directly as he desires at the proper and onely true naturall countrie of every worthy man, whose haven is heaven and the next life, to which this life is but a sea, in continuall aesture and vexation."[35]

This note is important because it reveals Chapman's faith that moral or philosophical truths lie hidden beneath the literal surface of the *Odyssey*—that Odysseus in struggling toward Ithaca is actually Everyman reaching with yearning for the shores of heaven. Even more significantly, it indicates Chapman's belief in an allegory that is *dynamic,* whose meaning and hero continue to develop through twists and turns of the plot. Chapman, like the Stoic and Neo-Platonic commentators on Homer stretching back two thousand years before him, tends to view human emotions as entanglements, as distractions from the true path indicated by reason or piety. He differs from them, however, in stressing Odysseus's originally passionate and unruly nature. As George Lord writes in what could be regarded as the thesis statement of his *Homeric Renaissance,* "the ethical bias of Chapman's *Odyssey* does not inhere in any attempt to make Ulysses a morally-perfect hero, but rather in the explicit emphasis which Chapman gives to the values which Ulysses must recognize before he can attain happiness."[36]

This ethical bias also allows for fair treatment of problematical goddesses. Chapman, as will become evident, was tempted by the orthodox allegorical Circe, but his own more complicated moral view and his loyalty to Homer prevented him from passing her on. He would have come across this Circe in his chief reference, the parallel Greek-Latin edition of Homer printed with the commentary of Jean de Sponde (Johannes Spondanus), a continental humanist.[37] In his "Argument" heading book 10, Chapman gives a rhymed synopsis of what is about to occur. "All save Euryloches" are

> to swine
> By Circe turned. Their stayes encline
> Ulysses to their search, who got
> Of Mercurie an Antidote,
> (Which Moly was) gainst Circe's charmes,
> And so avoids his souldiers' harmes.
> A yeare with Circe all remaine,
> And then their native forms regaine.
>
> (p. 169)

These lines contain an inaccuracy not found in his translation itself: the information that the Greek sailors wallowed in her sty for a year. They suggest that Chapman might have liked to have made the Homeric Circe worse than she really was, but felt duty-bound to follow the master in having her retransform Ulysses' companions within the day. This tension between what Circe was supposed to be for two thousand years and what Homer shows her to be animates his handling of her character.

For instance, Chapman is somewhat ambiguous concerning her status as a goddess. Though he continually shies away from translating the *thea* in her formulas—*Kirke euplokamos, deine theos audéessa* is rendered by him as "faire-haird, dreadfull, eloquent Circe" (10.175)—he is lavish with the adjective "divine." Her house and her presence are each so described. Generally, Chapman either ignores Homeric formulas or gives nonliteral translations of them, so his repeated balking at translating the *dia theaon* formula may merely be in keeping with this habit. His rendering of *Odysseus polytropos*—literally "Odysseus of many ways" or "moves"—as "the man / Of many virtues—Ithacensian, Deepe-soul'd Ulysses" (10.441–43) is an entirely typical shifting of meaning from the surface to the spirit that Chapman discerns beneath it.

Throughout book 10 and the poem as a whole, Chapman suppresses some of the sensuous details of the great feasting and bathing rituals in Homer. Perhaps these seemed merely repetitive to him; perhaps he saw no particular need for one of Circe's handmaids to massage Ulysses with olive oil after she had lavishly bathed him, or for another to pour water from a golden pitcher into a silver basin. In omitting details like these, however, Chapman changes the quality of Homer's verse, lessening its celebration and acceptance of the delights of the physical world. Because Circe's power is so grounded in these delights, Chapman subtly, perhaps unwittingly, undermines it.

In still other passages in book 10, Chapman devalues what is bodily or physical by adding disparaging judgments not found in the Greek text. When Eurylochus and the twenty-two scared sailors who have been chosen by lot to explore the island with him leave Odysseus and the others by the shore, Homer merely tells us that the former were "crying" (*klaiontes*) and the latter "lamenting" (*goöntas*). Chapman's Ulysses remarks: "All . . . tooke leave with teares, and our eyes wore / The same wet badge of weake humanity" (10.278–79). Homer's hero would never say such a thing, for in the Greek text masculine tears are a simple fact of nature, like breath or thunder or tides. Similarly, when Chapman's Ulysses is invited to mount Circe's bed, he thinks of his men and hesitates, afraid "that I might likewise leade / A beast's life with thee, softn'd, naked stript, / That in my blood thy banes may more be steept" (10.452–54). In justice to Chapman, it should be pointed out that this is very likely *exactly* what Odysseus fears from mingling sexually with Circe and hence he makes her swear a great oath before he touches her. Homer, however, is not as explicit. All Odysseus says to the goddess is that he is afraid "you might place some evil on me while naked and unmanned" (10.341). The connotation of sexuality as bestiality does not emerge from the Greek text.

Whatever Chapman takes away from Circe by devaluing the bodily and the concrete, he gives back by emphasizing her importance as a moral teacher. Circe assumes this role in book 12 of the Greek text when she gives Odysseus sailing directions and tells him of the restraints he must impose on himself and his men if he wishes ever to see Ithaca again. Previous believers in the allegorical meaning of Circe had never dared to comment on this long and crucial passage, for to call attention to it would have been to destroy their own credibility. Because Chapman's vision of allegory is dynamic, emphasizing the spiritual education of Ulysses, he is comfortable with the positive teaching role Circe assumes here and even adds to the fullness of Homer's descriptions. In lines 25–27 of the Greek text the enchantress, having singled out Odysseus from the crowd feasting on her shores, tells him "I will show you the way and point out each [pitfall], lest you, suffering, come to grief on land or sea in some bad sack of trouble." Chapman's version is as follows:

> Your way, and every act ye must addresse,
> My knowledge of their order shall designe,
> Lest with your owne bad counsels ye encline
> Events as bad against ye, and sustaine
> By sea and shore the wofull ends that raigne
> In wilfull actions.
>
> (12.37–42)

She adopts here the rather patronizing tone of one who is perfectly sure she possesses superior knowledge, sounding like a mother chiding a son for his headstrong folly.

Chapman's translation of her warning against the Sirens makes clear that it is misguided *desire* that causes such folly:

> whosoever shall
> (For want of knowledge mov'd) but heare the call
> Of any Siren, he will so despise
> Both wife and children for their sorceries,
> That never home turnes his affection's streame,

Nor they take joy in him, nor he in them.
The Sirens will so soften with their song
(Shrill and in sensuall appetite so strong)
His loose affections that he gives them head.
                              (12.58–66)

Homer's passage is grammatically puzzling and difficult to translate in a way that is both literal and smooth. It goes something like this: "Whoever, enticed by folly, listens to the voice of the Sirens—his wife and small children will not take joy in him. Nor will he, returning home, stand near [them]. For the Sirens will charm him with their piercing songs to stay within their meadows" (12.41–45).[38] Chapman's interpretation of *ou ganuntai* as "despise" is pure license, and his translation of *ligurei* as "shrill and in sensuall appetite so strong" is an exaggeration that sheds more light on his own assumptions than on Homer's text. Clearly there is a pro-spirit, anti-senses bias to his translation. Yet in spite of this bias, Chapman reads the *Odyssey* freshly. If his Circe were the traditional allegorical one, the Queen of Lust, she would never be warning Ulysses against "sensuall appetites."

    The last of Circe's instructions I wish to examine is her advice to Ulysses about how to pass through the strait of Scylla and Charybdis with minimal losses. She tells him to steer close to the rock of Scylla, and not to pause to fight when the monster grabs six of his men to feed her six mouths. Ulysses does not readily accept this prescription for seemingly cowardly behavior. When he protests, Circe replies:

O unhappy! art thou yet
Enflam'd with warre, and thirst to drink thy swet?
Not to the Gods give up both Armes and will?
She deathlesse is, and that immortall ill
Grave, harsh, outragious, not to be subdu'd
That men must suffer till they be renew'd,
Nor lives there any virtue that can flie
The vicious outrage of their crueltie,
Shouldst thou put Armes on, and approach the Rocke,
I fear sixe more must expiate the shocke.
Six heads sixe men aske still.
                              (12.177–87)

Chapman here introduces some Christian overtones ("renew'd" in the sense of "redeemed," "expiated") but otherwise his version follows the original closely. In both Homer and his Jacobean translator the passage is important, for it points out the limits of military heroism. These limits chafe the nature of Ulysses, who arms for the encounter anyway:

> then even I forgot to shunne the harme
> Circe forewarnd, who willd I should not arme,
> Nor shew my selfe to Scylla, lest in vaine
> I ventur'd life. Yet could not I containe,
> But arm'd at all parts and two lances tooke.
>
> (12.336–40)

In both the original and in Chapman, he proves that he has half-learned from Circe in spite of himself, for he does not pause at Scylla's rock to strike back at her even though he has grabbed his weapons. After a few more violent misadventures, the rest of this lesson about human and heroic limits finally penetrates Ulysses' character. When, battered and brine-streaked, he finally comes to rest on the civilized earth of Scheria at the end of book 5, he kisses it in gratitude. And he realizes that he owes his safe landing to the river god to whom he has humbly prayed. Chapman emphasizes the difficult knowledge that Circe has helped Ulysses to gain by adding two lines not to be found in Homer to his hero's reflective speech: "But he that fights with heaven, or with the sea, / To Indiscretion addes Impietie" (5.642–43). As George Lord remarks, "by this interpolation Chapman calls the reader's attention to a major revolution in Ulysses' outlook and prepares us for his glorification of the hero as the essence of virtue."[39]

By emphasizing Circe's role as a moral and spiritual teacher, Chapman restores her lost dignity and casts her as a central character in the dynamic allegory he thought the *Odyssey* to be. Chapman's Circe is not quite Homer's—she does not reign with such splendid entitlement over the pleasures and forms of the flesh—but neither is she a distortion. With tension, verve, and a healthy loyalty to Homer, Chapman succeeded in bringing a magnificent epic into English.

What can we conclude from this survey of Circe in her Renaissance incarnations? Chiefly, the amazing tenacity of a stereotype when it serves a cultural need. Laden with the heavy freight of denied and therefore projected sexuality, the sinister seductress refused to disappear even when the ur-Circe, the goddess in Homer's foundation text, once more became accessible. How could she make her exit when she offered, at least in imagination, a way for men to be overwhelmed by sexual experience and still

remain entirely innocent? "She made me do it," the beasts in her menagerie might well have brayed in chorus. If we compare ancient and Renaissance allegorical readings of the Circe myth, we are struck by the proportionately greater emphasis Renaissance interpreters placed on Circe's
alluring lasciviousness and by their lesser emphasis on Odysseus as representing the triumph of reason. In pre-Christian and particularly pre-Au-
gustinean times, when sex was simply looked upon as part of nature, there
was much less need to use the myth as a source of titillation.

Almost as remarkable as the tenacity of the stereotype is the freedom
of a few thinkers and artists from its grip. Gelli, Bruno, Dossi, Carracci: all communicate their highly individual visions of the enchantress
in a way refreshingly unaffected by cultural conditioning. For them, Circe seems to have offered a figure of female power to hold in mind, approach, and explore without fear.

Of all the writers surveyed, only Chapman—who as translator could
hardly avoid her—seems to have been thoroughly familiar with, and
generally accepting of, *Homer's* Circe. Other readers saw in Homer's figure what they were preconditioned to see. Consider, for instance, the
response of Roger Ascham, the childhood tutor of Queen Elizabeth.
Ascham, who taught his brilliant pupil to converse with him in Greek
"frequently, willingly and moderately well,"[40] certainly read the *Odyssey*
in the original, for he quotes directly from book 10 in one of his essays,
"The Scholemaster." Yet he views Circe only as a figure who deflects a
man from his true path, not as the one who points it out. He warns
against what might happen to a young Englishman sent south on the
Grand Tour: "Some *Circes* shall make him, of a plaine English man, a
right *Italian*. And at length to hell, or to some hellish place, is he like-
lie to go: from whence it is hard returning, although one *Ulysses*, and
that by *Pallas* ayde, and good counsell of *Tiresias* once escaped that horrible Den of deadly darkenes."[41] Did the young Elizabeth share her tutor's jingoistic misreading? Or did she instead recognize in Homer's goddess a kindred spirit, a rare feminine model of great power effectively
wielded, a consummate woman on top?

We shall never know, for information about Elizabeth in the privacy
of her thoughts remains exceedingly scant. Far more frequent are cunningly embellished portraits of her by others, like Spenser's chivalrous
depiction of her as Gloriana, his overt muse in *The Faerie Queene*.

6

Spenser, the Witch, and the Goddesses

The best known Circe figure in English literature is not named Circe. Yet the ability of Acrasia, the seductress of the Bower of Bliss at the end of book 2 of *The Faerie Queene*, to turn the men in whom she has lost sexual interest into animals leaves little doubt about her mythological ancestry. Like Ariosto's Alcina in *Orlando Furioso* and Tasso's Armida in *Gerusalemme Liberata*—her more immediate kin—Acrasia is the negative feminine incarnate, the woman able to deflect men from their selves and their quests, all the more dangerous because she is at first so alluring. Acrasia carries the same allegorical message and weight as the Circe of the Renaissance mythographers but is infinitely more powerful because freshly and fully envisioned, because we as readers can *see* the dew that her "late sweet toyle" of lovemaking has left on her skin.

Acrasia's position within the overall structure of *The Faerie Queene* is as important as Circe's in the *Odyssey.* Both act and appear at a major (perhaps *the* major) hinge of their respective poems. Thoroughly lost before he finds Circe, Odysseus comes away from their encounter with a renewed sense of direction toward Ithaca. Guyon, the rather priggish Knight of Temperance who seeks out and defeats Acrasia, is not, as far as we know, changed or marked by the experience, but the imagination of Spenser himself seems liberated by what occurs in Acrasia's domain. Before this point, he keeps firm, even rigid, control of his allegories. There are few moral ambiguities in the Book of Holiness or, until its very last verses, the Book of Temperance. Each book centers around the successful completion of a quest proposed by Gloriana the Faerie Queene, who represents Queen Elizabeth within the poem.[1] Each contains a host of good or evil characters, but few that are morally complicated or neutral.

After creating and destroying the Bower of Bliss, having called forth and released the intense imaginative energies that these tasks demanded, Spenser seems to realize that there are more things in Faeryland than he had dreamt of in his previous philosophy of allegorical tidiness. He jettisons—temporarily at least—both his polarized view of the feminine and his loyalty to the one-fulfilled-quest-per-book scheme that was his poem's original plan. Instead of telling elaborate tales of dominance and submission, Spenser begins to explore the ways in which opposing energies may be brought into concord. And in the later books of *The Faerie Queene* he projects fresh images of feminine sexuality and power: complex images that recall both the great pre-Christian goddesses and the wordly, absolutist power of the Queen.

Let us look more closely at this dynamic and at Acrasia's place at its hinge. Is her defeat connected with the more open imaginative atmosphere that follows it? If so, in what ways? And what relation, if any, does Acrasia's humiliation have with Spenser's eventual revocation of this openness?

In books 1 and 2, Spenser's portrayal of the feminine is thoroughly polarized. The positive female figures, such as Una and Alma, are exemplars rather than women. Because they are already perfect, they contain no tension or conflict and therefore do not stimulate much response from the reader. Una's appeal is primarily iconographic: as she makes her slow way across the plain in the poem's first scene, leading her lamb with Red Cross at her side, she awakens archetypal images of Mary on the road to Bethlehem, of the precious, untainted feminine forever in need of protection. Actually, of course, she is a good deal stronger than Red Cross, the Knight of Holiness who acts as her protector, and by later forgiving his faithlessness and rescuing him from the self-destruction of Despair, she enables him to grow into his proper spiritual stature. Her act of forgiveness has no drama behind it, however, for Spenser imagines her as already far above self-divisons such as the struggle between judgment and compassion. Lovely as Una is, she is not particularly sexual because she is not believably human. The only positive feminine character in the first two books who is endowed with a physical lushness is Charissa in the House of Holiness, whose bodice is permanently loosened because she has so many babes to suckle. Her eroticism is clearly not meant to be important in itself, but rather for the *agapé* that it allegorically expresses. Though "full of great love," she hates "Cupids wanton snare as hell" (1.10.30).

The negative feminine in the first two books is far more interesting because more complex. Not until the appearance of Britomart, his feisty Knight of Chastity in book 3, does Spenser solve the problem of how to characterize goodness in a way that is neither static nor bland. Duessa, Phaedria, Acrasia—the bad women of books 1 and 2—have in common a complicated double nature that couples the appealing with the horrid.

This compounded negative feminine takes on progressively more subtle forms. Errour, the first enemy Spenser's armored Red Cross knight encounters, is a particularly crude representation of it. "Halfe like a serpent horribly displaide," Errour still retains a woman's shape in the upper half of her body (1.1.14.7), making her conformation similar to that of the Sirens whose nether parts Ulysses loathes in Geffrey Whitney's book of emblems. At one point she winds her coils around Red Cross's body in a way that makes unmistakably literal the archetypal threat of the female to the male: engulfment. But he manages to free himself and decapitate her, whereupon she spews forth "a streame of cole black bloud" (1.24.9)—an unsubtle image that nevertheless, like so many of Spenser's, gratifies the reader's eye. Having released some of the terrific energies of destruction that most of *The Faerie Queene*'s knights possess in abundance, Red Cross then rides off lightly to his next encounter. His battle with Errour has demanded no mature self-mastery or spiritual knowledge, only the ability to recognize the obviously vile as vile.

Duessa, the next horribly attractive female he encounters, exposes the shallowness of Red Cross's understanding, of a righteousness that can successfully defeat only external evils. When he meets her he is already fallen, having abandoned Una because he has believed in Archimago's false dream images of her. Duessa (costumed as Fidessa) does not have to work to seduce him; she merely gathers the spoils that have fallen her way.

Comparing Spenser's characterization of Duessa with Ariosto's portrayal of the enchantress Alcina (who also provides a source for Acrasia in 2.12) reveals how Spenser has heightened her loathliness. Whereas Astolpho, the treebound knight in the *Orlando Furioso,* dwells on the bliss of his lovemaking with Alcina for several verses, Spenser's similarly captive Fradubio merely says he "in the witch unweeting ioyd long time"

(2.40.2), and then goes on to describe how he first realized her ugliness when he spied her bathing during a witches' celebration. It was then, Fradubio tells us, that he saw her "neather partes misshapen, monstruous" (2.41.1)—a peculiarly unpleasant detail that the more tolerant Ariosto, writing in a country in which witch-hunting never reached epidemic proportions, does not include. Duessa, unlike Alcina, is unveiled twice, once in warning and once in actuality.

Surely this unrobing is one of the most unfortunately memorable passages of *The Faerie Queene.* What Ariosto accomplishes in one verse of description that never ventures below Alcina's neck, Spenser does in three that focus particularly on Duessa's breasts and "neather parts," including a dung-clotted tail. "Her sowre breath abhominably smeld," Spenser tells us, and "Her dried dugs, like bladders lacking wind, / Hong downe, and filthy matter from them weld" (8.47.5–7). *The Faerie Queene* is full of decapitations, hacked limbs, and other grisly details of physical description, but nowhere in its thousands of lines are any male character's sexual parts so contemptuously described. Spenser's animus here seems redundant, inexplicable, unless we keep in mind that he was writing during the period when witch persecutions in England were at their height, when it was considered acceptable for jailers to search the bodies of aging women for signs of the devil's mark.[2] At the time the first books of *The Faerie Queene* were published, witches were no longer regarded as heretical enemies of the Catholic Church but were prosecuted under secular law.[3] Spenser, in labeling Duessa unequivocally as a witch and in presenting her hidden reality as decrepit, appears to be influenced by the realities of Elizabethan justice.

During the witch hysteria of the sixteenth century, as virulent in England as on the Continent despite the fact that England had a female monarch, the negative bias toward women that had been endemic for centuries and sanctioned by almost all cultural institutions found a very focused expression: it was channeled toward those women who, for reasons of age or poverty, were least able to defend themselves. The bitter question posed by Dekker, Ford, and Rowley's *Witch of Edmonton* to a London theater audience could well have been asked by many of the thousands put to death:

> Cause I am poor, deform'd, ignorant
> And like a bow buckled and bent together . . .

Must I for that be made a common sink
For all the filth and rubbish of Men's tongues
To fall and run into?[4]

Only a few of the citizens of Elizabeth's England publicly protested the injustice of the persecutions; the best known among them was Reginald Scot, who, in his *Discoverie of Witchcraft,* described the witch-hunters' victims as "women which be commonly old, lame, bleare-eied, pale, fowle, and full of wrinkles; poore, sullen, superstitious."[5] Many of them, he said, were beggars who went "from house to house, and from doore to doore for a pot full of milke, yest, drinke, pottage, or some such releefe."[6] Historians who have painstakingly examined local census and court records for information about the witches and their accusers have turned up little that conflicts with Scot's analysis of the persecutions as the scapegoating of the weak.

Spenser's seductive and duplicitous Duessa-Fidessa hardly conforms to the type of women who, in reality, were persecuted as witches. She is neither aged, indigent, or sullen. But she certainly conforms to the profile of what the witch-hunters *said* they were looking for. According to the Dominican authors of the *Malleus Maleficorum,* the bible of these persecutors, carnal lust, particularly women's lust, was the cause of witchcraft. Liberated female sexuality was viewed by these clerics and their followers as the most concentrated source of the world's evil. Duessa and Acrasia—Spenser's predatory vamps—beautifully accord with the ideology, if not with the more cowardly actual practice, of the sixteenth-century witch-hunters. And so does the stereotypical Renaissance Circe.

The more ugly the naked Duessa is revealed to be, the more amazing it becomes that the Knight of Holiness once found her beautiful. In book 1 Spenser shows and explores the power that sexual jealousy and desire have to deflect a virtuous man from his true course; we might understandably but erroneously conclude from the limited evidence of this book that Spenser, like Augustine, views sexuality itself as sin, as the cause of the inevitable human lapse from grace. The saga of Red Cross's fall and eventual redemption, because it does not significantly depart from the doctrines of medieval Christianity, offers a secure, satisfying basis for allegory. Politically, Una may stand for the truth of Anglicanism and Duessa for the whorishness of the Church of Rome, but in a much more fundamental way these two represent the stereotypes of the spotless virgin and the soiled seductress. Spenser sacrifices his own rich response to the feminine by polarizing it in this manner, but in doing so he makes his allegory work.

As far as this polarization of the feminine is concerned, Spenser's switching of his main frame of reference from Christianity in book 1 to classical ethics in book 2 makes not one whit of difference. Once again the bad women are sexual and the good women are pure. Sinful, duplicitous Duessa is now replaced by Acrasia, whose name is the Greek feminine noun for "incontinence"—a word used by Aristotle in his *Nicomachean Ethics* and a concept much discussed by Aquinas in his synthesis of Aristotle and Christianity. Acrasia, Spenser's Circe figure, is the Aristotelean's Satan. By name and nature she is the chief antagonist to the self-mastery that classical writers considered the sign of the superior, rational man; all action in the Book of Temperance tends toward Guyon's final encounter with her. The fact that Spenser's view of the feminine in these first two books remains consistently split is not surprising: he accurately registers Western cultural history, wherein the power of female sexuality was as effectively distrusted by Platonists and Aristotelian rationalists as it was by the church fathers.

Foremost among the good women of book 2 is Alma, the presiding presence of the House of Temperance in canto 9. Paralleling in importance the House of Holiness canto within the Christian framework of book 1, the House of Temperance episode exhibits the limits as well as the tenets of the ideology upon which Spenser bases his second book's structure. Alma herself, representing the rational soul within the well-ordered body, is a bright but insipid figure. She has "not yet felt Cupides wanton rage" (9.18.2). We might well wonder how, with no firsthand knowledge of passion, she has been capable of finding the temperate golden mean between emotional extremes. Arrayed in lily white, Alma leads her visitors on a tour from room to room of her castle, as Spenser, beneath the literal surface, discourses upon the parts and functions of the well-ordered human body.

The first important point to note about this castle/body is that it is difficult to enter, for it has been under seige for seven years. Arthur and Guyon have to drive off a host of enemies before they are free to go in. Though the castle has numerous gates, each representing one of the senses, they are habitually barred to all outsiders. The disturbing but inescapable implication is that the self is a fortress in a hostile world and that the soul is a prisoner within it. Furthermore, the castle's walls are of Egyptian "slime," presumably constructed of the mudbrick common in the Mideast. Spenser's word choice here is very emphatic, forcing us to realize the basic, substantial weakness of the whole edifice. "Soone it must turne to earth," he remarks about the castle; "no earthly thing is sure" (9.21.9). Having emphasized this weakness, Spenser then chooses to concentrate instead on the building's many excellences and balances. Among these are its geometric design, based on the figures of the triangle and the circle, "the one imperfect, mortall, foeminine; / Th'other immortall, perfect, masculine" (9.22.4–5). Spenser's rhetoric here takes on a decidedly Aristotelean cast.[7]

Alma's tour is methodical, leading through the parts of the house analogous to the heart, the chambers of the brain, and most of the digestive system. Only after it is over do we realize that she has ignored the genitals and that perhaps this house has been denatured. A question of inspired common sense that Stephen Greenblatt asks in his commentary on the Bower of Bliss in *Renaissance Self-Fashioning* is also relevant here. "How exactly," Greenblatt wonders, "does one distinguish between inordinate sexual pleasure and temperate sexual pleasure?"[8] Although Spenser implicitly confronts this question in books 3 and 4, he skirts completely around it here. No sexual behavior more compelling than gracious flirtation has a place in the House of Temperance. How does its population get replenished? How, for that matter, do the inhabitants of the house *eat,* since it must be difficult to maintain a food supply while under siege? These abeyances of common sense seem not so much Spenser's as those of the ethical system he is intent upon allegorizing through Alma and her dwelling place. Classical ethics that exalt reason as the completely adequate guide to proper conduct inadequately address the mysteries of sexuality and generation and undervalue the physical basis of life.

The fierce, long-standing battle going on outside the gates of the House of Temperance is inevitable, given the unnaturally calm atmosphere within. Spenser seems to be imagining here what Freud later theorized: that the energies of life only appear to submit to repression, while in reality regathering their strength beyond the boundaries of acknowledgment. The castle's assailants, particularly those attacking the unnamed fifth gate with "darts of sensuall delight" and "stings of carnal lust" are described as bestial and distorted. They are "like Snailes" or "like spy-

ders," "like ugly Urchins thicke and short" (9.13.3–7). Within the allegorical framework of book 2—as within Comes' *Mythologiae*—purely
natural energies are presented as squalid and degenerate.

The climactic encounter of book 2 is, of course, that between Guyon and Acrasia. Since Spenser has now switched his main frame of reference from Christianity to classical ethics, he can no longer appeal to
grace (or revealed truth) as the primary bulwark against the temptation
to inordinate sexual pleasure offered by the seductive woman. All that
stands between Guyon and his surrender to Acrasia is the Palmer and
the reasonable part of himself that the Palmer represents. The battle between the Palmer and Acrasia—or between Guyon's reason and Guyon's lust—is in all respects a more equal encounter than that between
the opposing forces of book 1. Any thoughtful reader knows that this is
a battle that cannot be permanently won, that the best that can be hoped
for is an outcome that mediates the claims of both instinct and the repression of instinct demanded by civilization. Freud's formulation of the
unending hostility between the pleasure and reality principles comes
close to being an abstract rendering of the natural antipathy between
Acrasia and the Palmer, and perhaps for this reason, as well as for its
sexiness and lushness, there is no part of *The Faerie Queene* that modern readers find so persistently fascinating and relevant to themselves as
Guyon's journey through the Bower of Bliss.

Spenser seems to acknowledge tacitly that the outcome of the struggle in the Bower is in doubt, for he carefully controls the *terms* of Guyon's temptation. He handicaps Acrasia by allowing her neither a voice
nor the opportunity to directly confront and seduce his hero. Given these
advantages, Guyon is victorious, though his victory may strike us as
cheap and difficult to admire. What would have happened if Spenser
had allowed Guyon to discover Acrasia alone in her verdant glade, singing in her own melodious voice about the fleeting sweetness of love? if
Guyon had met Acrasia as openly as Odysseus comes to Circe's door?
Since Circe is Acrasia's ultimate ancestor, this comparison is not irrelevant. The high seriousness and mutual challenge that Circe and Odysseus bring to each other have no part in the drama between Guyon and
Acrasia. In order to snare this straw-seductress too carefully controlled
by her creator, the Knight of Temperance reduces himself to a creeping,
peeping Tom. Two thousand years of distorted cultural attitudes about
sexuality intrude upon their encounter.

Though he allows Acrasia herself only a limited role, Spenser does not otherwise constrict the force and allure of sensual pleasure in the Bower of Bliss. His poetry rises to the opportunity that the Bower presents, as if the landscape of that green isle had the power to evoke the excellences distinctive to the genre of poetry itself. Intensity, musicality, gorgeously physical imagery: all appear plentifully in Spenser's verse in canto 12. The Bower is a carefully crafted *locus amoenus,* "A place pickt out by choice of best alive, / That natures worke by art can imitate" (12.42.3–4), and its creation must have challenged Spenser to use all the resources of his own inescapably sensuous art. One of the chief paradoxes of the Bower canto is that in it Spenser himself acts as an Acrasia who lures the reader to become progressively more absorbed in the pleasures of his lines. As Camille Paglia points out, "*The Faerie Queene* often becomes what it condemns, nowhere more overtly than in its voyeurism, in which both poet and reader are deeply implicated."[9]

Not that Spenser puts morality aside, for the Palmer with his rod and his stern words is always present. The figure of the Palmer has no counterpart in Spenser's immediate sources, Ariosto and Tasso. In the *Orlando Furioso* Ruggiero travels to Alcina's isle alone; in the *Gerusalemme Liberata* Carlo and Ubaldo travel to Armida's palace together, but neither acts as mentor to the other. The Palmer's magical rod, which has the power to tame raging beasts,[10] is similar to Ubaldo's charmed staff and to the magic ring (given to him by the benign Melissa) that Ruggiero carries. The rod is important, for with it in hand the Palmer can stroke or smite into submission any force that threatens—even churning, towering seas (12.26.6–7). In the Bower, reason carries a big stick. An instrument with such powers would seem to need a divine provenance; Spenser rather coyly tells us that "Of that same wood it fram'd was cunningly, / Of which Caduceus whilome was made, / Caduceus the rod of Mercury" (12.41.1–3), but he stops short of saying it was the gift of a god. We are left with the paradox of a figure who allegorically represents reason being able to exercise at will suprarational powers. The Palmer's possession of the magic rod is one more instance of Spenser's adjusting the odds for the encounter that is about to take place. Not only does he deprive the Circe-figure of her voice, but he puts the instrument she originally possessed in her first literary incarnation into the hands of her opponent! With the rod to supplement his constant, stern vigilance and with his habit of morally interpreting each phenomenon as it appears, the Palmer offers Guyon a formidable kind of aid. He is like a superego that has magic to fall back upon.

Furthermore, Spenser has endowed the male Palmer with much of the positive side of the original Circe. On the voyage to Acrasia's isle, he functions as a warner and a guide, just as Homer's Circe does when Odysseus is ready to leave her domain. The Palmer steers straight and tells the meaning of each peril as it appears; he and the ferryman together see that Guyon safely voyages past the Gulf of Greediness, the Rock of Vile Reproach, the Wandering Islands, the horde of shapeless sea monsters. The Palmer, again like Homer's Circe, possesses the power to retransform, to bring beasts back to human shape by stroking them with his rod. Stripped of her positive side, the maleficent-beneficent goddess of Aiaia is simplified into a witch, which is the word Spenser uses repeatedly for Acrasia. The fact that she is a "faire Witch" (72.2) merely makes her negativity more dangerous.

Once arrived on the isle and past the raging beasts, the Palmer and Guyon come to the outer gate of the Bower, which is set in an encompassing wall. The function of this gate is not to bar, for it "ever open stood to all" (46.2), but rather to inform about the quality of life within its confines. Spenser follows Tasso in offering a full description of the scenes carved on its surface, but he deliberately changes the myths that Tasso uses as the source of these scenes. Both Spenser's and Tasso's gates are warnings. Tasso's gate is adorned with two mythological tales beautifully worked in silver. One shows Heracles effeminized, serving Omphale, the other the battle of Actium with Antony pursuing Cleopatra and dying in her arms. Of these, the second is emphasized, with its point about the power of a beautiful woman to distract a warrior from his proper task. The myth Spenser substitutes, about Jason and Medea, is altogether more sinister and more charged with male-female enmity. Medea's "furious loving fit" of jealousy issues in two dead children and a bride consumed by flames. "Beware of the death-dealing woman" is the primary message of Spenser's gate. It is a message that has already been hinted at in our preliminary glimpses of Acrasia's victims—in Mordant's name and in the image of Cymochles lying "in his ladies lap entombed" (5.36.3). The secondary meaning of the gate concerns the confusion of appearance with reality, for the waves through which the Argo sails are so artfully carved upon the unreliable medium of ivory (recalling the gate through which false dreams pass in both the *Odyssey* and the *Aeneid*) that they appear as "frothy billowes." Taken together, these messages suggest that within the confines of the wall what appears as the quintessence of life will be, in reality, death-serving.

Our intellectual mastery of Spenser's carefully developed symbology may be beside the point, however. "We can master the iconography, read all the signs correctly, and still respond to the allure of the Bower."[11] Or we can choose to curtail that response. But to say, as one critic has said, that "the Bower of Bliss is a dead thing, a painted artifice gleaming with gold and silver and crystal"[12] amounts to little more than an admission that it is possible, with blinkered senses, to progress through Spenser's lines as determinedly as the Palmer. Spenser's distinctive achievement in this canto is his success in drawing the reader into the conflict between the poet and the moralist in himself.

The signs of how we are *supposed* to interpret events in the Bower continue to multiply. The poet says forthrightly that the false Genius, the porter of the first gate, is "the foe of life" and

> Not that celestiall powre, to whom the care
> Of life, and generation of all
> That liues, pertaines in charge particulare,
> Who wondrous things concerning our welfare,
> And straunge phantomes doth let vs oft forsee,
> And oft of secret ill bids vs beware:
> That is our Selfe, whom though we do not see,
> Yet each doth in him selfe it well perceiue to bee.
>
> (47.2–9)

These lines, besides being the first intriguing hint that a healthy vision of sexuality may yet be found in *The Faerie Queene*, imply that the pleasures of the Bower are sterile and dead-ended. A few verses later we are told that Art (presumably Acrasia's art) "as halfe in scorne / Of niggard Nature, like a pompous bride / Did decke her, and too lauishly adorne" (50.6–8). Tasteless excess would seem to be the hallmark of Acrasia's style, along with a compulsion to meddle with the temperate perfections of nature.

When Spenser describes Excesse personified, however, the sensuousness of his poetry gets in the way of reader disapproval of her. We see her reaching for riper fruit "whose sappy liquor, that with fulnesse sweld, / Into her cup she scruzd" (56.3–4). The images of plenitude, of fruit yielding to the hand's pressure, and the long vowel sounds are so inherently appealing that it is difficult not to perceive Guyon's dashing of her cup to the ground as a spastic overreaction. His emphatic refusal of what she offers is markedly different from the behavior of Odysseus, who takes the cup Circe holds out and drains it, confident that a charm he already possesses (the moly) will protect him from the pernicious drug. Unlike Odysseus, Guyon seems to need violence as a release—probably because, also unlike Odysseus, he will not allow himself the release of pleasure.

Though Spenser tells us that Art and Nature work against each other on Acrasia's island, when we actually see or hear their mixed effects, it is hard not to delight in their harmony. The choir of human and natural sounds at the heart of the Bower is described as a tasteful, delicate blandishment of the ear in which "birds, voyces, instruments, windes, waters, all agree" (70.9). This water music, in which normally discrete sounds and instruments all blend into each other, is probably intended by Spenser as a metaphor for the morally unwholesome dissolution of boundaries that goes on in the Bower. If so, the archetypal association of water with the flow of life transcends and contradicts his limited moral meaning. What living, hearing person would not delight in "silver sounding instruments" that meet "with the base murmure of the waters fall"? To dismiss these harmonies as mere artifice is to undervalue the power and complexity of Spenser's imagination. C. S. Lewis, who emphasizes the rivalry between Art and Nature in his well-known commentary on the Bower, makes his point by selecting his evidence very carefully. Though Lewis dwells on the painted ivy found in verse 61, which he calls "metal vegetation as a garden ornament," he never mentions the beguiling water music.[13] The difficulty of interpretation springs from the inconsistency of Spenser's imagery, for some of it is cued to his moral stance and some of it seems the work of an inspired and freely delighting hedonist.

The main temptation Guyon confronts on the island is offered not by Acrasia (whose access to Guyon Spenser carefully controls), but by two "wanton Maidens" splashing in a streaming fountain. These nymphets, who originate in the fifteenth book of *Gerusalemme Liberata*, are appropriate seductresses for the inexperienced Guyon. Whereas Carlo and Ubaldo pass by them unmoved, Guyon slackens his earnest pace and feels secret pleasure in his "stubborne brest." Spenser, while retaining most of the details of Tasso's description of the bathing girls, heightens the episode's lascivious tone.[14] His girls respond to the awareness that they are being watched with behavior that is teasingly obscene, further kindling Guyon's lust and causing him to incur a firm rebuke from the Palmer. Since Spenser is not willing to allow Guyon to confront Acrasia one-to-one, the bathing girls episode represents the height of his hero's personal temptation in canto 12. Guyon proves himself capable of lustful response and proves himself even more capable of immediate, thoroughgoing repression. In Tasso this episode has a lesser importance, for the relationship between Armida and Rinaldo, her temporarily captive knight, is complex, emotionally charged and thoroughly developed; the splashing girls are just a lively part of the landscape on the way to the enchantress's garden. The adolescent titillation they offer cannot compare to the drama of adult sexuality, even love, between Armida and Rinaldo in the sixteenth and later books.

When Acrasia finally appears upon her bed of roses, we begin to see why Spenser shields Guyon from her allure. Her gaze and touch have the power to draw forth or "sucke" the "molten" spirits of her lovers. Spenser seems to know his demonology well, for this power of Acrasia allies her with the supposed succubi, then being hung or burned in record numbers, who were thought to take possession of men's souls. It has nothing to do with Homer's Circe, who left the consciousness of her victims intact. We see the young knight Verdant lying in a posture of postcoital surrender, his head cradled in Acrasia's lap. His armor, the hard surface that defines correct male personality in Spenser, is hung on a nearby tree. He is like Lucretius's or Botticelli's Mars, who casts aside his military equipment, the better to be ravished by Venus. So completely has Verdant abandoned himself that "ne for honour cared hee, / Ne ought, that did to his aduancement tend, / But in lewd loves, and wastfull luxuree, / His dayes, his goods, his bodie he did spend" (80.6–9). What Acrasia offers is not only erotic pleasure—"long wanton joys"—but the dissolving of the will and the end to all quests.[15] Here the linearity of male ambition gives way to engulfment, embowerment, a soft surrender within a leafy cave.

The Bower of Bliss, in spite of the Palmer's insistence to the contrary, is aptly named. In this tableau of the lovers Spenser vividly shows the power of a moment of pleasure and abandonment to take on an aspect of eternity, to deliver those that share it from all consciousness of goals and of time. That this sense of timelessness is partially illusory—that Acrasia will tire of Verdant within the hour, day, or year—is indisputable; nevertheless, Spenser pictorializes here a common human experience that threatens the orderly, sequential arrangements upon which civilizations are built. Certainly it threatens the accomplishment of quests specified by Elizabeth-Gloriana.

Guyon is only a voyeur to this experience of bliss, yet he reacts to it with a passion of destruction that shows that he has been deeply stirred. Perhaps we most fear what we most desire. Guyon's excessive violence is that of someone threatened at his core. With his heavy sword he turns their bliss to balefulness: "Their groves he feld, their gardens did deface, / Their arbers spoyle, their Cabinets suppresse, / Their banket houses burne, their buildings race, / And of the fairest late, now made the fowlest place" (83.6–9). In destruction he achieves the release that he has otherwise denied himself.

Guyon's razing of the Bower also destroys the allegorical framework of book 2. He reveals himself to be as volatile as Pyrochles (a knight Spenser has earlier introduced to represent the excesses of anger) and therefore a travesty of the Knight of Temperance Spenser has heretofore presented him as being. Guyon's incendiary fit amounts to a tacit—and perhaps not fully intended—admission on Spenser's part that classical ethics cannot adequately contain or address the realities of human passion and need. In this sense, the razing of the Bower is profoundly truthful. Spenser, in apparent contradiction to his original plans for the book, is saying "no" to a system of ethics and allegory that represses full humanity. Is he also saying "no" to a distorted vision of feminine sexuality? In a sense he is, for at the end of book 2 the Renaissance Circe figure, with her age-old allegorical pedigree and her projection-swollen libido, is led away in chains of adamant. Mercifully, she does not appear again in *The Faerie Queene*.

Spenser has now, almost, cleared the ground for construction of a more comprehensive symbolic narrative. A central theme in the following books is "the effort to free the feminine from masculine tyranny."[16] Britomart, the Knight of Chastity,[17] inaugurates this effort by her easy defeat of the proud Guyon in the first verses of book 3. Repression is no match for the power of virtuous love. Although Guyon lingers in the narrative for a few more cantos, he is soon enough gone for good.

Though this study affords space to sketch them with only the briefest of strokes, the remaining books of *The Faerie Queene* offer an unparalleled opportunity to discover what happens when a major artist sweeps cultural stereotypes concerning man-woman relationships out of his mind and attempts to imagine this territory anew. The flames that consume the Bower of Bliss burn away constrictions, thickets of bias that prevent Spenser from convincingly envisioning any nourishing, life-promoting ground of feminine power in books 1 and 2. Never again in

The Faerie Queene does Spenser follow the age-old model of stereotyping the feminine as Lust that must be properly subjugated by masculine Reason.

Goddesses can and do flourish in the later books, whose most memorable character is a beautiful, magnificently nervy, actively seeking *female* knight. Who, having read the complete *Faerie Queene,* could fail to remember with pleasure the sense of sanctuary, sexual celebration, and fertile peace that imbues the garden of Venus and Adonis in 3.6 and the garden surrounding the temple of Venus in 4.10; the atmosphere of reverence and compassion within the hushed temple of Isis in 5.7; the dance of the Graces, turning like a mandala of delight upon the peak of Mt. Acidale in 6.10? These cantos, set like jewels in the midst of their narratives of anxiety-ridden quest and often bearing only a tenuous relationship to the plots of those narratives, offer a vision of the energies released when opposites are resolved and brought to concord. Concord, in fact, is personified by Spenser as the guardian of the threshold to Venus's inner sanctum. Only those tempered by her moral art can advance into the presence of the great goddess, his resurrected Aphrodite, whom Spenser describes as "Mother of laughter, and welspring of blisse."

Spenser seems to know intuitively that if he wants to find a healthier basis for feminine power and sexual relationship he has to return to pre-Christian mythic sources. But, having heard Elizabeth hymned as Diana and Venus virgo, he was also unquestionably aware of the opportunities for inspired Queen-praising these sources afforded.[18] Do Spenser's lovely, bountiful goddesses spring from his share of the collective unconscious, from his own wordly ambitions, or from a tangling of both these sources? Like so much else relating to *The Faerie Queene,* the answer to this question is impossible to ascertain. In any case, Spenser was highly successful as poet-courtier, receiving (after the publication of the first half of *The Faerie Queene*) a yearly pension more generous than that offered to any of his literary contemporaries.

Thoroughly knowledgeable about the hierarchies of power, Spenser was implicated in these hierarchies through his service as Secretary to Lord Grey, Elizabeth's highest imperial official in Ireland. His choice of the "holy Virgin chiefe of nine" as his muse in the Proem to book 1 was shrewdly chivalrous. This clever ellision of Elizabeth with the inspirational goddesses of mythology, however, had its price. Spenser's invocation is not like Homer's ("Sing in me, Muse, and through me tell the story . . .") a straightforward prayer for his verbal powers to be divinely augmented; it is also a plea for the royal ear to attend to his song. This paradox of poet as courtier to a female Prince, and the energy simultaneously evoked and constrained by it, shimmers and veers throughout *The Faerie Queene*.

Elizabeth as goddess, Elizabeth as woman-on-top: these tropes impinge upon Spenser's perception of the mythic feminine, but they do not determine it. For he also excels as poet-explorer of the imagination's archetypal stores, seemingly blessed with unimpeded access to the collective unconscious. This access is clearly not only to the letter of ancient myth (easy enough to come by in this age of popular mythographies), but also to its vivifying spirit. As C. S. Lewis has perceptively observed, Spenser excels nearly all other poets in his ability to translate "into the visible feelings else blind and inarticulate," for he has a profound sympathy with that which makes symbols, "the fundamental tendencies of the human imagination as such."[19]

Nowhere is the tension between these two stances or capabilities (poet-courtier and poet-explorer) more plain than in book 5, the Book of Justice, wherein Faeryland comes perilously close to Elizabethan realpolitik. As Jonathan Goldberg points out, the narrative of *The Faerie Queene* "relentlessly undoes itself"[20]—mainly, I would suggest, because of the conflicting pulls and loyalties within Spenser himself. The remainder of this chapter will focus briefly on one particular undoing, the way in which Spenser's apprehension of the feminine, liberated after the narrative moment when his Circe figure is chained and led away, later becomes repolarized.

The mission of Artegall, the book's knight and the beloved of Britomart, is to liberate Irena (Ireland) from Grantorto (the Pope and Catholicism), who—so Spenser tells us—is forcibly and unjustly depriving her of her heritage.[21] Before he can accomplish this mission, Artegall is taken captive by the Amazon queen Radigund, whose slave he remains, ignominiously forced to twirl a distaff until he is liberated by Britomart. Britomart herself comes under the influence of the goddess Isis, at whose church she spends a night when she is on her way to rescue Artegall. In this configuration of Amazon, female knight, and merciful goddess Spenser explores many possibilities of feminine power; his plot, unfortunately, ultimately reduces these possibilities to one stale pattern.

Britomart, a favorite of feminist readers because she is one of the few actively questing female heroes to be found in pre-nineteenth-century literature, is imagined by Spenser as an ancestress of Elizabeth. Her royal blood exempts her from the behaviors of practiced passivity prescribed for other women in Faeryland as in England. Trained from infancy to wield spear and shield, Britomart disdains "the fine needle and nyce thread," the conventional pastimes of noble ladies. She forthrightly seeks and fights for what she wants—union with Artegall, the man she loves—and thus is the only one of the knights of *The Faerie Queene* whose quest is identical with her heart's desire.

In creating an actively seeking and loving heroine, Spenser recreates an ancient archetypal pattern that had fallen out of favor in Western culture. Britomart's mythic forebears are Psyche laboriously performing her tasks and enduring her ordeals so that she may be reunited with Amor, and Isis wandering through Egypt in search of the parts of Osiris's body so that she may put them back together and make his dead bones live. For Britomart personally, the Great, inspiring Goddess is not Venus but Isis, with whom she identifies unconsciously in a dream she has during the night she spends in her church. Spenser emphasizes the strong affinity between Britomart and Isis by having the cult statue of the goddess reach out to bless the visiting knight and by having Britomart later show mercy—the quality that, above all others, Isis emanates and represents—to her enemies in battle. Spenser's Isis is Venus ethically refined, the female life-giving principle informed by compassion.

The nobility of Spenser's vision of Isis and Britomart, however, does not survive confrontation with Elizabethan sexual and imperialist politics. As book 5 draws closer to its bloody denouement in Ireland, Britomart becomes increasingly part of a positive-negative configuration she shares with Radigund, the Amazon leader who holds Artegall captive. Like Acrasia, like Duessa, Radigund is the nasty witch behind a face so beautiful that it causes helpless males to swoon. Artegall's reaction to his first sight of her when he unlaces her helmet exactly parallels the way he responds to his initial glimpse of Britomart: both times he figuratively unmans himself by involuntarily dropping his sword. Radigund is the Jungian shadow to Britomart's moral radiance; she is her double, "split off from her as an allegorical personification of everything in Artegall's beloved that threatens him."[22]

Of what, precisely, does Radigund's threat consist? Nothing other than her improper acting out of the woman-on-top fantasy—improper since she lacks the royal blood that Britomart and Elizabeth enjoy. Spenser presents her as vengefully overturning a sexual hierarchy that he apparently accepts as natural and ordained. Wearing an apron and holding a distaff, the captive Artegall is a sight meant to wound the eyes and the spirit. Britomart rescues him and restores the proper sexual order with an absolutism that seems to spring not from her own character, but directly from Spenser's ideology. While Artegall is resting and recovering his self-esteem,

> she there as Princes rained,
> And changing all that forme of common weale,
> The liberty of women did repeale,
> Which they had long vsurpt; and them restoring
> To men's subiection, did true Iustice deale:
> That all they as a Goddesse her adoring,
> Her wisedome did admire, and hearkned to her loring.
>
> (7.42.3–9)

One of the most distasteful details here is the Amazon women's *love* for their own loss of freedom. Another is the willingness of such an exceptional woman as Britomart to impose subjection upon them.

From this point on in the narrative, Britomart's connection with Isis, goddess of mercy, is forgotten. Neither the Knight of Chastity nor her favorite goddess is around to lay her gentle, tempering hands on Artegall's warrior's arm when he is meting out "justice" to the Irish rebels at the end of this Book of Justice. Britomart's efficiency in restoring proper hierarchical order to the Amazon lands has, in fact, enabled him to ride off on this imperialistic mission. And once he is gone, he does not come back to her. Britomart's quest, despite her courage and energy and beauty, remains unfulfilled. In his creation of Britomart, Spenser offers—for the first time, perhaps, in centuries—a vision of female magnificence that is nourished by the magnificence of goddesses in the past. Then he subordinates that vision to the thinly symbolized imperatives of contemporary foreign policy.

Pressured by the self-imposed task of justifying Elizabethan imperialism in Ireland, by tensions connected with his ambition to please his very earthly and particular muse, Spenser allows his portrayal of the feminine to move from polarization to wholeness to polarization again. He casts out the Circe stereotype, but not, finally, the habits of thinking that produced her. Acrasia comes back as Radigund, refusing to stay banished.

What would have been the outcome, one wonders, if Guyon had been less scared, if Spenser had allowed his Knight of Temperance to touch the negative feminine with anything other than his sword?

7

The Lovelorn Temptress

Spenser stands out as the Renaissance poet who most strenuously wrestled with the hold of the stereotypical Circe upon patterns of masculine thought. The poets who recreated the enchantress in the decades following him shunned this kind of questioning engagement. Never was Circe so trivialized as in the seventeenth century. Never was she so magnified. To Calderón, the great playwright of Counter-Reformation Spain, she was lovely and lethal as Sin itself, which is the name he gives her in *Los encantos de la Culpa,* a drama that pushes the standard Christian interpretation of her myth to its flesh-denying extreme. But to a host of now-forgotten musicians and writers whose ambition was to provide aristocrats and plutocrats with a satisfying night's entertainment, she was merely the star of a popular story particularly well suited to displaying some of the more flamboyant contemporary theatrical conventions. In the masques, operas, and ballets they created, her magic never really imperils men's souls; it does, however, enable her to fly through the air in ingeniously designed mechanical chariots, to create hybrid beasts who will rise and lumberingly dance to orchestral melodies. The Circe of these entertainments is tamed, declawed, and frequently stricken with unrequited passion for Ulysses, who knows that "two words of love and five or six sighs" from him are enough to keep her behaving properly and well.[1] No longer the self-sufficient goddess or the irresistible succubus reclining in her lair, she is merely a deviant but lovelorn female in need of masculine direction and control. The potent eroticism of the Renaissance Circe, so perilous to its perceivers, is now diluted by submissiveness. Pretty, pliant, and frequently stricken to the heart, the trivial seventeenth-century Circe is *never* a woman on top.

Why this shift in the *maga*'s image, this change from fearsomeness to fragility? It had nothing to do with any actual change in the status or competence of women, who were certainly as capable and strong during the seventeenth century as their female forebears had been. English women during this era, as Antonia Fraser makes clear in *The Weaker Vessel,* succeeded as merchants, writers, scientists, and defenders of landed estates during the Civil War. Their rate of literacy was higher than it had ever been, thanks to the emphasis sectarians placed upon Bible reading. Whatever motivated the fantasy of feminine weakness that was then so prevalent, it was not grounded in fact. Why, exactly, the tides of eros—at least insofar as they are reflected by literary figures—should have shifted in the seventeenth century remains mysterious.

The lovelorn, trivialized Circe was a more familiar figure on the Continent than in England. At least ten musical entertainments in which she was a main character, as well as many others that featured her mythological descendants, Alcina and Armida, were produced in France, Italy, and Belgium during the seventeenth century.[2] The texts of only two English masques featuring Circe survive: William Browne of Tavistock's *Inner Temple Masque* and Aurelian Townshend's *Tempe Restored;* in both she resembles her Continental sisters in being a woman of dangerous gifts but susceptible charms, willing to sheathe her powers in order to please Ulysses, the man she adores. Both could be dismissed as dated trifles, were it not for *Tempe Restored*'s somewhat obscure connection with John Milton's *Comus,* whose title character is her son and probably the only male Circe figure in Western literature.

In seventeenth-century England, masques were the most aristocratic of dramatic productions, not only because their staging, with its emphasis on elaborate sets, lavish costumes, and mechanical contraptions, required huge outlays of cash, but also because they traditionally ended with the restoration of order from above and with a presentation of participants before the reigning authorities in the audience.[3] One of their conventions required that a dance of "antimasquers," country louts or other unruly sorts who represented the forces of disorder, be followed later in the drama by the measured quadrilles of "masquers," seemly nymphs or gentlefolk who were associated with the superior forces of order. Circe's uncouth menagerie had obvious potential as antimasquers and it is probably for this reason above all others that her myth was adapted to the form.

The *Inner Temple Masque,* produced for an audience of law students and teachers in 1614, features a Circe who knows the standard repertoire of enchantress tricks—raising the dead, walking on water, pulling down the moon—but who limits herself to casting a spell of sleep over Ulysses and his men.[4] When she wishes to wake him because she desires him, she squeezes moly over his eyes. Then the two proceed to watch a series of dances, indefinitely postponing their lovemaking. Browne's fluent but desultory verse lacks both conflict and allegorical ambition; it is no more than the verbal occasion for a series of songs and dances.

Browne's Circe, however, has one important quality in common with that of Townshend in *Tempe Restored,* produced at court seventeen years later: each voluntarily cedes her transforming rod, the phallic symbol of her power, to another character (to Ulysses in the first instance, to Minerva in the second). Who could be less threatening, more scintillating and suited to a night's elegant entertainment, than a Circe who freely gives her magic away?

The Circe of *Tempe Restored* does so because she has to be true to her part in Townshend's Neo-Platonic allegory.[5] Instead of representing unadulterated lust or passion, she personifies "desire in general . . . which hath power on all living creatures . . . being mixt of the Divine and Sensible."[6] She is a malleable character capable of renovation because she represents the whole Neo-Platonic (or Ficinian) continuum between the sensual and the ineffable. She becomes so attached to one of her pet beasts that she yields to his pleas to be regranted human form, whereupon he immediately escapes from her domain. At this point, lovelorn and enraged, her pain makes her seek diversion. Her nymphs arrange a pageant for her, a kind of masque within the masque, which features Divine Beauty descending on a cloud with her sixteen male and female attendant spheres and stars. Voilà. Circe, who as Desire is always susceptible to Beauty, realizes the depravity of her former zoological tastes and voluntarily gives up her magical rod. Celestial Harmony floats down from above, Heroic Virtue dances in from the wings and all bow or curtsy before the king.

Clearly, *Tempe Restored* is Platonism in the service of royal ostentation.[7] The transcendental aspects of the masque required the ingenious devising of clouds sturdy enough to support seventeen people in a con-

trolled descent to the stage floor and must have challenged the ingenu-
ity of Inigo Jones. "This sight altogether was for the difficulty of the
Ingining and number of the persons the greatest that hath been seene
here in our time," Townshend proudly boasted.[8] Charles I's queen, Henrietta Maria, deigned to play the role of Divine Beauty, appearing in an
elaborately silvered gown whose luminescence was designed to contrib-
ute to the play's overall moral effect. Townshend thought it likely that
"Corporeal *Beauty* consisting in simetry, colour, and certaine unexpress-
able Grace, shining in the Queenes Maiestie, may draw us to the con-
templation of the Beauty of the soule, unto which it hath Analogy."[9]
Thus philosophy was used to rationalize the squandering of the nation's
wealth. With production costs per masque presented at the royal court
in the 1630s approaching 20,000 pounds, it is small wonder that the
Civil War was only a few years off and that the masque as a genre did
not survive this upheaval.[10]

Tempe Restored also beautifully illustrates another of the masque's conventions: the reconciliation of opposing characters and forces by the end
of the drama. In *The Tempest* and *The Winter's Tale,* late plays with
masque-like elements, Shakespeare himself partially bends to this convention. In Townshend's bauble, the intractably wicked Renaissance Circe is re-characterized so that she can do her share of reconciling. Perhaps watching such entertainments helped members of the Stuart courts
convince themselves that the deepening factionalism in their country
could, after all, be smoothed over. If they could really believe in the king
as the tamer of nature he was often portrayed as being onstage; if they
could believe in the queen as Divine Beauty, then problems about Ship
Money or Puritans or Ireland might recede to insignificance.[11]

As an anti-royalist, John Milton must have had mixed feelings when
he was invited by Henry Lawes, musician at court and music tutor to
the children of the aristocratic Egerton family, to write the text for a
masque to be produced at the family seat, Ludlow Castle, in 1634. He
was then twenty-six and unknown, attracted, one can well imagine, by
the guaranteed audience for this potential work and by the opportunity
to collaborate with an accomplished musician. But the reconciliation
convention in particular would have been anathema to Milton—unac-
ceptable for reasons of both politics and temperament. Almost certainly, Lawes suggested the Circe myth to him as the subject for the new
work; Lawes and young Alice Egerton, the fifteen-year-old daughter of
the family, had participated in the production of *Tempe Restored* three

years earlier and the experience would have been relatively fresh in their minds. The refined and sinuous poetry of *Comus,* however, possesses nothing in common with that of *Tempe Restored.* Milton also makes two important plot changes: first, he ignores the reconciliation convention entirely; and second, he makes Circe a man.

The heart of this drama is a debate about virginity and promiscuity that is a standoff, with neither the Lady nor Comus convincing each other or ceding rhetorical ground. Scenes of temptation or trial, rather than of reconciliation, were what inspired Milton's deepest creative engagement; the great works of his maturity all center around such scenes. Believing (as he was to state later in the *Areopagitica*) that "that which purifies us is trial, and trial is by what is contrary," Milton was not about to create an adversary whose will would go limp at a crucial moment and thus leave the purity of his young Lady protagonist insufficiently challenged. Comus, his male Circe, combines the indefatigable appetites of his father, Bacchus, with his mother's knowledge of sorcery. "Much like his father, but his mother more" (l. 57), he is more than a match for the hapless young Lady.

Why the sex change of the sexual tempter? Before Milton gave him new life, Comus was an obscure character in classical mythology whom Ben Jonson had presented as "the god of cheer or the belly" in his masque of 1618, *Pleasure Reconciled to Virtue.*[12] Why, with "the great and famous allegorical figure of Circe . . . one of the best-known symbolical figures of the Renaissance"[13] available to him, did Milton spurn her for the role of sexual tempter and chose instead her much less illustrious son? The obvious reason is the constraint of casting. Alice Egerton, who must have been destined for the leading role before the masque even existed, could not play against a female tempter without their dialogues being construed as ludicrous or, worse still, scandalous.[14] The invention of Comus as Circe's son enabled Alice virtuously to star while still making the myth, with its attractive potential for temptation scenes, available for Milton's exploration. The change of sex of the Circe figure may also have been, for Milton himself, a kind of psychological masking and protection since it put a woman, not a man, in the vulnerable position. Not until almost three decades had gone by and he was composing book 9 of *Paradise Lost* did Milton allow himself to express the consequences of a fully sexual woman's assault upon a virtuous man's resolve.

Whether or not we agree with it, Milton's view of sexuality in *Paradise Lost* seems to derive from lived experience; in *Comus* it has the rigid insubstantiality of theory. Sexuality in this masque is not a force Milton associates with civilized human life. He views it as belonging to the domain of Comus and his routers, as something properly expressed only in the dark depths of the forest or in Comus's palace within the forest's clearing. Though he does not deny the reality of the forest—an age-old symbol of the mysterious and the unconscious—Milton presents its reality as dangerous. It is a place in which to get lost, not to live. And so the Lady, in the midst of her adolescence, becomes as disoriented in the dark wood at the beginning of this play as Dante does at the beginning of the *Commedia.*

Before we even see or hear her, Milton gives us Comus in his full power and voice. He enters with "charming-rod in one hand, his glass in the other" and urges his beast-headed followers to dance:

> We that are of purer fire
> Imitate the starry choir,
> Who in their nightly watchful sphere,
> Lead in swift round the months and years.
> The sounds, and seas with all their finny drove
> Now to the moon in wavering morris move,
> And on the tawny sands and shelves,
> Trip the pert fairies and the dapper elves;
> By dimpled brook, and fountain-brim,
> The wood-nymphs decked with daisies trim,
> Their merry wakes and pastimes keep:
> What hath night to do with sleep?
> Night hath better sweets to prove,
> Venus now wakes, and wakens Love.
>
> (ll. 111–24)

These lines hardly sound like the utterance of a rapacious brute. Comus shows himself here to be capable of delicacy and even aware of that most hallowed of Pythagorean and Neo-Platonic concepts, the music of the spheres. To dismiss the dance of Comus and his followers as "riot, and ill-managed merriment" (as the Lady later does) or as "barbarous dissonance" (as the Attendant Spirit does) fails to convince the reader whose ear has already been blandished by Circe's son. For the reader, the dynamics of experiencing *Comus* are very similar to those of experiencing Spenser's Bower of Bliss: the sensuousness of the poetry itself leads one way while the moral cues intended by the poet point to another. Because sensuousness is more timeless than moral stance, the verse of Milton and Spenser has become more seductive with age.

The young Lady, with her impervious chastity, represents the other half of the play's debate. Marshalled on her side are the Elder Brother, the Attendant Spirit, and the moral convictions of John Milton himself. The argument for chastity that these characters present is essentially an argument for the virtue construed in its narrow sense as celibacy or virginity. Only in the lines about Venus and Adonis and Cupid and Psyche that Milton added to the Spirit's epilogue for the printed version of 1637 does he favorably allude to sexual life of any kind. In 1634 he seems to have been flirting with the idea of celibacy as the only path to virtue; the attitude toward sexuality in marriage that he expresses in the "Hail wedded Love" panegyric in *Paradise Lost* was still decades away. Thus, when the Elder Brother delivers his speech praising "saintly chastity" he uses the virginal Diana and Minerva as examples. According to the Brother, this virtue is so dear to heaven

> That when a soul is found sincerely so,
> A thousand liveried angels lackey her. . . .
> Till oft converse with heavenly habitants
> Begin to cast a beam on the outward shape,
> The unpolluted temple of the mind,
> And turns it by degrees to the soul's essence,
> Till all be made immortal
>
> (ll. 453–54, 458–62)

Though the boy speaks gracefully, he has been sternly tutored, thoroughly indoctrinated in the austere patristic notion that to free the spirit one must renounce the flesh.

And what if one does not renounce the flesh, but "by lewd and lavish act of sin, / Lets in defilement to the inward parts"? Then, the Elder Brother asserts, "the soul grows clotted by contagion" (ll. 464–66). This image of the once-liquid and lambent soul sourly solidifying reveals at once Milton's puritanical priggishness and his poet's attunement to the senses.

The Lady, who has by now naively followed Comus to his palace, behaves once there in a manner her brother would certainly applaud. She refuses Comus's cup or touch, choosing instead to act as the exemplar of "the sun-clad power of chastity," of "the sage and serious doctrine of virginity" (ll. 781, 785–86). When Comus seeks to persuade her, she turns a deaf ear to his eloquence. She does not want to hear that "Beauty is nature's coin, must not be hoarded, / But must be current, and the good thereof / Consists in mutual and partaken bliss, / Unsavoury in the enjoyment of itself" (ll. 738–41). Comus's verbal brilliance delights the reader, but it leaves her unmoved, and the debate becomes a stalemate.

Before Comus resorts to rape, her two brothers burst in, brandishing swords and a magical herb that the Attendant Spirit has given them. Haemony, whose name combines the Greek words for blood and wine (*haima* and *oine*) and thus carries a Christian connotation, is Milton's version of moly. Though a scraggly version of the plant grows on earthen soil, it comes into full golden flower only "in another country," presumably the Platonic "broad fields of the sky" that the Spirit speaks of in the epilogue and from which heavenly grace proceeds. The grace that haemony allegorically represents has limited powers; it can protect against enchantments but not undo them. As Comus leaps up to escape from the boys, he points at the Lady with his rod and causes her to lose all power to act or move. Her brothers are powerless to rescue her, perhaps because her paralysis is an accurate representation of her moral position, of the repressive chastity that can preserve her virtue but not her vitality. Her alienation from her own body is complete.

At this point Milton would seem to have written himself into a rhetorical corner. But *Comus* is a masque, not an academic disputation, and poetry and music accomplish what moral philosophy has failed to do. The Spirit, who earlier has boasted of his Orpheus-like power to "still the wild winds when they roar / And hush the waving woods," now demonstrates his musical abilities. At his delicate and lovely call, Sabrina, the nymph of the river Severn, comes forth. Who could fail to respond to such a song?

> Sabrina fair
>   Listen where thou art sitting
> Under the glassy, cool, translucent wave,
>   In twisted braids of lilies knitting
> The loose train of thy amber-dropping hair,
>   Listen for dear honour's sake,
>   Goddess of the silver lake,
>   Listen and save.

Beneath its lyricism and refinement, the song draws upon images of hair and water that are often archetypally associated with fertility and sexual life. Sabrina, even though Milton has been careful to first describe her as "a virgin pure," represents a type of potent grace that comes from below, from the direction of the earth and the genitals, not from above.[15] Her waters sprinkled on the Lady release the enchantment, bringing her back to the experience of her own body. They also rescue Milton himself from completely rejecting Nature within the allegorical scheme of *Comus*.

The masque ends traditionally, with the presentation of the leading players to the resident powers that be, in this case the parents at Ludlow Castle. The Attendant Spirit proclaims that the children have been tested and found steadfast and now are ready "To triumph in victorious dance / O'er sensual folly, and intemperance" (ll. 973–74). The delicate symbolic resolution that Sabrina brought to the Nature versus Virginity debate has seemingly been forgotten. Milton allows the Spirit to have the last word and the Spirit beckons enticingly to a paradise "up in the broad fields of the sky." His message is that you too can follow if you "Love virtue, she alone is free, / She can teach ye how to climb / Higher than the sphery chime" (ll. 1018–20). Since the whole conceptual framework of the play suggests that repression is the better part of virtue, this advice is less appealing than it seems. The Spirit's message, essentially, is that you too can enter paradise if you deny a large part of your own nature.

When Milton prepared the script of *Comus* for publication three years after the masque's performance, he may have belatedly wished to find some reconciliation between the forces of sexuality and repression. He added a passage to the epilogue that locates the Garden of Adonis up in the celestial fields (though, instead of reaping sweet pleasure of each other, as in Spenser, this Adonis recovers from his wounds in slumber while Venus watches sadly over him). Perhaps by then Milton felt the play's moral stance to be too rigid and looked to Spenser, whom he acknowledges in the *Areopagitica* as "his original" and "a better teacher than Scotus or Aquinas," for guidance. Spenser's garden, however, is located on earth; its imagining involved an acceptance of both divine and human sexual nature. Milton's garden is in some transcendent neverneverland where babies appear, like Cupid and Psyche's twins, out of their mother's "fair unspotted side."[16] No messy, anxiety-producing processes are involved. The reference to the Garden of Adonis in *Comus* is an adornment that reveals the young Milton's uneasiness about the place of sexuality in his poems or in life.

Thirty-odd years and three marriages later, Milton securely locates his archetypal garden on earth and identifies it as the locus of both pleasure and disaster. In *Paradise Lost* there is no reversal of the tempter's sex; nor does Milton shy away from imagining an erotically persuasive woman. To what extent does Milton's characterization of this erotic Eve draw upon the allegorical Circe with which he would have been familiar? The answer is not much—until she bites the apple. Then and only then, does the dangerous enchantress who has haunted the fringes of his imagination come into her own.

Eve's tasting of the fruit of the Tree of Knowledge in book 9 of *Paradise Lost* upsets the hierarchical relationships that Milton, with his Platonized Christianity, has presented as proper and ordained. In the over-under terms of this framework, Eve's act asserts human will above divine will, the feminine above the masculine, appetite above reason. Her plucking of the apple gives her the power to alter the order of Creation and transforms her—temporarily—from a patriarchal woman to a Circean figure. Just before the serpent begins speaking with Eve, Milton associates Circe's powers with hers and refers to the sorceress for the only time in his poem. We are told that Eve heard the sound of the serpent approaching through rustling leaves, but paid no attention, for she was used "To such disport before her through the Field, / From every Beast, more duteous at her call, / Than at Circean call the Herd disguis'd" (9.520–22). The reference is ironic, for Eve is in no way in control of the serpent, but it does show the association Milton made at this point in the poem's composition.

When the serpent begins speaking, he addresses Eve with the sort of titles once reserved for Kubaba or Isis or Artemis of Ephesus. "Sovran Mistress," he calls her, "Queen of this Universe" . . . "Empress of this fair world." He appeals to the woman who marvels at her image in the pool (in her nativity scene in book 4), who feels the affinity between her own bounteousness and the garden's, who is aware of the effect her beauty has on Adam: to the creature whose existential reality has been masked by her position in a hierarchy. Eve's taste of the fruit seals her connection with the snake and the tree—both familiars of the goddess in ancient Cretan and Near Eastern art, though Milton could not have known that—and brings her into a sense of her own power.[17] A heightened, aggressive eroticism is a large part of this power; her eyes dart "contagious fire" that Adam cannot resist. She becomes like Apollonius's Circe, like one of the children of the Sun whose lineage tells in the rays of golden light flashing from their eyes.

At his crucial moment of decision, Adam behaves far more like Attis or Adonis, whose lives have meaning only in relation to the beloved feminine, than like the more pious Aeneas, who unhesitatingly resolves to abandon the beloved woman so that he may remain obedient to the gods. In *Paradise Lost* the fall into Original Sin is a fall out of patriarchal hierarchies and back into the ethos of a time when no transcendent deity ruled over the immanent force of Nature. "I feel / the Link of Nature draw me," Adam avows to Eve: "Flesh of Flesh / Bone of my Bone thou art, and from thy State / Mine never shall be parted, bliss or woe" (9.913–16). Adam's words very beautifully speak for union, rather than for the gradations so important to the poem's Platonically influenced conceptual structure. The knowledge that he and Eve gain from the fruit of the Tree is, at first, a heightened knowledge of desire. Who could have imagined that the young poet of *Comus,* so intent on telling his characters and his audience how they might learn to sport in the broad fields of the sky, would one day write the most famous lines in English poetry in favor of earthly, sexual love?

By the time Adam and Eve awaken from their lovemaking following the Fall, however, Milton has reimposed in all their strength the hierarchies that he seemed temporarily to suspend. Henceforth Adam and Eve cannot innocently submerge themselves in passion; their guilty self-consciousness signals the supremacy of mind over body even when they choose to obey the dictates of their bodies. Milton as narrator keenly describes this war between consciousness and physical nature, in which high passions sorely shake Adam and Eve's

> inward State of Mind, calm Region once
> And full of Peace, now toss't and turbulent:
> For Understanding rul'd not, and the Will
> Heard not her lore, both in subjection now
> To sensual Appetite, who from beneath
> Usurping over sovran Reason claim'd
> Superior sway.
>
> (9.1125–31)

It is an old, old story, this tale of sensual appetite coming from beneath to overcome *sovereign* reason, and it expresses, I believe, the nearly uni-

versal human uneasiness at the fact that consciousness, with all its possibilities, flowers from nature and is subject to bodily imperatives and
constraints. Not since Homer's time, when the seat of intelligence was
believed to be located somewhere in the chest, has Western culture been
able to accept consciousness matter-of-factly as a function of physical
being. Since then, women, like Eve, like Circe, have often been regarded as the enemies of what is most precious and distinctive in human
nature because they themselves have been too identified with the flesh.
Milton's Eve, in his own terms, represents the power of the low over
the high; herself "th' inferior, in the mind and inward Faculties" (8.540–
41), she embodies the downward pull toward mortality, sexuality, earth.

In Adam's temptation scene Milton expresses the power of this pull
as eloquently as it has ever been expressed. He is not like the Homeric
allegorists who sweep half a myth and all its human drama out of their
tidy interpretations so that Odysseus, representing the radiance of Logos or Reason, may remain untarnished by Circe's dark female powers.
Adam engages with Eve as fully as Odysseus engages with Circe, but
she has the power only to make him lose his home, not to help him
find it again. That power belongs to Milton's Christ, who, by extend-
ing his gifts of grace from on high, holds out the promise of an eternal,
transcendent home. Unfortunately, death is its gate.[18]

The great Spanish contemporaries of Milton, Lope de Vega and
Calderón, were much more directly fascinated than he by the implications of the Circe myth. Lope wrote a long narrative poem and a sonnet bearing her name, both published in 1624. Calderón wrote two dramas based on the story: one a *fiesta, El mayor encanto, amor* (1635), and
the other a sacramental *auto, Los encantos de la Culpa* (after 1650). Their
Circes, though often magnificent, share one important quality with the
trivial ones then adorning the stage in other European countries: they
are consumed by love for Ulysses and made vulnerable by their passion.
This vulnerability can be regarded as the distinctive twist that seventeenth-century writers give to the myth; in their work the terrible and
potent Renaissance Circe (who apparently could no longer be abided)
falls in love and sheathes her claws, though she may bare them again to
retaliate when she finds she cannot get what she wants. She behaves, in
short, like a woman—more like the *Odyssey's* yearning Calypso than its
mysterious Circe. If Ulysses were presented as a character of equal vulnerability in these works, the ways in which the sexes pierce, comple-

ment, and enlarge each other could have been insightfully dramatized. In Calderón's dramas, such mutuality almost occurs. But most seventeenth-century versions of the myth seem shaped by their writers' unexamined assumptions that sexual love weakens and that females are the sex more prone to this weakness.

Lope de Vega, for instance, turned to the Circe myth at a time when he was seeking to change the nature of his love relationship with Marta de Nevares (a married woman twenty-five years younger than himself, acclaimed for her intelligence and musicality as well as her beauty) from an actively sexual one to a purely spiritual one. The birth of their daughter in 1617, three years after he was ordained as a priest, intensified his desire for this transformation.[19] In the edgy but admiring relationship of Circe and Ulysses, Lope seems to have found a way of shaping his own experience toward a desired end. "To Circe," the prefatory sonnet to the narrative poem, is addressed to a female presence who seems as personal, as much Marta, as she is mythic. He asks her to "consecrate your beauty and my desires" to the great light whose daughter she is, to act as the muse of his poem by suspending "the lyre on the branch of peace."[20] In return, he gives her the longer poem, which contains "a greater wisdom with which to understand yourself."

What is this greater wisdom? Seemingly, that she must become resigned to not getting what she wants. The Circe of Lope's plot, in spite of her beauty, her divinity, her emerald eyes blazing with lascivious fire, never succeeds in bringing Ulysses to her bed. He is willing to love her "with that recognition / which I owe to your regal beauty / and to your clear, divine mind," but not to make himself sexually available and therefore vulnerable to her. All the while this Ulysses holds to the thought of Penelope and Ithaca shimmering in the distance, in his past and future. At the end of their encounter, Circe has, in effect, turned into that far safer figure, Calypso. She spends hours before her mirror, trying to make herself more beautiful, wondering what she lacks. When he tries to leave, she angrily clings, even conjuring up a sea storm to detain him. And even as she holds on, Ulysses' men—whom she has promptly returned to human shape at his request—compound the insult to her pride by succumbing to the charms of her handmaids.

Lope's Circe is rendered powerless by the strength of Ulysses' resolve to eschew sexual engagement—a resolve he shares with his creator, who hints of it in the poem's second stanza. In these lines Lope, in his own voice, pays homage to Circe's ability to bestow form. He asks her to deliver him from the shape that nature has given him, to "turn me into a new form, a Platonic swan." Like Yeats three hundred years later, who claims at the end of "Sailing to Byzantium" that he wishes to take on the form of a bird made "Of hammered gold and gold enamelling," so that he can sing of the turbulent human scene while gazing down on it from above, Lope wishes to remove his love to some graceful, suprasensual realm where it can be celebrated and maintained apart from the risk of grave personal conflict. He begs his Circe to use her powers over the flesh to deliver him from the flesh, to make him into a large, floating, mythical bird. What use would she have for such a creature? No wonder this simultaneously spurned and honored goddess suffers acute pain.

If Lope's solution to the vulnerability and suffering that almost inevitably accompany sexual love is male sublimation, Calderón's is male renunciation. He appears to have been more powerfully attracted to the Circe-Ulysses myth than any other seventeenth-century writer, working with it in two plays written over an interval of at least fifteen years. The first, secular play, *El mayor encanto, amor*, illustrates nothing so much as Calderón's opulent sense of the Baroque and his wide acquaintance with ancient and Renaissance literature; the allegorical *auto*, *Los encantos de la Culpa*, is entirely more serious, using the tenets of a conservative Christianity to probe human nature acutely and dramatize its deficiencies.[21] Calderón's *auto* is more extreme than other allegorical interpretations of the Circe myth but more enlightening for just this reason. It does not stop short of dramatizing the tale as an ideological struggle between the forces of life and the forces of death—with sexuality aligned with death.

Before he matured as an artistic defender of the Counter-Reformation, Calderón served a lengthy stint as court playwright for Philip IV, responsible for providing sophisticated entertainments liberally financed by the royal treasury. With Inca gold to back the staging of his creations, Calderón was in a position Inigo Jones would no doubt have found enviable. What theatrical designer at the court of the Stuarts would have dared to command the building of an island, complete with parapets and waterfall and a small, peaked mountain, in the midst of a royal lake? Such was the set of *El mayor encanto*, whose audience gathered on a June evening around the illuminated pond of the Buen Retiro palace near Madrid.[22] In many ways Calderón's account of the relationship between Circe and Ulysses follows Homer closely, but he transforms her originally scrubby island into an atmosphere worthy of *The Arabian Nights*.

This Circe is a formidable combination of erudition and voluptuous beauty, fully capable of challenging Ulysses in every way. She boasts of her mastery of both the liberal arts and the black ones. Like Ovid's lustful sorceress, she can summon mists, earthquakes, and lightning at will; like Ariosto's Alcina, she can change spurned lovers not just to animals, but also to plants and trees. However, when Ulysses proves immune to her potion (because he carries a bouquet of magical flowers given to him by Iris, who plays Hermes) and draws his sword, she immediately falls at his feet and offers to retransform his men. Then follows an interlude of mutual courtliness and of mutual struggle with the conflicting interior voices of love and pride. Calderón's most original contribution to the myth in this play is his depiction of how Circe and Odysseus mirror each other. Since both are arrogantly aware of their sexual and intellectual powers, they are a good match for each other. And both eventually surrender their pride to their passion.

The remainder of Calderón's plot in *El mayor encanto* is Homer modified by Tasso and Virgil. A conflict between passionate love and duty now replaces the more subtle interior conflict between pride and love. As in the *Odyssey*, Ulysses' men remind him of his obligation to resume their journey. Just as Tasso's Carlo and Ubaldo clank a suit of armor to summon the spellbound Rinaldo to his martial duty, so here Ulysses' men blow trumpets and clatter Achilles' weapons to shock their leader out of his sensual dream. They underestimate Circe's attractions. It takes the dire, threatening ghost of Achilles himself to send Ulysses on his way. Once he moves, he moves quickly, telling his men that "flight today / Is an act as brave as prudent, / Since the sorceries of love, / He alone who flies, subdueth" (*LGE*, pp. 134–35).

Calderón's Ulysses does what Virgil's more upright Aeneas may well have longed to do: sneak away from the seductive woman without any final scene of farewell. Circe, no longer valuing her powers since she knows the greatest of them is love—and love has failed her—consumes her own palace in flames and goes down with it. She ends her life as Dido does. Whatever sympathetic understanding Calderón has previously extended to her is now irrevocably withdrawn. The stereotypical conflict between love and duty with which the play concludes can be described in more archetypal terms as that between a male whose sense of identity ultimately depends upon journey and conquest, on exploits performed away from the secure center, and a female whose identity lies (as she is rather surprised to discover) at that center. "Thou effeminate Greek" is the taunt from Achilles that finally stings Ulysses into action.

Calderón's fascination with this myth of opposing but approximate-
ly equal male and female forces lasted for at least two decades. In *Los
encantos de la Culpa,* a drama of greater unity and depth, he recasts the
conflict in traditional Christian terms. Like Calderón's other allegorical
autos, Los encantos was first performed during the Corpus Christi festival and was intended to dramatize the value of the sacraments, in this
case the Eucharist. It is an Everyman play, with Ulysses bluntly renamed
"The Man" (El Hombre) and Circe christened "Sin" (La Culpa). El
Hombre, according to one of the play's more acute critics, J. Richards
LeVan, "feels and does as a character on the stage what the will feels
and does as a faculty of the soul."[23] Circe here represents much more
than just sexual lust; she is a figure for all the earthly delights that,
Calderón believes, cause human beings to turn away from the love of
God toward an idolatrous lust for life.

Many of the play's scenes correspond to those in *El mayor encanto,
amor* and follow Homer in pattern, if not in meaning. *Los encantos* opens
with a terrific sea storm. The Man's ship, piloted by his Understanding
(El Entendimiento) and crewed by his Five Senses, barely makes it to
harbor at Circe's island. No sooner are they there than the impetuous
senses, traveling ahead of the Man (who has fallen asleep), become enslaved. The Hearing, enticed by Sin's handmaid Flattery, is turned into
a chameleon; Smell, by Calumny, into a Lion; Taste, by Gluttony, into
a pig; Touch into a bear, by Lasciviousness; and Sight into a tiger, by
Envy. Even Understanding finds it difficult to resist the assaults of Pride
with her poisoned cup. Playing the role of the wary Eurylochos, Understanding comes back to report the extent of the disaster to Ulysses.
He describes Circe as "most beautiful," as speaking in a voice that is
"softly bland, yielding swift to pity's law" (*SS,* p. 169); yet he recognizes
her as "Sin, that fierce and fell Monster full of ravening rage." Her attractiveness, in Calderón's allegorical scheme of things, is proof of her
loathsomeness. She can be delicate and radiant as Dawn (a metaphor
he later uses repeatedly to describe her) and still be deadly.

In this play Iris with her saving flowers is identified as Penance. She
appears when the Man, on his way to Circe's palace, prays for forgiveness for his failure to supervise his own senses. The bouquet she drops
is "all dappled o'er with virtues from the life-blood of a lamb" (*SS,* p.
175). It protects Ulysses from Circe's brew, but not from her personal
attractiveness. One by one he drops the flowers as he succumbs to her
seductions. Her allure is by no means purely physical, for she promises
to share with him the full, heady range of her powers: "Thou wilt see

my deep researches,— / Thou my wonders wilt examine. / All the se-
crets of my science / Will be bared to give thee answer" (*SS,* p. 184).
These enticements, complemented by her "raptures, ravishments, en-
trancements, pleasures, blisses, fondest favors," quite overcome the curious Greek. The two sit down at a sumptuous table that has miracu-
lously appeared in Sin's garden of earthly delights.

At this point Understanding and Penance reenter and the drama in-
tensifies to a crescendo of counterpoint. Music, who is Circe's most seductive servant, continually advises the Man "Oh! forget that thou must
die! / And but think that thou dost live!" while Understanding and Penance repeatedly counter "Oh! forget that thou dost love! / And remember thou must die!" (*SS,* p. 194). In this most basic of contests, it is the
fear of death that finally wins. As the Man repents of his pleasure-seek-
ing lust for life, the lavish foods on the table disappear into thin air and
are replaced by the plain, substantial bread of the Eucharist—which
alone, according to Calderón, has power to satisfy. At the play's end Sin's
palace itself goes down in an earthquake. Her powers are as nothing compared to those of Penance and of Christ. Sin, finally, is just one more
defeated, lovelorn female.

The Sorceries of Sin is the last allegorical interpretation of the Circe
myth that I know of, and also the most intense and inclusive. Like the
ancient Stoics' Circe, Calderón's has the power to subvert the faculty of
reason in human nature, for "man by sinning / Is transmuted to a brute
. . . / In whose soul no reason dwells" (*SS,* p. 170). Like the Circe of
Porphyry and the Neo-Platonists, his Sin is the goddess of *this* world,
presiding over a realm of appearances vastly inferior in value to an otherworldly domain of Reality. And like the Eve of Judeo-Christian myth
and of Milton, she has the power to deflect humanity from God and
from its true, transcendent home.

Calderón's allegory, unlike many of Spenser's, is flawlessly consistent
and can be attacked only by those who stand outside its assumptions.
The chief of these assumptions is that natural life has no value per se,
but only as preparation for participation in an otherworldly Kingdom
of God to which the doctrines and sacraments of the church offer the
only routes. Calderón is heaven-bent on rejecting the intrinsic value of
earthly, bodily existence. He reconciles Christianity and Plato by devaluing the ordinary human appetite for life.[24] In his metaphysical scheme
of things, the human fear of death is the most valuable trait in our psyches, for it acts as a spur to piety.

To anyone not sharing Calderón's conservative brand of Christianity, his identification of life with death and death with life is a delusion per-petrated by sleight-of-faith. Freud's comments on religion in *Civiliza-tion and Its Discontents* seem particularly applicable to Calderón's au-thoritarian faith: "Religion . . . imposes equally on everyone its own path to the acquisition of happiness and protection from suffering. Its tech-nique consists in depressing the value of life and distorting the picture of the real world in a delusional manner—which presupposes an intim-idation of the intelligence. At this price, by forcibly fixing them in a state of psychical infantilism and by drawing them into a mass-delu-sion, religion succeeds in sparing many people an individual neurosis. But hardly anything more."[25] In Freud's terms, the crowds by the stage at the Corpus Christi festival were being intimidated as they were en-tertained: taught to discount the firsthand experience of their senses in favor of an ideology that severely compromised the pleasure principle that was their birthright. It is hardly surprising that Calderón's plays, and particularly his *autos,* have fallen out of favor in the skeptical twen-tieth century.

In his thoroughgoing rejection of natural life and of the authority of the senses, Calderón is much more extreme than Milton, but in his cast-ing of Woman as the primary impediment to spiritual ascent he is iden-tical. He can afford, paradoxically, to create the most attractive Circe since Homer's. Sin is passionate, generous, intelligent, and imbued with a freshness and beauty metaphorically associated with wildflowers, bird-song, and dawn. She is in every way (except eschatologically) a fitting mate for the wily and curious Ulysses, for she represents earthly life at its best. By deliberately making his Circe so attractive, this master play-wright of the Counter-Reformation emphasizes the strength of the faith that is able to reject her. He hands back to the archetype most of its ancient powers. Calderón's Circe is goddess of this world, resplendent with beauty and danger.

She is also, spectacularly, a loser in love, because this world, in his Platonic scheme of things, is not the one that counts. In this regard, she stands first among equals in the company of her seventeenth-cen-tury sisters.

8

Whore and Femme Fatale

The less eschatologically oriented cultural climate of England never produced an interpretation of the Circe myth as extreme as Calderón's. In fact, in England myth itself was shortly to go out of style. Awed by Newton's mathematically demonstrated celestial mechanics and by the powers of human reason to which the discovery of such mechanics attested, English intellectuals of Samuel Johnson's generation had little use for associative, mythopoeic thinking and tended to regard the accumulated heritage of myth merely as a collection of bizarre and pretty stories suitable for decorating the walls of elegant country houses. Johnson himself found dramas based on these age-old stories boring. He wrote in criticism of a contemporary play about Ulysses: "We have been too early acquainted with the poetical heroes to expect any pleasure from their revival; to show them as they have already been shown is to disgust by repetition, to give them new qualities or new adventures, is to offend by violating received notions."[1]

This mid-eighteenth-century view of myth as a closed and exhausted system with no relevance to contemporary life was soon to be ably attacked by Blake and later Romantics. Blake went on to create his own system of myth, refusing to be enslaved by what he regarded as the "single vision" of the rationalists. Shelley, Keats, and many of their contemporaries found the old Greek myths still imaginatively stimulating and expressive of human truth. Like artists of any other era, nineteenth-century writers and painters brought their own issues and feelings to their reworkings of myth.

As a result, the archetypal image of the dark, dangerous woman proliferated in nineteenth-century, and particularly late nineteenth-century, literature and visual art.[2] Femmes fatales such as Lamia, Delilah, Judith, Salome, and Keats's Belle Dame Sans Merci expressed the evil, sexual half of the good-evil polarization into which nineteenth-century culture forced the feminine. Spenser's Una-Duessa and Britomart-Radigund pairings were, in a sense, prophetic, for they prefigured the kind of dualistic objectifying of women that became habitual in English-speaking cultures three hundred years later. For every chaste, subservient, and spiritually radiant Angel of the House (or Household Nun, as Bram Dijkstra calls this stereotype in *Idols of Perversity*), shadow figures of monstrous devil-women existed in imagination if not in reality.[3]

Such polarization, of course, reflects an extreme discomfort with sexuality. It was as if the spirit-body dualism that had permeated Western culture from Plato's time onward, and in which the female sex had generally been assigned the part of the body, were now cast in a slightly different way. In this imperialistic and thoroughly patriarchal century, women were permitted to represent spirit if they were sufficiently amenable to male hegemony. Those who represented body were anything but tame: wild, power-hungry creatures who turned unwary men into their sexual thralls. Once again males were perceived—as they had been during the Renaissance—as the more vulnerable sex. The lovelorn temptress had become passé.

One would expect Circe to be a popular figure in such a climate of thought. Several well-known painters of the time, including Louis Chalon in France and Edward Burne-Jones, J. W. Waterhouse, and Arthur Hacker in England, produced canvases depicting her powers. Louis Chalon's painting (figure 22), which was exhibited in the Salon of 1888, suggests the iconography of ancient goddess art. His stylized Circe sits, like the goddess of Çatal Hüyük, on a throne flanked by lions, before a blazing elemental sun that bathes her nude body in light. Her right arm is outraised in salute, as if demanding homage to her powers. A few perfectly normal-looking pigs loll in the dark foreground as necessary reminders of her identity, but the viewer's eye rests upon them only in afterthought. This Circe is both fierce goddess of light and radiant, voluptuous woman. Chalon's portrait of her suggests that the single fact of her myth that most impressed him was her descent from Helios—a fact omitted from many allegorical interpretations. His painting is testimony to the

Figure 22. "Circe," painting by Louis Chalon, 1888.

power of the Circe myth, or of any genuine myth, to strike the mind afresh
and to brush away centuries of intervening interpretation.

Chalon's painting almost certainly influenced J. W. Waterhouse's "Circe Offering the Cup to Ulysses" (figure 23), first exhibited in 1891, for
there are strong similarities of composition and iconography in these
works. Waterhouse's Circe, like Chalon's, sits on a golden, lion-flanked
throne and raises her arm against the background of a huge, light-filled
disk. But the disk is mirror rather than sun, and she herself lacks all
hieratic quality. What she possesses instead is a gorgeous freshness, a
quickness that makes her far more seductive than Chalon's figure and
that makes the goblet she holds in her right hand look truly enticing.
Waterhouse clothes her in a transparent garment of shining, tissue-like
fabric that might have come from the loom of Homer's Circe. Of all
the visual representations of this enchantress, from any era, she is the
hardest to resist. Ulysses, whose reflection appears to one side of the
mirror, looks understandably very wary.

The invitation that Waterhouse's 1891 Circe holds out is rescinded by
"Circe Invidiosa," his 1892 painting of the sorceress. Though this figure
too is abundantly dark-haired—how could Circe be blond?—Waterhouse
appears to have used a different model for her. He captures the *maga* as
she pollutes Scylla's pool, pouring out the green, disfiguring liquid from
a shallow glass bowl. Perhaps he was inspired to catch her in the act of
poisoning by Edward Burne-Jones, who had earlier painted her as a stat-
uesque vamp bent over her bowl of brew, measuring out drops of the
pharmakon kakon to add to it, as two black panthers intently watch.
Waterhouse's Circe Invidiosa is drawn into herself, gathered around the
core of her malicious power. The painting possesses an integrity of line
and makes striking use of the greens and blues for which Waterhouse
was famed. When held in mind together, Waterhouses's Circes prompt
the viewer to pose the very same question that Eurylochos and his men
asked as they approached her stone dwelling: is she goddess or woman?

Far less painterly and more voyeuristic is Arthur Hacker's depiction
of the enchantress. In Hacker's "Circe" a voluptuous, September Morn-
like woman sits displaying herself before a herd of creatures in various
stages of the man-to-hog metamorphosis (figure 24). The ground around
her is strewn with flowers, which Hacker has arranged like droppings.
The painting is a classic example of Victorian hypocrisy, for though the
artist has composed it in such a way that the viewer's eye is drawn primarily to the naked flesh of his model, it pretends to be a parable about

Figure 23. "Circe Offering the Cup to Ulysses," painting by J. W. Waterhouse, 1891.

Figure 24. "Circe," painting by Arthur Hacker, 1893.

sexual depravity. M. H. Spielmann, the critic who wrote the commentary for the *Royal Academy Pictures* volume of 1893, when the painting was first exhibited, was impressed and taken in by its overt moral message. He believed Hacker had "sought to accentuate the degradation of bestiality and sensual depravity, the depth of which is clearly sounded by the indifference of the human beings to the horrible change which is taking place around them."[4]

Two women artists of the period, Alice Pike Barney and Elenore Plaisted Abbot, also produced Circes; in both of their images the figure's sexual powers are hinted at by her long, wild, wind-dishevelled hair. Glamorous, possessed of an energy disturbingly feral, these Circes are of one nature with the beasts who surround them. Abbot's print was, fittingly, one of the illustrations for a new edition of Keats's poems, where she could take her place alongside Lamia and La Belle Dame Sans Merci. Neither of these images suggests any reassessment or positive transformation of the concept of the feminine promulgated by the fin-de-siècle male establishment. Barney and Abbot, though reveling in the enchantress's sheer vitality, seem not to question the prevailing dogma that to be female and fully sexual was perforce to be malevolent. Better known women artists of the period, like Suzanne Valadon and Mary Cassatt, were not drawn to the femme fatale as a subject for painting; instead, they concentrate on the domestic, daily side of female experience.

Curiously, I have not been able to find any figure named Circe in nineteenth-century English or American literature. Although a cultural climate that severely polarized the feminine would have been ripe to receive her, she seems to have appeared only to visual artists, not to writers.

When Circe reemerges in literature, in the Nighttown episode of James Joyce's *Ulysses* and, later, in the work of Margaret Atwood and Eudora Welty, she has been imaginatively transformed. Joyce's nominal Circe, the brothelkeeper Bella Cohen, shares the profession that Servius had centuries before used to stigmatize the enchantress in his commentary on the *Aeneid*. But Joyce turns this nasty bit of traditional allegorizing inside out. In *Ulysses,* Bella's brothel becomes the stage upon which, in Freud's terms, the superego is assassinated and the sexual fantasies of the id are freely played out. This purgation acts as the climax and turning point of the novel; following it, Leopold Bloom and Stephen Dedalus recognize each other, albeit temporarily, as spiritual father and son and together head unerringly toward their Ithaca. Whore though she is, Bella's presence in the novel is positive in its effects.

Joyce's choice of Leopold Bloom, the uncommonly decent common man, as his Ulysses says much about the moral understructure of his work. How ironic that this novel, whose hero—in an unprepossessing way—habitually behaves more charitably toward the other human beings he encounters than any other hero of modern fiction who springs to mind, should have been censored as morally decadent on both sides of the Atlantic. Joyce never idealizes Bloom and insists throughout on his hero's sometimes messy and ridiculous humanity, but there can be little doubt that he intended him to be exemplary. When Joyce first mentioned his epic work in progress to his friend Frank Budgen, he stressed that he considered his Ulysses to be both a complete man and a good one.[5] Indeed, Joyce seems to have been attracted to the idea of writing a modern *Odyssey* because he considered Odysseus to be the only complete hero in literature, as well as "the first gentleman in Europe."[6]

Joyce's Bloom shares a core of identity with Homer's Odysseus. They are both wanderers—Bloom all the more so because he is connected by ancestry with the Jews of the Diaspora—and the wanderings of both are seen in relation to a fixed center occupied by a loved woman: Penelope in the palace at Ithaca, Molly in the bedroom at Eccles Street. Just as important, both display an attunement to the feminine that more stereotypically masculine heroes such as Achilles or Aeneas lack. In the Circe episode Bloom undergoes a phantasmagoric change of gender that makes overt an androgynous strain in his nature latent throughout the novel. He is given to pondering women's woe, sympathizing at various times with the beleaguered motherhood of Mrs. Purefoy, Mrs. Dedalus, and Mrs. Dignam and with the general condition of women subjected to domestic tyranny. His attunement to the feminine, like that of Odysseus, makes him extremely attractive to the women he meets. Even after her adulterous afternoon with the prodigious Boylan, Molly reaffirms her choice of Bloom, made on Howth head sixteen years before. She liked Bloom and chose to say "yes" to him, she says, "because I saw he understood or felt what a woman is."[7]

In both Odysseus and Bloom this emotional sensitivity seems to be connected with vulnerability and with a capacity to bear pain. In his poem's first lines, Homer introduces his hero as having experienced many woes, and he derives his very name from a verb connected with the noun for "pain" or "grief."[8] Odysseus's identity is furthermore connected with the long gash on his thigh made by a boar's tusk when he was an adolescent.[9] This near-wound to generativity is suffered figuratively by Bloom, who has been gored, in a sense, by death, for he has been impotent with Molly since the death of their infant son eleven years earlier. Bloom's conditional impotence is one of the great mysteries of the novel; it seems brought on by an expectation of loss and by a perhaps unconscious desire to avoid the further biological fatherhood that would expose him anew to the possibility of such a loss. This impotence exposes Bloom to the masochistic elements in his own nature, for he cannot defend himself effectively against the internal voices jeering him as a "womanly man" or cuckold. It also connects him with a long tradition of mythic heroes, including Adonis, Attis, and the Fisher King, who suffer wounds to their generativity. Joyce may well have intended Bloom to be seen as part of this tradition.

Although Joyce could hardly be more aware of the vulnerability of male sexuality, he does not endorse the standard allegorical position of blaming women for this vulnerability. Bloom lives with the consciousness of this psychic wound every day, powerless to heal himself but courageous enough not to blame anyone else for his pain. In his refusal to indulge in the psychic relief of projecting anger—or of viewing Molly as a witch who has somehow unmanned him—Bloom is as much the self-master as Odysseus when he keeps his wits and his self-possession through one dangerous situation after another.

The ways in which Joyce chose to make Bloom *unlike* Odysseus also illustrate a great deal about the values on which the novel rests. Bloom is no king. He speaks in no councils, he has no servants or goddesses to conveniently watch over him. Instead we follow him on his daily round to the butcher shop, the privy, and the public baths, a round in which he moves as one human atom among others in the swirl of a great city. Only in fantasy, during the psychic catharsis of the Circe chapter, does Bloom briefly dominate his fellow men—first as Lord Mayor of Dublin and then as the acclaimed (and later pilloried) Leopold the First. But even as a dominator, at the top of the political heap, Bloom shows himself to be concerned with the betterment of his kind. In the new Bloomusalem he proclaims that "free money, free love and a free lay church in a free lay state" will be available to all (462). Social and political hierarchies exist in *Ulysses,* but they are hardly condoned by Joyce, and they are not bolstered by the position of any of his central characters.

Similarly, Joyce stripped away Odysseus's sometimes indulged and sometimes restrained proclivity for violence when he refashioned the hero as Bloom. Although the *Odyssey* is a poem of relationship and by no means a paean to might, the capacity to dominate through force is an integral part of Odysseus's heroic character. Before he learns, through Circe's tutelage and his own bitter experience, the limits of military prowess, Odysseus is not above sanctioning episodes of mass destruction like the sack of Ismaros. Ismaros has no parallel in Bloom's adventures. Nor is the way Odysseus initially encounters Circe—with a sword held to her throat—duplicated by the more masochistic and less confident Bloom.

Bloom's renunciation of violence is a central part of his character, based not only on inclination but on conviction as well. In the Cyclops episode Bloom stands up to the mean-spirited narrator and to the xenophobic and anti-Semitic Citizen. While the others seem to be awed by what happens at "the business end of a gun," Bloom sees that kind of power as of "no use." "Force, hatred, history, all that," he tells them and us, is "not life for men and women. . . . And everybody knows that it's the very opposite of that that is really life." When asked what is really life, Bloom replies "Love . . . I mean the opposite of hatred" (331). His vision of history as a saga of hatred and domination dovetails with

Stephen's earlier statement that "history is a nightmare from which I am trying to awake" (40). Bloom's defense of love causes the brutes in the pub to mock him and question his masculinity, but it stands out as one of the clear acts of courage in the novel. In this episode Joyce questions the norms of heroism and maleness that have prevailed for centuries. Both he and Bloom recognize that a history based on destruction and domination is not worth prolonging.

It is important to know and remember that Joyce considers Bloom the complete and good man, because otherwise we as readers can easily lose our bearings in the relativistic world of *Ulysses*. As a result of Joyce's ingenious and varied techniques of narration, we see both Bloom and Stephen from many points of view. Joyce himself is Proteus, transforming his voice and vision from the sniping of the anonymous narrator of "Cyclops" to the pulp romanticism of Gerty MacDowell to the verbal river roll of Molly. Each of these and other narrators communicates a piece of the truth, but we would be foolish to accept any single narrative voice in the novel as the bearer of the final truth about the characters. Relativity—and the questioning, anti-authoritarian stance that relativity implies—are built into the very structure of *Ulysses*.

Often the multiple narrational voices have the effect of complementing each other. In chapter after chapter we see Bloom's moral excellence and Stephen's intellectual excellence displayed, even though the narrator (the Thersites-like character, for example) may not appreciate what is displayed. Also in chapter after chapter, in fantasy if not in fact, we see an abundance of sexual behavior. Sexuality is one of the few givens in Joyce's relativistic world.

It is appropriate, therefore, that the climax of the novel takes place in a brothel. The Circe chapter, set in and on the streets outside of Bella Cohen's establishment in Nighttown, is the most important of all to the plot, for in it Bloom and Stephen find each other. Bloom's loss of a son is assuaged in this and the following chapters, for a few hours at least, by his protection of Stephen. And Stephen's need for a spiritual father who will take his well-being to heart and who will model a more complete humanity is met briefly by Bloom. The first moment of union between them takes place inside the brothel when they look into the hall mirror, surrounded by a hat rack, and jointly see the face of the antlered, cuckolded Shakespeare who has figured in Stephen's theories but who is more appropriate to Bloom's experience.

This moment of shared vision is not discussed by Bloom and Stephen, so it is hardly a moment of communion. Only we as readers, as the audience for the dramatic script that is the Circe chapter, know about it. "Circe," as a surreal play within a novel, is artifice compounded and at two or three removes from verisimilitude. Joyce's choice of the dramatic format for the chapter has the effect of giving him as playwright-director even greater freedoms than those he has assumed in previous parts of the novel. No longer is he content with the dazzling, Protean changes of voice and perspective that have accounted for much of the complexity and richness of *Ulysses* up to this point. Now he tampers with the very givens of existence. Axiom One: language is a human prerogative, not accessible to inanimate objects. In "Circe," a button, a cake of soap, or whatever else Joyce wills to speak, speaks. Axiom Two: human beings are doomed to carry their identities, somewhat shaped and battered by experience, from birth to grave. In "Circe," male can become female, human can become flying insect, the dead can rebecome the quick. Axiom Three: items from one character's exclusive personal experience are not accessible to the memory of another. "Circe" functions as the memory-bank of the novel, wherein details of thoughts or events that occurred to one character can, and do, pop up in the speech or vision of another. Bloom's beholding of the antlered Shakespeare of Stephen's full-blown theory is a case in point.

Joyce himself is the Circe of "Circe." As writer-director he preempts the *maga's* magic, her ability to change given forms at will. As on Aiaia, in "Circe" anything can happen, and the episode's atmosphere of vaudeville tinged with terror results from this fact. In this chapter Joyce, as Robert Newman has remarked, "seeks to dissolve distinctions by collapsing *Ulysses* into a memory where the laws of intellect are no longer operative . . . the network of connections within *Ulysses* grows and becomes increasingly elaborate until we realize that everything somehow connects with everything else."[10] It would be foolish to regard Joyce's nominal Circe, Bella Cohen, as the figure who presides over this vast network of possibility. She is merely one character in a script with others, on a par with Bloom, Stephen, and the dubiously young women who work for her.

As the *magus,* Joyce pulls fantasies from his characters' unconscious minds like rabbits from a hat. They are complete, surprising, suddenly there in all their fullness. Bloom's psyche provides most of the content for these fantastical dramas, and yet Bloom himself—the chief actor within them—does not seem to be aware that they are taking place. The nineteen pages (455–68) during which Bloom progresses from Lord Mayor to Martyrdom, fit neatly between two of Zoe's sentences as she goes on talking to him.[11] Bloom would need a psyche that worked at the speed of light to call up all these dynamic images within the requisite flash of time. And to learn from these elaborate masquerades, to profit from the psychic release that is taking place, he would seemingly have to be conscious of what is happening. Joyce as authorial wizard is doing nothing less than suspending the laws of psychodynamics that had been recently pioneered by Freud and Jung. Or rather, he is bringing to bear on these laws the Everyman concept, the literary trope in which one person's experience can stand for all of humanity's and all of humanity's can become relevant to that one person's. As already noted in the instance of Bloom's and Stephen's looking into the mirror and jointly seeing Shakespeare, in "Circe" individual experiential boundaries do not necessarily hold. Nor, in Bloom's case, is it necessary for a character to be conscious of the psychic release that is taking place in order to be freed by it. But more about that later.

Within the "anything goes" atmosphere of "Circe" the rigid proprieties of Irish Catholic culture regarding sexuality are predictably demolished to rubble. On Mecklenburg Street maidenheads go for ten shillings each (433), one commodity among others in a nightmare world that exposes all that has been hidden or repressed. In "Circe," characters' sexual feelings and fantasies are objectified, set out on the stage of the reader's mind to be seen for what they are. These feelings, Joyce believed, provide common human ground. About the time that he first began composing *Ulysses,* he commented on this commonality in a letter to his brother Stanislaus:

> Anyway, my opinion is that if I put down a bucket into my own soul's well, sexual department, I draw up Griffith's and Ibsen's and Skeffington's and Bernard Vaughan's and St. Aloysius's and Shelley's and Renan's water along with my own. And I am going to do that in my novel (inter alia) and plank the bucket down before the shades and substances above mentioned to see how they like it: and if they don't like it I can't help them. I am nauseated by their lying drivel about pure men and pure women and spiritual love and love for ever: blatant lying in the face of truth.[12]

In "Circe" Joyce's lowering of the bucket into his own psyche brings up a host of sexual impulses that are typical, not just of himself and of Bloom but of turn-of-the-century European culture.[13]

All of Bloom's dramas in "Circe" have a strong masochistic element: he is advertised as a cuckold; pilloried for his social reform schemes; publicly diagnosed as "a finished example of the new womanly man" (464); and—worst of all—ridden by the she-man Bello, who throws him on a flaming pyre when she finally tires of him. Male masochism was a phenomenon not much written about or labeled before the late nineteenth century, when the sexologist Krafft-Ebing justified his naming of it after Leopold Sacher-Masoch, author of *Venus in Furs*, by claiming that before that novel was published in 1870 "this perversion . . . was quite unknown to the scientific world as such."[14]

Joyce used Sacher-Masoch's fiction as one of his sources for the Circe chapter and even describes Mrs. Bellingham, one of the elegant society viragos who denounce Bloom at a mock-trial for his perversions, as "a Venus in furs" (448). In *Idols of Perversity* Bram Dijkstra points out that male masochism was a logical consequence of the extreme and simplistic polarization of women that took place in the last half of the nineteenth century.[15] In a cultural climate that considered only evil, power-hungry women to be fully sexual, men interested in reciprocal sex would be willing to seek victimization. Bloom's perversions of imagination are not so much his own as his time's; they actually attest to his normality. They also provide the measure of the cultural conditioning he has to overcome within himself in order to see, accept, and cherish Molly as she is.

Having made these general remarks about the chapter, I want now to focus on that moment when Bloom meets its nominal Circe, Bella Cohen, and on the dynamic scenes that follow. Joyce's casting of this archetypal figure as whore sports with a centuries-old tradition—the motto over the 1621 Alciati emblem of Circe had warned readers to "Beware of Prostitutes." But Joyce does not accept this tradition uncritically, and he does not allow his hero to heed the Alciati motto. Bloom engages with Bella as thoroughly in imagination as Odysseus had engaged with the transforming goddess in actuality. The guilt and fear he feels in her presence spring from the depths of his psyche and bring the entire syndrome of Bloomean sexuality to the surface of our awareness.[16]

This Circe is "a massive whoremistress" (485), a formidably vulgar figure. She has kohl-rimmed, glittering "falcon" eyes: a detail that suggests Joyce's awareness that her name means "hawk" in Greek. In place of the bowl of transforming brew and of her driver's stick, she carries a black horn fan that immediately springs into a life of its own. This, in Joyce's version, is her instrument of phallic power. The fan keeps tapping Bloom until he pays homage to its holder, hailing her as "powerful being" and declaring that he "enormously" desires her domination (486). The fan demands that he kneel and lace Bella's shoes. Bloom at once complies, thus assuming the old Greek posture of surrender, the posture that Circe had assumed at her doorway with Odysseus.

This sex reversal shortly becomes an overt fact of the drama. Bella becomes Bello and Bloom becomes a female slave avidly participating in an orgy of humiliation. As he becomes female he also figuratively becomes a pig. She (or he) exclaims "Truffles!" and Joyce's stage direction at this point reads "with a piercing epileptic cry she sinks on all fours, grunting, snuffling, rooting at his feet" (488). Perhaps these transformations or degradations would not have happened if Bloom had held on to the potato he habitually carried in his pocket because it was his grandmother's preventative against disease. But when he entered the bordello he gave it to the whore who greeted him, Zoe, and he realizes too late that "I should not have parted with my talisman" (486–87). Surrendering it, he surrenders to the inevitability of women's emotional domination over him.

Is the potato Joyce's version of the Homeric moly? Superficially, yes. Joyce must have enjoyed inventing this homely equivalent of Homer's mysterious plant. But the notion of moly as a protective and beneficent influence Joyce, like the Homeric allegorical commentators, took figuratively as well. He wrote to Budgen in 1920, when he was working on the Circe episode, that "Moly is the gift of Hermes, god of public ways, and is the invisible influence (prayer, chance, agility, *presence of mind,* power of recuperation which saves in case of accident. This would cover immunity from syphilis—swine love). . . . In this special case his plant may be said to have many leaves, indifference due to masturbation, pessimism congenital, a sense of the ridiculous, sudden fastidiousness in some detail, experience."[17] Though Joyce does not list Molly in this catalogue of Bloom's guardian influences, surely the similarity between her name and that of the Homeric herb is not accidental. Joyce as master wordsmith probably named Molly after the magical plant; above all, it is Bloom's love for his wife and his desire to return to her that enable him—though he gives up his potato—to pass through Nighttown fundamentally unscathed.[18]

Once Bloom's fantastical orgy of humiliation with Bello has begun, Joyce plays it through to its sacrificial end. Bello tells Bloom that "what you longed for has come to pass. Henceforth you are unmanned and mine in earnest, a thing under the yoke" (490). He becomes a "wigged, singed, perfume-sprayed, ricepowdered" whore: the person at the very bottom of the nineteenth-century European power structure. After suffering various indignities, including having his pelvic capacity measured, he finally submits to death on command. To find the ultimate humiliation visited upon women, Joyce had to go outside of European culture altogether. He (and Bello) transform Bloom at this point into a Hindu widow doomed to die on her husband's pyre. Only when the suttee smoke rises does Bello finally disappear for good.

Her place is immediately assumed by an ethereal nymph who takes form out of the smoke. This is the nymph from the picture hanging above Bloom's and Molly's bed (a vantage point that this household goddess has found very bruising to her chaste sensibilities). "What have I not seen in that chamber?" she asks (497). "What must my eyes look down on?" The timing of this pure nymph's appearance is significant, for it attests to Joyce's recognition that the impossibly pure woman and the voracious virago are interdependent, that they are two faces of the same sick cultural mentality. Whereas Bella-Bello inspired in Bloom a passion of self-mortification, this nymph evokes his feelings of sexual guilt. Bloom feels he has to apologize to her for his "soiled personal linen," and he confesses that he has been "a perfect pig" (497). The more guilty Bloom becomes, the more removed and ethereal the nymph becomes, until she eventually garbs herself in the habit of a nun.

At this point Bloom is rescued by complete happenstance, by the popping of his trouser button. "Bip!" the button exclaims, recalling him to the moment and his senses—much as Odysseus, immersed in the delights of Circe's palace, was suddenly recalled to a memory of Ithaca by the prompting of one of his men. Bloom remarks to the nun-nymph coldly, "you have broken the spell." He then asks her a question that someone should have asked St. Augustine in his later years, when he was intent on denouncing sex: "If there were only ethereal where would you all be, postulants and novices?" (501). In desperation the nymph strikes at Bloom's loins with a poinard. He seizes her hand and she "flees from him unveiled, her plaster cast cracking, a cloud of stench escaping from the cracks." This stage direction can be interpreted as Joyce's comment on the repressed sexuality he saw festering everywhere beneath the hard mask of Christian piety. To put it mildly, he was not fond of the Platonic element in Christianity and saw no point in valuing spirit that did not dwell in flesh.

Once Bloom has defeated the nymph in this fantastical drama, he finds the actual Bella Cohen much less formidable. The whole time the drama has been going on he has been staring at her without seeing her. Now he does, and he curtly dismisses what meets his eye as "mutton dressed as lamb" (501). For the rest of the chapter and the book neither of the polarized stereotypes of women have any hold upon him, although he still reveals himself to be extremely sensitive to Molly's adultery and given to masochistic bouts of fantasy about it.

Stephen's encounter with the fantastic feminine in the Circe chapter is of a different nature than Bloom's.[19] Instead of engaging with the specter his mind calls up, he tyrannically rejects it and thus reveals his comparative unreadiness and immaturity. His reaction is completely understandable, however, for his vision of his mother risen from the dead, "her face worn and noseless, green with grave mould" (515), is more visually terrifying than anything Bloom has had to face. When Stephen asks her to tell him "the word known to all men," she doesn't answer him directly. Instead she gives him advice he does not want to hear: the standard Irish Catholic admonitions to pray, to repent, and to beware of the fires of hell. He reacts to these clichés with a fury of self-assertion, shouting out "Non serviam!" as if it were a war cry (or moly) that could save him. Then he raises his ashplant and, waving it as if it were Siegfried's sword, brings it down upon the chandelier. In the ensuing confusion the ghoulish Mrs. Dedalus vanishes. Stephen has for the moment rescued himself, but he has not begun to come to terms with his mother, with the feminine she represents, and with his guilt for abandoning her when she was dying.

Richard Ellmann remarks of this scene that "in Stephen's case the saving grace is 'the intellectual imagination,' which preserves him from surrender to mother Dedalus, mother church, mother Ireland, mother England, all demanding his filial allegiance."[20] I cannot agree, for it seems to me that an intellectual imagination that projects onto the mother the whole weight of the cultural authority that he is in active rebellion against makes it harder, not easier, for Stephen to acknowledge his own emotional identity. I can find no instance in *Ulysses* in which Bloom indulges in this kind of projection onto Molly. Bloom, from whom Stephen has much to learn, is Stephen's moly in the Circe chapter. Or perhaps, more accurately, Bloom is Stephen's Hermes, the soul-guide who points him in the direction of a more complete humanity.

Joyce's Circe episode ends with the overt rescue of Stephen by

Bloom—an incident that was based on an actual event in Joyce's life which, more than any other biographical event, provided the germ of *Ulysses*.[21] When the drunken Stephen is knocked down by a British soldier whose girl he has flirted with and whose king he has supposedly insulted, Bloom dusts him off and takes him home. As Bloom approaches the supine Stephen, he is confused by the mumbling he hears. He catches a few words of a poem he does not recognize (Yeats's "Who Goes With Fergus," which, as we have learned from the Telemachus episode, Stephen recited at his mother's bedside). That these words should be on Stephen's lips when he is semiconscious strongly suggests that his earlier rejection of his mother's ghost was an act of superficial bravado. He is still entangled with her in "love's bitter mystery."[22]

Bloom stands over Stephen, his bearing "silent, thoughtful, alert . . . his fingers at his lips in the attitude of secret master" (532). Suddenly a figure appears on the dark wall opposite him: "a fairy boy of eleven . . . dressed in an Eton suit," with "a delicate mauve face." The child reads a book of Hebrew from right to left and kisses its pages. Bloom calls out "Rudy" in wonder and recognition, but this apparition of his son gazes back at him with unseeing eyes. Ellmann calls Rudy's appearance "the seal upon Bloom's Good Samaritan act" and says that the triad of chapters that "Circe" concludes ends with a recovery of life stronger that that which occurs at the ending of any other triad.[23]

Certainly the chapter ends with promise: that Stephen will recognize and assume his own deep emotional bearing; that Bloom, through his own acts of charity, will cease to be paralyzed by loss. But because Joyce, for all his stupendous wordplay, is an emotionally reticent writer, we do not know if these promises will ever be fulfilled. Though we can strongly suspect that Stephen will meet his Nora and turn into Joyce, that Bloom will at last be able to banish the shadow of death from his marriage bed, Joyce gives us no such easy satisfactions.

Nor can we say with complete assurance that it is *because* of the psychic release that has occurred in the Circe chapter that Bloom and Stephen are able to realize the father-son bond that is potentially healing for both of them.[24] In "Circe" all the walls come tumbling down—primarily the thick masonry that Irish Catholic culture set up between appearance and the psycho-sexual realities of people's lives, but also individual characters' walls between the conscious and the unconscious. At the end of this chapter, which dramatizes the expression of wild and dynamic energies, Bloom and Stephen emerge with a firmer sense of direction, whether coincidentally or consequently. Their encounters in "Circe" seem to help each toward the resolutions he needs to make.

In any case, the direction they assume is toward Molly. Molly almost certainly represents "the nonrational sense of being which supports us all, which impels us to stay alive even when life seems a blight."[25] Her "yes" to Bloom among the rhododendron on Howth head is an ecstatic version of the inarticulate yes of our hearts when they keep on beating. Joyce described her to Budgen as "the flesh that always affirms," a line meant as a deliberate travesty of Goethe's Mephistopheles' boast that his is "the spirit that eternally negates."[26] Of all the characters in *Ulysses,* Molly is the least individual and most symbolic. She is Woman as Natural Force, Woman as Goddess, and only secondarily Marion Bloom of 7 Eccles Street. As Marilyn French points out, "no real human being could ever have Molly's absolute and blind ignorance of all events except sexual ones."[27] Earthy, lyrical, and well aware of her own powers, Molly has at least as much in common with Homer's immortal Circe as she does with his mortal and individual Penelope.

For Leopold Bloom, the archetypal feminine and the personal feminine are one and the same woman and he is married to her. After the brief moment in the Ithaca chapter when he and Stephen stand side by side in the garden looking up at the light in Molly's window, he goes in and performs the bravest of all his acts: crawling into her adulterous bed. To get there he, like Odysseus, has had to slaughter suitors. The suitors, for Bloom, are not really Boylan and the host of other men to whom Molly has been attracted.[28] They are the culturally conditioned temptations in his own head to see Molly as a sexual possession who has humiliated him or to view her as the polarized evil woman. We know from the Circe chapter that these are strong temptations, but Bloom, with his scrupulous moral nature and his abundant charity, has been able to defeat them. Ithaca ends with him curled like "a manchild in the womb" beside the ample earth of Molly, who lies "in the attitude of Gea-Tellus" (658). Quite simply, he accepts her as she is. He chooses love rather than hatred.

Joyce must have been aware that this ethic of responsibility for one's own demons and acceptance of the life of others was foreign to any culture he knew. He had written to Nora in 1912, two years before he started *Ulysses,* "I am one of the writers of this generation who are perhaps creating at last a conscience in the soul of this wretched race."[29] From our vantage point, with two world wars, the destruction of the European

Jews, and two obscenity trials for *Ulysses* intervening between 1912 and the present, Joyce's Stephen-like conviction that art can create conscience looks somewhat naive. Certainly, however, *Ulysses* demonstrates conscience in an imaginatively compelling way, demonstrates that there could be an alternative to the saga of domination and subjection that Stephen recognizes as the nightmare of history.

Ending as it does with Molly's voice, a voice that moves "slowly, evenly, though with variations, capriciously, but surely like the huge earthball itself round and round spinning,"[30] *Ulysses* is like a return to ancient spirituality. It recalls a time when woman and earth were revered as the sources of life. This simple but radical idea of giving the ancient feminine a present, living voice has more recently been explored by several women writers. Margaret Atwood and Eudora Welty allow their Circes, at last, to speak for themselves.

9

Her Voice

For all her magic, immortality, and perilous allure, Circe's fate through the centuries has, in one important respect, been similar to that of her ordinary sisters. Her point of view and voice have remained for the most part unexpressed. From Homer to Joyce, the male writers and artists drawn to her myth have been interested primarily in the effects of her powers on men; they have not allowed themselves to wonder how it feels, from the inside out, to wield such awesome control over others' bodies. In most of her literary incarnations, Circe has been as mute as the Virgin Mary, that other magical shaper of flesh and blood whose ponderings of heart remain unworded. Only Calderón endowed the enchantress with a reasonably full voice, secure in his knowledge that before either of his plays ended it would be silenced, defeated.

In recent decades, the literary and visual artists attracted to the Circe-Odysseus myth have been predominantly female,[1] and they have not hesitated to imagine its historically missing point of view. Both Eudora Welty, in "Circe," which appeared in *The Bride of the Innisfallen and Other Stories* in 1955, and Margaret Atwood, in her twenty-four poem cycle of "Circe/Mud Poems," published in *You Are Happy* in 1974, gaze out at the world through the *maga's* eyes and speak in her knowing voice. At least two other women writers, Katherine Anne Porter and Toni Morrison, touch upon the myth but do not use Circe as narrator.

Porter's lyrical and spirited essay, "A Defense of Circe," follows Homer very closely, cleansing his story of centuries of tedious allegorizing and correctively emphasizing Circe's role as generous host, lover, and guide.

Porter mentions Circe's "gentle remoteness," "her divine amiability and fostering care";[2] she calls attention specifically to the beauty of detail in the bathing and feasting rituals that take place in the enchantress's palace. Yet when she discusses the transformations, her conviction that Circe dispenses a kind of revelation-therapy takes her far beyond Homer's text. Circe's "unique power as goddess," Porter writes, "was that she could reveal to men the truth about themselves by showing to each man himself in his true shape according to his inmost nature." Perhaps—but Porter fails here to distinguish her interpretation from Homer's intentions and thus repeats the misstep of the ancient allegorists. The assumption that seems to lurk behind Porter's view of the transformation—that men are really pigs—does not appear to be any more enlightened than the bias of most of the myth's male interpreters during the past two millennia to regard a powerful woman solely as a witch.

Toni Morrison's Circe—an old servant of that name who dwells with a horde of Weimaraners in a decrepit mansion in central Pennsylvania—is unambiguously a creature of the novelist's own imagination. She appears in the midst of *Song of Solomon,* a richly embellished quest novel published in 1977. As keeper of true names and pointer of true directions, Morrison's Circe enables Milkman Dead, the novel's protagonist, to discover what he is searching for: the facts of his own ancestry. Significantly, she is also a midwife, thoroughly acquainted with female rituals and lore. In all of these respects, she is as effectively instrumental a character as the enchantress of Aiaia. But she is not a main focus of Morrison's attention or imagination, and so her own history and sensibility are not thoroughly explored. To enter the consciousness behind the *maga*'s magic, we must turn to Atwood and Welty.

Why was Welty attracted to the material of "Circe," which remains her only explicit use of Greek myth? Her native Mississippi, which had served her well as a setting for fiction, could hardly be further from the ancient Aegean. Adept at finding the extraordinary in the midst of the commonplace, Welty would seemingly have had no need to range into distant mythic territory. Yet the persona of Circe proved irresistible to her—probably because it offered a model of a solitary, powerful female figure as transformer, as shaper. Through the words and eyes of Circe, Welty explores the aspirations and limits of her own craft and art. The question of Eurylochos and his mariners in the *Odyssey*—is she goddess or woman?—when they first hear the piercing notes of Circe's song is relevant to Welty's story and also to Margaret Atwood's cycle of poems. For insofar as woman creates, whether as artist or mother, she is goddess; and insofar as she opens her heart to love or grief, she is mortal woman. Both Welty and Atwood touch and explore the seam between these roles.

Thematically, Welty's "Circe" probes the differences between mystery and magic. Mystery, as Welty states in a later essay entitled "Writing and Analyzing a Story," is the stuff of both life and fiction; it dwells particularly in the currents of feeling *between* people: "Relationship *is* a pervading and changing mystery; it is not words that make it so in life, but words have to make it so in a story. Brutal or lovely, the mystery waits for people wherever they go, whatever extreme they run to."[3] The very greatest mystery, according to Welty, "is unsheathed reality itself."[4] As a writer, her intent is to pay homage to this mystery by fixing it precisely but delicately upon the page, so that it may once again take wing in the reader's imagination.

Within the story, Welty's lovely, arrogant Circe recognizes mystery as the birthright of mortals, something she herself wants (if only to destroy) but does not understand. As she gazes upon the sleeping Odysseus, she realizes that "they keep something from me, asleep and awake. There exists a mortal mystery, that, if I knew where it was, I could crush like an island grape. Only frailty, it seems, can divine it—and I was not endowed with that property. They live by frailty! By the moment! I tell myself that it is only a mystery, and mystery is only uncertainty. (There is no mystery in magic! Men are swine: let it be said, and no sooner said than done.)."[5] Her meditation here is the heart of the story, which scrupulously delineates both the sorceress's initial disdain of mortals and her increasing dissatisfaction at being unable to share Odysseus's fate. Even as this Circe stands in awe of mystery, she also longs to possess it, to hold it within the palm of her power like a child seeking to grasp a soap bubble. But because she herself will never die she cannot truly comprehend a reality that is evanescent. Like it or not, she is stuck with immortality and its attendant magic.

What is this magic? As Welty shows it, a total control over the natural and human environment. This control has its comical moments ("Outside!" Circe exclaims to the swine, "No dirt is allowed in this house!"), but maintaining it is exhausting. She needs to draw back periodically into privacy, "deathless privacy that heals everything, even the effort of magic" (532). Bored, compulsive, and alone, Circe at the beginning of this story is like an artist gone stale in her art. Her island existence can be seen as a metaphor for the plight of the writer too thoroughly enmeshed in her own intelligence and thus starved for material. Odysseus's immunity to this Circe's drugs comes as a pleasant surprise, for it offers her the company of a seeming equal and the opportunity to escape from routine and control into passion.

Passion—with its impersonality, its awakening of the elemental—is the one territory in this story that gods and mortals share. Circe thinks of Odysseus as a "strange man, as unflinching and as wound up as I am. His short life and my long one have their ground in common. Passion is our ground, our island—do others exist?" (534). Her posing of this question is a sign of her immortal ignorance, for at this point she knows nothing of love or loss, the other experiences usually recognized as existential ground.

Welty's story is about the evolution of Circe's consciousness, not Odysseus's. He may well get sailing directions from her—she possesses the requisite foreknowledge; he is off to Hades by the end of the narrative—but this kind of guidance is not what Welty cares about. She focuses almost exclusively on the tension between Circe's arrogance and her yearning.

Both these emotions quicken in her as Circe listens to Odysseus tell the story of Polyphemos while an owl outside her window critiques his narrative: "He told me of the monster with one eye—he had put out the eye, he said. Yes, said the owl, the monster is growing another, and a new man will sail along to blind it again. I had heard it all before, from man and owl. I didn't want his story, I wanted his secret" (533). Clearly she's bored with hearing butcheries woven into legend, with the conventions of heroism. The bones of past heroes (the "old, displeasing ones") hang like wind chimes from the willows fringing her island.[6] She compares Odysseus's verbal performance here with the behavior of her father the Sun, who calmly and constantly goes his way shedding light, "needing no story, no retinue to vouch for where he has been" (ibid.). Helios's sufficiency unto himself is his prerogative as a god. What Circe completely fails to grasp, however, is the relationship between secret and story, between the mystery of mortality and the desire to create and share meaning. Stories, Welty seems to imply, are our light.

Let us return to the scene in which Circe is gazing down on the sleep-tossed form of Odysseus. Only mortals, she thinks to herself, can discover where the mystery lies in each other, "can find it and prick it in all its peril, with an instrument made of air. I swear that only to possess that one, trifling secret, I would willingly turn myself into a harmless dove for the rest of eternity!" (ibid.). What is this "instrument of air"? Welty is too delicate to pin down her metaphor, preferring instead to trust her readers' guesses. It might well be the sympathetic imagination: that faculty, usually grounded in love, that enables us to bridge the gulf between our separate beings.

By the story's end Circe has been marked by the passion she and Odysseus have shared. When she hears that he is about to leave, she suffers a night of torment in which she roams distractedly around the island and wakes up in her own sty. She is pregnant with the son (Telegonos) whom she knows will grow up to kill Odysseus. No longer satisfied with the impersonal and elemental, or with her own ability to control, she seems, like Homer's Calypso, painfully caught between the divine and the human. She stands on a rock, staring out at his ship, which is "a moment's gleam on a wave." And she wishes for grief, whose "dusty mouth" she cannot find. Quite simply, Welty's Circe cannot sustain her own suffering. Grief, she thinks ruefully, is "only a ghost in Hades" (537). Perhaps she means to disparage human grief and sensibility with this remark, but it also amounts to a veiled confession that she now believes love is sufficiently real or substantial to cast grief as its shade. Welty's Circe thus pushes against and confronts the limits of her powers: love and loss remain human prerogatives that she can yearn for but not fully experience.

The sophisticated, elegant lyricism of this story does not completely disguise its parabolic nature. In adopting Circe's persona, Welty seems to explore what her own art would be like if the emotional bonds that support it were to be undervalued or severed. Having inhabited the *maga*'s consciousness, she recognizes arrogance as an impediment to storytelling, and the total control of magic as a block to art.

In her initial boredom, her saltiness, and her risk-taking, Margaret Atwood's Circe strongly resembles Welty's. Both retain most of the archetype's traditional powers, and both cast a cold eye on the conventions of heroism and quest myths. But Atwood's instinct is to explore the story's sexual politics, rather than its implications for art making. She seems to have been attracted to Homer's telling of the Circe-Odysseus myth because she saw in it a metaphor for the meeting (or collision) of patriarchal manhood and feminine power occurring in her own time.

The "Circe/Mud Poems" are part of *You Are Happy,* Atwood's sixth book of poetry. Much of her earlier work had revealed a heightened sensitivity to sexual politics and to the consciousness of the oppressed. In *Power Politics* (1971) one of Atwood's speakers expresses the stereotype of male domination and female victimization as strongly as anyone probably ever has. She tells her lover "you fit into me / like a hook into an eye / a fish hook / an open eye."[7] The exposed, unflinching stance of this speaker represents a gain in consciousness over the withdrawal and non-engagement of some of Atwood's earlier poetic personae, but her role as an aware victim advertising her wounds—or rather, her sexuality as wound—did not satisfy Atwood for long. By the time of the publication of her second novel, *Surfacing* (1972), Atwood, although still keenly interested in the consciousness of the oppressed, had already realized the pitfalls inherent in dwelling on victimization. In the novel's last pages its anonymous narrator sums up an important insight she has painfully grasped: "This above all, to refuse to be a victim. Unless I can do that I can do nothing. I have to recant, give up the old belief that I am powerless and because of it nothing I can do will ever hurt anyone. A lie which was always more disastrous than the truth would have been" (191). Atwood's adoption of the Circe persona, rich with power but lacking in innocence, represents the next step in this evolution.

This Circe both resembles and differs from Homer's. Like the goddess of Aiaia, she is connected with sacred natural forces, with the moon—to which she has built temples—and with the earth—to which she keeps her head pressed, hoping to collect "the few muted syllables left over."[8] Yet for all her foresight and intuitive understanding, she is a priestess rather than a goddess. She shares the same order of being as Odysseus and their meeting is an affair of equals. Atwood has no need for Hermes and his gift of moly in her version of the myth, for the power between the lovers is already evenly balanced. Her Odysseus comes to the encounter well armored in a "shell of confident expectation."[9] In one regard her perceptions are closer to Homer's than those of any intervening interpreter of the myth: she focuses on the issue of trust between a man and a woman and on the relationship of trust to sexuality.

Atwood's cycle tells the story of a love, an intense but brief affair that goes through many seasons of feeling during its short span of time. The series is framed by beginning and ending poems in italics that seem more obviously metaphorical than the others. The first poem I interpret as a comment on the disaster of patriarchal history (46). Odysseus approaches

Circe through a charred landscape, where the trees are sparse and blunt-ed. Atwood does not tell us explicitly what disasters have seared this Aiaia, made it into a place that can barely sustain life; she assumes that we already know. Because Circe is identified with her island's landscape throughout the series, the wounded state of the environment reflects her own condition and, even more widely, that of other powerful women for whom history has been a wasteland. Though she sees that Odysseus represents "power, power / impinging," Circe does nothing to turn him away. The remark she makes about him in the last line—"You find what there is"—could be said with equal truth about a skilled lover or a force-ful imperialist. Which does she consider him to be? As we are to find out, roles shift like tides between them.

In the next three poems Circe describes her life before Odysseus. Giv-en her boredom with manufacturing pig-men and "men with the heads of eagles" who no longer interest her, we begin to understand why she has done nothing to hinder Odysseus's arrival. He might be one of the new kind she is looking for, one of "the ones who have escaped from these [prevailing] / mythologies with barely their lives" (47). These new, imagined men "would rather be trees" than participate in the power games that have enabled her, with male connivance, to turn men into beasts. Circe clearly recognizes in the third poem that transformation requires mutuality, that it is not her work (or fault) alone. Indeed, the fur and hides and tusks and snouts spontaneously materialized when she refused to communicate with the wandering men who approached her. Is male bestiality here dependent on female lack of response or vice versa? Atwood makes clear that they are two moves in the same game.

Then Odysseus arrives. The sixth poem, addressed to him, is Atwood's most trenchant critique of patriarchal ideology. Her Circe has no respect for Odysseus's supposedly heroic deeds. "There must be more for you to do," she tells him

> than permit yourself to be shoved
> by the wind from coast
> to coast to coast, boot on the boat prow
>
> to hold the wooden body
> under, soul in control.

(51)

She perceives the poverty of the dualistic, over-under way of thinking and living that has resulted in a massive devaluation of body, woman, and nature in Western culture. "Don't you get tired of killing?" she asks; "Don't you get tired of saying Onward?" Instead of filling his life with hollow victories and predatory wandering, she advises him to "Ask who keeps the wind / Ask what is sacred" (51). In just over a hundred words Atwood's Circe thus dispenses with the ethos of domination and progress that has prevailed for millennia. Her voice here is flawlessly intelligent and assured. But her radiant self-possession, as Atwood shortly makes clear, depends upon distance, upon her position on the periphery, on an island almost lost in the mists of the horizon.

Once this Circe and her Odysseus draw closer in attraction, her self-possession becomes at risk. As in Homer's version, she is the first to surrender; she permits Odysseus to become close enough to assume the posture of a rapist holding down her arms and hair. "Let go, this is extortion," she tells him in Atwood's tenth poem (which occupies the same position in this twenty-four poem cycle that the Aiaia episode does in the twenty-four book *Odyssey*): "You force my body to confess / too fast and / incompletely, its words / tongueless and broken" (55). With this mock-rape as the beginning of their experience as lovers, understanding between them does not flower fully or naturally. Probably because of the more than 2,500 years of women's subjection intervening between Homer's Circe and Atwood's, the latter extends no gracious invitation to Odysseus to mingle with her in lovemaking and trust. Indeed, he has to *order* her to trust him in the twelfth poem, and she has to sacrifice in order to comply.

Up to this point she has worn a sacred talisman around her neck, a withered fist whose fingers rub together in the "worn moon rituals" of goddess-based religion. This charm may well be Circe's moly. Now Odysseus unbuckles the fist, symbolically breaking her connection with the angry ancient powers that have protected and sustained her.[10] Odysseus is clearly the aggressor here, making her give up her protection before he takes off his own armor. He plays safe, while she experiences the sacrifice as an amputation, a severance from the powers that have thus far preserved her. She opens "like a hand / cut off at the wrist" (58). And yet she does open, showing herself after this point to be capable of pleasure and of wonder.

The fifteenth poem is the jewel of the series, the one that most fully reveals this new range of feeling in Circe. Freshly vulnerable herself, she is at last able to see Odysseus's vulnerability and to acknowledge the man beneath the hero role. She speaks to Odysseus with all her old precision, but now also with a lover's tenderness:

Your flawed body, sickle
scars on the chest, moonmarks, the botched knee
that nevertheless bends when you will it to

Your body, broken and put together
not perfectly, marred
by war but moving
despite that with such ease and leisure

Your body that includes everything
you have done, you have had done
to you and goes beyond it

This is not what I want
but I want this also.

(60)

With these words she acknowledges his past, his suffering, the grief implicit in his name. Perhaps she too wants to be regarded in this way, with full acknowledgment and acceptance. Perhaps she desires the surrender to be mutual, as it eventually becomes in Homer's version. If so, she does not get what she wants and she herself is as much to blame for this failure as Odysseus.

Fear shortly intrudes upon her mood of tender clarity. No two poems in the series are more dissonant in tone than the delicate fifteenth and the cynical sixteenth. For the reader, to move from the one to the other is to pull back the antennae of feeling and to take refuge once again in sociohistorical analysis. In the latter poem Circe recalls a story once told by "another traveller, just passing through" (61). He and a boyhood friend constructed a headless woman out of mud, a kind of life-sized Venus of Willendorf, whose sun-warmed earth-flesh they fucked repeatedly, with flawless satisfaction. "Is this what you would like me to be?" she wonders of Odysseus. "Is this what I would like to be? It would be so simple." Given the tendency of patriarchy to deny women's voices and of Western culture to equate the feminine with the material and corporeal, Circe's fear here (which seems to include a fear of her own complicity) cannot be dismissed as paranoia. Though she has opened herself to Odysseus, she does not trust him to want more than her body. She is haunted by this image of the mud woman, who seems also to haunt Atwood, for "Mud" figures in the series' title.

Not until the final, twenty-fourth poem is Circe's voice as unguarded as it is in the fifteenth. Her tone shortly becomes, in the eighteenth poem, that of someone who knows herself too well, who knows that the most subtle and effective of impediments to love is her own temptation to retreat from engagement back into the witch or goddess role expected of her: back into invulnerability, omniscience, seeming immortality. Musing to herself, she admits that it is not Odysseus she fears "but that other / who can walk through flesh, / queen of the two dimensions" (63). That other is her Persephone-like other self, the arrogant one who thinks she is acquainted with the borders of life, the one who "knows the ritual" and "gets results," who closes herself off to any feeling from the outside world. This Circe catches herself in her own power game, revealing that she can judge herself as harshly as she judges all the tiresome heroes saying "Onward." This ruthless self-consciousness and honesty give Atwood's Circe a complexity and believability beyond that possessed by any of the others, except for Welty's.

Having predicted her own retreat from intimacy, she goes on to demonstrate it. But by this time Odysseus is in retreat too, safely ensconced in a study where he is writing down his version of his adventures—a more patriarchal verson of the *Odyssey*, perhaps. She tries to warn him that the saga is not finished, that "fresh monsters are already breeding in my head" (64), but he fails to listen. And why should he? As she admits, "it's the story that counts" (68), and he thinks he has control of the story. By the end of the twenty-third poem the love once alive between them has all but disappeared in the wake of each of their separate retreats into the strategies of defense, control, survival. The series up to this point bears out the truth of Carl Jung's description of the seesawing relationship between the desire to love and the will to dominate. "Where love reigns," Jung wrote, "there is no will to power; and where the will to power is paramount, love is lacking. The one is but the shadow of the other."[11]

The final, framing italicized poem softens the series as a whole because it suggests an alternative to the endless cycles of sexual power struggles and lost love. In its first lines Circe allows herself to conceive of a landscape other than the charred forest she has known. "There are two islands / at least," she says, "they do not exclude each other" (69). On the first, familiar one she is "right" and in control; her affairs happen over and over, running through her mind and experience like a bad film through a jerky projector, their repetition demanded by compulsion. But on the second island, the one she admits "I know nothing about / be-

cause it has never happened," the atmosphere remains alive with possibility. Here the land is not charred or "finished," but fully capable of
supporting life. Here her own body is not "reversible," but inescapably
mortal. She imagines herself and Odysseus walking through a field in
November, licking melted snow from each other's mouths, stopping to
examine the track of a deer in the mud. (The mud here is only mud,
not some pornographic building material.) This vision seems as fragile
as its flakes of snow, untested, evanescent. Yet its evanescence is its point.
The island, miraculous in an ordinary way, exists potentially in any
moment and is the magnification of a moment. As such it represents
an escape from the relentless compulsions of individual and cultural history, a leap into the timelessness of love.[12]

Atwood's Circe is able to realize this moment in imagination only.
Her ability to call it to mind, however, points the way for the lovers in
"Book of Ancestors," the last and most perfect of the poems in this volume. These lovers are well aware of scenes of violence in the collective
past; they have toured a Toltec temple where they have seen a fresco of
a priest cutting out the heart of a sacrificial victim.[13] But their intense
trust for each other gives them faith to believe that they are not doomed
to recreate this scene figuratively. For them "History is over" (95); they
"take place / in a season, an undivided space" similar to that of the island Circe has imagined. In that space of reality, they meet in front of
a fire at midwinter and gently open to each other in love. The woman's
words in the poem's last lines connect their encounter with the sacred
rites of the priests:

> what
> they tried, we
> tried but could never do
> before . without blood, the killed
> heart . to take
> that risk, to offer life and remain
>
> alive, open yourself like this and become whole
>
> (96)

What necessitated slaughter in the past now has been chosen freely, thoroughly and mutually transformed.

This transformation into wholeness is not one that Atwood's Circe,
for all her clarity, wit, and power, has been able to achieve on her own.

Nor has she been able to provide direction to Odysseus, who chooses not to listen to her. Atwood's adoption of the Circe mask may well have provided the poet herself, however, with the direction she needed. It allowed her to speak in the voice of a woman unashamed of her strengths and unwilling to confine herself to a victim's role. It allowed her to explore the condition of such a woman on the periphery of patriarchy and in relationship to a male equal. And finally, it enabled her to discover and express the limits of power conceived as the will to dominate rather than as the capacity to love.

After all their words have been spoken, both Welty's Circe and Atwood's Circe remain in an attitude of yearning. Both want what they do not have and cannot control: the mystery inherent in mortality, in relationship. Instead of imagining the *maga* as the terrifying Other, Welty and Atwood have entered her consciousness and allowed that consciousness to develop beyond the confines of its former craft. Their Circes are ready, or almost ready, to drown their books, to settle if possible for the wonder of being human. Of all the writers and artists who have touched this myth since Homer, Welty and Atwood have most distinctively pointed a direction in which it can evolve.

Conclusion: Transformations

What a long slog through centuries of misogyny. Yet Homer's story of Circe and Odysseus, our foundation text and the starting point of this book, could hardly be less tendentious and ideological, or more fascinating. He sings of the meeting between a goddess who wields awesome power over flesh and blood and a Mycenaean hero who does not shrink from her power, of the trust that evolves between them. He also tells of reversal, of how what is negative and terrifying can become positive and illuminating if courage keeps the leash on fear.

In Homer's version, the archetypal core of Circe's character is pristine, undamaged. Like Kubaba, like Kybele, like the pre-Homeric Artemis, she is the goddess who gives form to life and the goddess who takes it away. She acts from the center of her power, and her throne is her flawless bed. The sexual relationship between Odysseus and her is redemptive, bringing into trust and balance all that is negative and imbalanced in the first part of the myth. Odysseus begins by holding a sword to her throat, but he ends by taking her knees in the gesture of entreaty and surrender—as she has already surrendered to him. She responds generously and truthfully, with directions that are essential to his voyage home. This competent, patriarchal hero, representing the new order, confronts an exemplar of the old, female-centered one and eventually opens to her and receives her blessing.

Would that history had followed the course of Homer's myth and that all patriarchal heroes were as receptive as Odysseus to the wisdom of the feminine. He receives from Circe a whole set of instructions that have to do with the acknowledgment of human limits, with the recognition that some powers (Scylla, Helios and his oxen) are too potentially destructive to tamper with and must be respected and left alone. Odysseus returns to Ithaca because he is no Faust or Alexander, because he finally believes that the will to control and dominate everything he encounters—a drive that he has already ruthlessly acted out during the sack of Ismaros—will in the end destroy him too. Any alert and fair-minded reader of the *Odyssey* recognizes Circe's primary role in teaching Odysseus this difficult lesson. His willingness to listen to her appears to spring from the bond of pleasure established between them.

So, what happened? Why was a sense of the wholeness of this myth lost for well over two millennia and the liaison between Circe and Odysseus regarded as too dangerous even to acknowledge? We are faced here with a phenomenon that would seem hard to believe: one of the most important episodes in one of the bedrock works of Western literature was consistently and grossly misread for centuries. Only the existence of persistent, pervasive, and unacknowledged biases can account for this fact.

These biases include, I believe, a profound distrust of the body and a fear of the loss of rational control that is an integral part of sexual experience. Furthermore, this uneasiness about carnality and sexuality was projected on to Woman, who, in the words of Dorothy Dinnerstein, "serves her species as carnal scapegoat-idol."[1] These biases do not show up in Homer's poem because he lived and wrote in a time when the experience of being human seems still to have been unitary, when consciousness was not conceived of as a refuge removed from harsh experience, or distanced from the body's keen pleasure and pain. Homer's heroes possess a bright sentience that is inseparable from their life-embracing, death-facing flesh. They share "the seeming identity of body and mind . . . and thence the loveliness of the former" that Coleridge noticed in infants,[2] probably because they are described by Homer in a language that had not yet developed the abstract vocabulary that can and often does pull intelligence away from sense experience. Every Homeric character exists forthrightly in his or her bodily vulnerability, open to the currents of danger and pleasure and divinity that press from within and without. The great feasting and bathing rituals in Homer are hymns to this wondrous existence in the body, which is abruptly snuffed out by death.

Plato and his followers, or perhaps the Pythagoreans and Orphics before them, made a profound change in the legacy of cultural attitudes that have been passed down to us. Their longing for the eternal and absolute led them to postulate the existence of a pure realm of Being that had its muted, imprisoned echo within the soul of every human being. The body—so bright and cared for and prized in Homer—was viewed by the followers of Plato and Pythagoras as a prison or tomb. The resulting body-soul or body-mind dualism readily lent itself, in the generations following, to misogyny, for how could eternally pregnant, lactating, and menstruating women be considered creatures preeminently of mind? The male/soul, female/body typology was a large part of the climate of thought in which Homeric allegory developed and in which, later, Christian belief was codified into doctrine.

Like cowbirds making use of the nest already there, the ancient allegorists preempted Homer's story, shoving what they didn't like out beyond the boundaries of acknowledgment and fledging a new myth, one about the Triumph of Reason, from the part that remained. Now Odysseus's ability to drain Circe's cup and remain unchanged certified him as an exemplar of *logos*. "I am the master of my fate," this new Odysseus might have boasted to her, "I am the captain of my soul." It was a boast that has proved as disastrous to the course of our culture as the original Odysseus's one about blinding Polyphemos was to his personal journey home. In this new myth, which gave symbolic form to developing Western attitudes toward body, women, and nature, all that was beyond human control either receded to insignificance or was labeled as evil. Circe, who represented to Diogenes of Sinope, in 350 B.C.E., the voluptuousness that enslaves the soul and distracts it from its true course, became even more sinister to post-Augustinian interpreters of her story. Now she represented that brand of sin upon human nature, sexuality itself.

Contemplating these developments in the centuries following Homer, how can we not feel sad that the longing for transcendence, for some contact with Being that feels absolute, which is so poignantly and universally human and so beautifully expressed in Plato, became so thoroughly entangled with existing gender and power arrangements? And this entanglement proved extraordinarily long-lived. A metaphor Plutarch uses to describe marriage—as the bonding of the governing soul, represented by the man, with the governed body, represented by the woman—was still current in England in the seventeenth century.[3]

Though Circe's persona has passed through a multitude of minor metamorphoses since antiquity, virtually all of her pre-twentieth century guises ratify the great change in the way her character was seen that took place between Homer's time and that of the early allegorists. I can find no other essential transformation in the reading of her myth until the twentieth century, until after Freud and Jung and their followers had illuminated the interconnection and dependency of conscious mental systems on organic, unconscious ones and it was no longer tenable to view consciousness as a phenomenon that existed *apart* from nature. Although feminist thinkers have attacked Freud for his patriarchal assumptions concerning female development, they have not honored him sufficiently for helping to destroy the old, pernicious body-mind (or body-soul) dualism that so efficiently buttressed misogyny. In this new climate of thought, the old certainties of allegory began to look feeble, and the dualistic reading of the Circe myth, which persisted in all its strength at least through the seventeenth century, seems at last to be expiring.

The basic pattern of seductive Woman impeding starry-eyed Man in his pursuit of distant glory obtained, however, for a very long time; it can be found in Calderón as in Virgil and Spenser. Whether that glory is seen as the Kingdom of God, the glittering imperial city, or the favor of the Fairie Queene, the renunciation of sexual pleasure, because it is seen as the most powerful impediment to this glory's realization, can be found in all three writers. In Virgil this renunciation is so strong that Circe's island occupies only a score of lines and is safely skirted around by Aeneas, who has already piously sailed away from Dido's flaming pyre. In Spenser the renunciation is not easy or secure, for it conflicts with the neo-paganism so congenial to his poetic imagination and with his temperamental openness to the feminine. Nevertheless, Guyon does manage to turn Acrasia's bliss into balefulness and Artegal does slip out of Britomart's embrace to go off and subdue the Irish rebels. To read *The Faerie Queene* is to watch a major poet *almost* break out of two thousand years of cultural conditioning and follow his own instincts about what promotes life and what does not. This same tension between pleasure and its renunciation is skillfully allegorized and dramatized in Calderón's *Los encantos de la Culpa,* but the outcome of the contest there is never fundamentally in doubt. How else could a luxuriant character named Sin end her stay on the Corpus Christi festival stage than by going down in quake and flames?

All three of these writers, we should note, are quite honest about the *cost* of renouncing pleasure and sexuality in favor of distant, imagined glory. The *Aeneid* ends with carnage and violated trust; book 2 of *The Faerie Queene* with a merciless, incendiary fit; Calderón's *auto* with apocalypse.

This destruction is symptomatic of what happens when we pursue some vision of the eternal and absolute (even if we insist on mingling this vision with worldly power, as in the case of "eternal" Rome) while dishonoring our earthly, finite, inescapably sexual and mortal roots. As Carol Christ points out, "our religious and philosophical traditions since Plato have attempted to deny finitude and death and have prevented us from fully comprehending our connections to this earth. . . . We must learn to love this life that ends in death. . . . Our task is here."[4] The radiant sentience and courage of Homer's characters, their willingness to embrace life and face death in the moment, speak of another possibility for our lives, yet we cannot go back to their time before the development of abstract thought and language, before consciousness learned to stand back from experience and from nature.

Perhaps part of what Joyce meant when he wrote of "creating at last a conscience in the soul of this wretched race" was the use of artistic consciousness to expose the whole folly of the body/soul dualism and to acknowledge the harm this rift has caused. How else than by acknowledgment of damage and pain can the process of healing begin? Joyce's Dublin in *Ulysses* is the mirror of a society inured to a fractured way of life. In it, sexual feeling is everywhere, but everywhere denied, made to retreat into romantic euphemism or shameless cynicism by the combined forces of the Catholic Church and of the scientific rationalism with which Mulligan and his cohorts are heavily dosed. Molly Bloom's ability to shed all contradictions, to maintain her own luxuriant vitality in the teeth of these forces of denial, certainly testifies to Joyce's belief in the power of the feminine to endure with health and élan.

Yet Joyce does not view the feminine as the Other, as the possessor of mysterious powers of transformation inaccessible to half of the human race. In his Circe chapter he as author makes use of this power, endowing inanimate objects such as buttons with language, a Jewish grandfather with wings, and his humane but masochistic hero with a sex change. He uses the power to transform to effect a massive exposure and detonation of cultural hypocrisies and contradictions. Bloom and Stephen walk away from the Circe chapter and the chaos of Nighttown with a much firmer sense of where they are going. Home to Molly, as it turns out, to a cherishing of sexuality and of life that has always been there to come back to.

Similarly, in Margaret Atwood's cycle of Circe poems, Circe herself is not the sole possessor of the power to transform. Although on her island men do take on animal forms, the transformation is the result of a collaborative effort: she permits to happen what they secretly will. Atwood's series, like Joyce's chapter, is really an exposure of the dualism, of the whole folly of projecting on to Woman the burden and delight of the carnality that we all bear. This Circe is bored and heartsick with the role into which she has been born—as Eudora Welty's Circe is rapidly becoming. Neither of these two knows how to free herself from the role, though the last words of Atwood's Circe are a renunciation of it and a wistful imagining of what life and relationship would be like if men and women cast aside the securities of power hierarchies and together faced the mystery of their existence. What if? she asks.

I wish to second her question. What would our tenure on this planet be like if we wholeheartedly accepted our identity as spiritual animals who long for the transcendent but who are capable of finding it only in the moment in which we stand rooted? If we acknowledged that within our own natures spirituality and sexuality are inextricably connected? Perhaps then we would have no need for Circe myths, with all the freight they carry concerning sexual hostility and vulnerability and control, and no need for Circe's emphatic reminder to those who come to her door that they are, unmistakably, creatures. Perhaps then the stereotypical Circe would suffer a death as gentle and natural as the one that Homer's Tiresias predicts for Odysseus, and the archetypal core of her power would be freed for us to use in creating new myths to dream onward.

Notes

Introduction

1. Lucy Hughes-Hallett, in her introduction to *Cleopatra: Histories, Dreams and Distortions,* draws this clarifying distinction between the use of fiction as evidence for social history and as evidence for the imaginative life of a culture (3).

2. See particularly Eliade's *Myth and Reality,* Wheelwright's *Metaphor and Reality,* and Campbell's *The Power of Myth.* There is plenty of room for mystery, also, in Carl Jung's conception of myth, but Jung sees the mysteries that mythic narratives confront as being primarily *within* the human being. To Jung, "myths are first and foremost psychic phenomena that reveal the nature of the soul . . . they are symbolic expressions of the inner, unconscious drama of the psyche which becomes accessible to man's consciousness by way of projection" ("Archetypes," 6). Jung's is thus an idealist view, which sees inward reality (psyche) as more important than outward event or matter.

3. Jung, "Archetypes," 19–20.

4. Ibid., 32.

5. For excellent critiques of this aspect of Jung's thought see Demaris Wehr's *Jung and Feminism: Liberating Archetypes,* and Annis Pratt's essay "Spinning among Fields: Jung, Frye, Lévi-Strauss and Feminist Archetypal Theory," in Lauter and Rupprecht, eds., *Feminist Archetypal Theory.*

Chapter 1: Homer's Story

1. Campbell, *Occidental Mythology,* 172.

2. The name of the island might derive from the name of Circe's brother

Aietes; or from *aiai,* an exclamation of extreme distress (in which case it would mean "wailing"); or from *aia,* an alternate form of *gaia,* the Greek word for earth, which Homer sometimes uses. It might also derive from the West Semitic *ayya,* which means "hawk." They all seem appropriate.

3. 10.136. Although Homer once applies this phrase to Calypso (12.44-9), he otherwise reserves it for Circe; it is her most distinctive epithet.

4. This and all other translations from the Greek, unless otherwise indicated, are mine.

5. Homer knew the Argonaut myths, which he describes as "of interest to all" (12.70). In Apollonius Rhodius's Hellenistic version, Circe, as aunt to Medea, is an active part of the cast.

The Italians, from Virgil's time to the present, have been eager to claim Circe and have named a mountain and a national park after her. Locating the island off the west coast of Italy is unconvincing, however, because for the Greeks the sun does not rise over the Tyrrhenian Sea. Also, Homer describes the island as low-lying, not mountainous. All attempts to trace literally the geography of the *Odyssey* are doomed, of course, to uncertainty. Long ago Eratosthenes warned that "the scenes will be found when you find the tailor who sewed the bag of the winds, and not before" (quoted by Robert Brown, Jr., *Myth of Kirke,* 97).

6. Homer also refers to Circe once as "nymph," in a line repeated from the Calypso episode. The word *thelkter,* meaning magician or charmer, was probably current in Homer's time—the related verb *thelgo* is used several times in book 10—but he never applies it to Circe. Most translations give alternate readings for at least some of the usages of *thea,* so most readers do not get an accurate impression of Circe's status as a divinity.

7. So W. B. Stanford argues in "That Circe's ῥάβδος Was Not a Magic Wand," *Hermathena* 66 (1945): 69–71.

8. Hermes is father to the master-thief Autolycos, Odysseus's maternal grandfather and giver of his name; see Robert Graves, *Greek Myths* 1:65.

9. For over two millennia etymologists have been searching for this plant, which has linguistic affinities with an old Greek word for wild garlic. But since this garlic has yellow flowers it does not seem ideal.

Gabriel Germain treats the subject of moly thoroughly in *Génèse de l'Odyssée,* 216–20. Other plants that have been suggested as the magical herb are purslane, white grape, marjoram, buckthorn, wild celery, and mandrake.

10. In locating Odysseus's will or consciousness (*nóos*) in his breast (*stethos*) rather than his head, Circe is consistent with Athene, who later praises the hero by telling him "always there is some thought in your chest" (13.330). Homer generally locates the organs of consciousness in the torso; there is no separation between the corporeal and mental life of his heroes.

11. Robert Fitzgerald's translation as "flawless" seems apt, even though

it does not suggest the visual quality that the Greek word connotes. No one else in the *Odyssey* has a bed that is flawless, *perikalle.*

12. See ll. 108–10 of "To Aphrodite" in *The Homeric Hymns,* trans. Athanassakis.

13. Fitzgerald's translation of the first part of this sentence—"wild regret and longing pierced them through"—though inspired English, seems to imply that Odysseus's men did not wholly desire this second transformation. This implication is nowhere to be found in Homer. I agree with Paolo Vivante's reading of *hypedu* as "emerged from within," for it fits the context perfectly. See Vivante, "On Homer's Winged Words," 7.

14. Hesiod, in lines 1111–14 of the *Theogony,* mentions three sons born to Odysseus and Circe. E. A. Butterworth, in *Some Traces of the Pre-Olympian World,* states that several late Greek writers refer to a poem called the *Telegony,* which tells the story of the murder and its aftermath (57). Apparently, Telegonos, when he saw what he had done, brought Penelope and Telemachos and the body of Odysseus to his mother Circe, who made them all immortal. In another version, Telegonos marries Penelope; Telemachos, Circe.

15. The word that Homer uses, *Kimmerion,* has been disputed for centuries. Some editors have read it as *Cheimerion,* meaning Land "of Winter," and justified their choice by pointing to Homer's mention of the long days of darkness in this country. The word has also been associated with a historical people named the Cimmerians, whom Herodotos (4.11) locates in the Crimea beside the sea of Azov and who invaded Ionia in the mid-seventh century B.C.E., sacking the primitive temple of Artemis at Ephesus. These people may or may not be the same as those who appear earlier in Hittite and Assyrian inscriptions as the Gimirri. I am inclined to identify the Kimmerioi as the Cimmerians, because of their proximity to the Black Sea region, where many scholars place Circe. For a review of the dispute, see Stanford's note on 382 of the first volume of his edition of the Greek text.

16. The point that Odysseus has to *earn* this additional information from Circe is convincingly made by Seyfi Karabaş in "The *Odyssey* and the Turkish Quatrains," 141–42.

17. Jung, "The Transcendent Function," in *Collected Works* 8:68.

18. Hillman, *Anima,* 61.

19. Hillman mentions, as one of his many defining descriptions of this Jungian archetype, that she is "mediatrix of the unknown" (*Anima,* 129). The phrase very accurately describes Circe's role in the *Odyssey.*

20. "This central symbol is the *vessel.* From the very beginning down to the latest stages of development we find this archetypal symbol as essence of the feminine. The basic symbolic equation woman = body = ves-

sel corresponds to what is perhaps mankind's—man's as well as woman's—most elementary experience of the Feminine" (Neumann, *Great Mother,* 39).

In his chart on p. 83, Neumann locates Circe at the end of the Negative Transformative pole of the archetypal feminine; he admits, however, that she was originally a goddess who became a witch when her myth became "patriarchally colored" (288).

Neumann also stresses that "when an ego approaches a pole [of the archetypal feminine] along one of its axes, there is a possibility that it will pass beyond this pole to its opposite. This is to say that in their extremes the opposites coincide or can at least shift into one another" (76). His observation well explains Circe's shift from malefactor to benefactor of Odysseus.

21. Ibid., 31.

22. Robert Bly very memorably expresses this connection between the beginning of cultural life and the beginning of individual life: "Just as every adult was once inside the mother, every society was once inside the Great Mother" (from "I Came Out of the Mother Naked," in *Sleepers Joining Hands,* 29).

23. The insight that Circe and Penelope complement each other and are attuned is expressed in an unusual way in Dino de Laurentis's otherwise undistinguished 1954 film, *Ulysses.* In it, Silvana Mangano doubles these parts, playing both enchantress and wife.

24. Frank Budgen, *Making of Ulysses,* 17.

Chapter 2: Where Did Circe Come From?

1. For discussion of the scope of this religion, see E. O. James, *The Cult of the Mother Goddess;* Erich Neumann, *The Great Mother;* Merlin Stone, *When God Was a Woman;* and especially Marija Gimbutas, *The Language of the Goddess.* Gimbutas prefers the term "Great Goddess" to "Mother Goddess" as "best describing her absolute rule, her creative, destructive and regenerative powers" (316).

2. Martin P. Nilsson mentions two antithetical strains in Greek religion, the Olympian and the chthonic. He thinks that "the antitheses are of a racial character" (*Minoan-Mycenaean Religion,* 633).

3. Gimbutas, *Language of the Goddess,* xix.

4. Apuleius, *The Golden Ass,* trans. Graves, 228.

5. A suggestion originating with Victor Bérard and developed further by Michael Astour in *Hellenosemitica,* 284.

6. Gimbutas, *Language of the Goddess,* 322.

7. Buffie Johnson, *Lady of the Beasts,* 8.

8. Nilsson, *Minoan-Mycenaean Religion,* 491.

9. Gimbutas, *Language of the Goddess,* 322.

10. Mellaart, "Excavations at Çatal Hüyük, 1963," 65, 75.

11. Gimbutas, *Language of the Goddess*, 187.

12. Mellaart, "Excavations at Çatal Hüyük, 1962," 70.

13. For impressive visual documentation of this continuity in design motifs, see Balpinar, Hirsch, and Mellaart, *Goddess from Anatolia*, vol. 1.

14. Machteld J. Mellink, "Comments on a Cult Relief," 351–54.

15. Charles Picard, *Éphèse et Claros*, 496.

16. R. D. Barnett, "Early Greek and Oriental Ivories," 22.

17. Aelian, *On the Characteristics of Animals*, 12.4.

18. One statue of Kybele unearthed from the ruins of a shrine at Pergamon has a multiplicity of breasts, like those of cult statues of the Ephesian Artemis. This sign of their kinship, however, is a Hellenistic innovation; in their older forms the goddesses are less encumbered. See Maarten J. Vermaseren, *Cybele and Attis*, 27.

19. Hogarth, *Excavations at Ephesus*, 95, 237.

20. Paul Jacobsthal, "Date of the Ephesian Foundation-Deposit," 85–95.

21. Hogarth, *Excavations at Ephesus*, 1. The Amazons loom large in the post-Homeric Greek imagination, particularly in classical sculpture, where they are often warred against and inevitably defeated. This encounter is fraught with symbolism: male against female; patriarchy versus matrilineal society; reason, perhaps, against nature. An anti-Amazon bias is not noticeable in Homer, though he has clearly heard of the legendary tribe and includes their queen Penthesileia among the cast of the *Iliad,* as a respected warrior on the Trojan side. Historically, Amazon legends may have originated from the encounter of the patriarchally organized Greek colonists with still-matrilineal segments of the local population in Asia Minor. See note 55 in this chapter.

22. Apollonius Rhodius, *Argonautica,* iii.310ff.

23. Burkert, *Greek Religion,* 12.

24. Mellaart, "Excavations at Çatal Hüyük, 1961," 64–65.

25. Both Henri Frankfort, in *The Art and Architecture of the Ancient Orient,* and Johnson, in *Lady of the Beasts* (82), speculate that she is Lilith, the mysterious and uncompliant companion of Adam who is later supplanted by Eve in Hebraic myth.

26. Germain, *Génèse de l'Odyssée,* 262.

27. Pictured in Johnson, *Lady of the Beasts,* 203.

28. Lewis Farnell, *Cults of the Greek States* 2:425; Nilsson, *Minoan-Mycenaean Religion,* 503.

29. Farnell, *Cults of the Greek States* 2:448.

30. M. S. Thompson, "Asiatic or Winged Artemis," 295.

31. Hogarth, *Excavations at Ephesus,* 176.

32. Germain, *Génèse de l'Odyssée,* 262.

33. *De Dea Syria*, 41; quoted by Germain, 262–63.

34. Gimbutas, *Language of the Goddess*, xxii, 146.

35. Gimbutas, *Gods and Goddesses of Old Europe*, 211.

36. Burkert, *Greek Religion*, 242.

37. Gimbutas, *Gods and Goddesses*, 214; Nilsson, *Minoan-Mycenaean Religion*, 312.

38. Germain, *Génèse de l'Odyssée*, 144.

39. Katherine G. Kanta, *Eleusis*, 13.

40. George Mylonas, *Eleusis and the Eleusinian Mysteries*, 223.

41. Johnson, *Lady of the Beasts*, 262.

42. Mark Golden discusses the post-Homeric usage of *choiros*, meaning "young pig," to refer to a woman's genitals and suggests that the dual wild/tame nature of the pig may explain why fifth-century Athenians connected this word with female sexuality, which they regarded as a dangerous force unless properly tamed in marriage ("Male Chauvinists and Pigs," 1–12). Such usage is common in Aristophanes, particularly in *Acharnians*. Eva Keuls notes that in Attic the use of pig words to refer to women "acquired overtones of contempt" (*Reign of the Phallus*, 353).

43. Germain, *Génèse de l'Odysée*, 131–32, 149–50; Germain does not explain, however, why this "initiation" does not also involve the hero, Odysseus.

44. Not all taboos on pork were Judaic. At the temple at Hierapolis in Syria, pigs were never eaten because they were sacred to the Goddess. Lucian, *De dea Syria*, quoted by Germain, 135.

45. Samuel Kramer, *Sacred Marriage Rite*, 64–65.

46. Ibid., 101.

47. Ibid., 105.

48. *Epic of Gilgamesh*, trans. Sandars, 86–87. In this and other modern versions the Goddess appears as Ishtar, for translations are based primarily upon the Assyrian tablets.

49. Sandars, "Introduction" to *Gilgamesh*, 12.

50. The *Odyssey* shows possible influences from *Gilgamesh* at other points as well. See Germain, 420ff. Like Gilgamesh, Odysseus travels to the Land of the Dead (also after being given directions by a female) and returns to rule his kingdom. Gilgamesh was the primal epic hero; it seems likely that Homer, as an Ionian poet, would have known about him.

51. Nilsson, *Homer and Mycenae*, 253.

52. Graves states that Iasion is a Titan (*Greek Myths* 1:89).

53. Herodotos tells us that in at least one part of western Asia Minor, Lycia, citizens identified themselves by their mothers' rather than their fathers' names (1.173). If what he says is true, then a matrilineal system of social organization, with its relatively greater freedom for women, lingered there into the fifth century B.C.E.

54. Greek legend dates this repression to the time of Cecrops, revered

as the first king of Athens and the founder of the institution of marriage. To placate the wrath of Poseidon, who was angry at the women of the new Athenian kingdom because they chose Athene rather than himself as its tutelary deity, Cecrops decreed that women could no longer take part in political assemblies and that newborn children must be known by their fathers' names. Identification by patronymics necessitated the curtailment of women's sexual freedom and the bestowing of one woman upon one man. The surviving version of the Cecrops legend is late, dating from the Roman scholar Varro in the first century B.C.E.

55. According to William Blake Tyrrell, no historical evidence exists to either prove or disprove the existence of the Amazons and therefore speculation about who they might, in actuality, have been is pointless. He reads the myth as an inversion of patriarchy, as the Athenians' dire picture of what women would be like if they were not confined within marriage (*Amazons: A Study in Athenian Mythmaking*).

George Thomson remarks that the Amazon legend developed "as a symbol for the matriarchal institutions of a theocratic Hittite settlement at Ephesos, dedicated to the Anatolian mother-goddess" and "continued to expand in response to the expanding acquaintance of the Greeks themselves with the still matriarchal peoples with which they were everywhere brought in contact" (*Prehistoric Aegean*, 182–83). Thomson is wrong when he confuses matrilineal societies with matriarchies and when he misdates the Hittites, but these inaccuracies of detail need not discredit his general idea.

Chapter 3: From Myth to Allegory

1. See Snell's *The Discovery of the Mind*, trans. Rosenmeyer.

2. Liddell and Scott's *Greek-English Lexicon* makes clear that the old usage survived even as new usages developed.

3. These ancient commentators habitually assumed that their own intentions were also Homer's. "There is a general failure in antiquity to make a clear distinction between allegorical expression and allegorical interpretation. What we call allegorical interpretation in this context normally takes the form of a claim that an author has expressed himself allegorically in a given passage." Robert Lamberton, *Homer the Theologian*, 20.

4. E. R. Dodds remarks that the Homeric man's ability to *hear* his *thymos* as an independent inner voice "must have opened the door wide to the religious idea of psychic intervention, which is often said to operate . . . on [the *thymos*'] physical seat, his chest or midriff" (*Greeks and the Irrational*, 16).

5. Many of the observations in this paragraph are drawn from Snell, *Discovery of the Mind*, 6–9.

6. Ibid., 1–2.

7. Dodds points out that *psyche* had many shades of meaning in the work of fifth-century Attic writers. It could connote the seat of courage, of passion, of anxiety: broadly the range of the Homeric *thymos*. On the lips of "an ordinary fifth-century Athenian," Dodds writes, the word lacked "any suggestion of metaphysical status" (*Greeks and the Irrational,* 139). That status was the innovation of the Orphics and Plato, with whom my discussion will primarily be concerned.

8. Snell, *Discovery of the Mind,* 17.

9. W. K. C. Guthrie, *Orpheus and Greek Religion,* 11.

10. Ibid., 49–50.

11. The doctrine of transmigration of souls, current in Indian philosophy before the Buddha's time, may have spread into Asia Minor and influenced Orphism in Thrace. The Greek Orphics' insistence on *liberation* from the cycle of reincarnation may then, possibly, have spread eastward. Erwin Rohde, in his book on the history of the concept of *Psyche,* states that "at a certain period in Greek history, and nowhere earlier or more unmistakably than in Greece, appeared the idea of the divinity, and the immortality implicit in the divinity, of the human soul. . . . Thence it has affected all subsequent ages and has transmitted to East and West the elementary principles of all true mysticism" (254).

12. Burkert, *Greek Religion,* 300.

13. Dodds, *Greeks and the Irrational,* 152.

14. Ion of Chios, a fifth-century authority, says that Pythagoras composed poems under the name of Orpheus. Ibid., 149.

15. Quoted in Iamblichus, *Life of Pythagoras,* trans. Taylor, 267.

16. Ibid., 30, 37.

17. Ibid., 37, 162–63.

18. Dodds, *Greeks and the Irrational,* 209; *Oxford Classical Dictionary,* 2d ed., 839.

19. Plato, *Phaedo,* 64C, in *Great Dialogues of Plato,* trans. Rouse, 467. Further references will be included in the text.

20. Plato, *Phaedrus,* 247D, trans. Hackforth, in *Collected Dialogues of Plato,* ed. Hamilton and Cairns. Further references will be included in the text.

21. This apt phrase derives from Elizabeth Spelman, who in her extremely lucid article, "Woman as Body: Ancient and Contemporary Views" (8, 109–31), analyzes the connection between Plato's views on soul and body and his references to women.

22. Evidence for the seclusion of citizen women in Athens is both literary and archaeological. Helene B. Foley, who has reviewed the relevant surviving prose, notes that orators praised the modesty of female relatives who were embarrassed to dine even with male kinsmen. She further notes that

"in some law court cases witnesses had to be produced to certify the existence of a respectable wife, a woman who was referred to only by the name
of her husband and father." See "The Conception of Women in Athenian
Drama," in *Reflections of Women in Antiquity*, ed. Foley, 130–31.

House plans of the time, as they have been reconstructed by archaeolo-
gists, place the *andron*, or men's dining room, near the street and far removed from the women's quarters, suggesting that respectable women did
not attend *symposia* even in their own households. Plans are included in
Susan Walker's article "Women and Housing in Classical Greece," 81–91.

23. In his Funeral Oration, Pericles praises as most virtuous those modest women who have acquired no public reputation whatsoever, either for
good or ill; Thucydides, 2.46.

24. Marylin B. Arthur, "Early Greece," 50.

25. *Symposium*, trans. Joyce, in *Collected Dialogues of Plato*. Plato's diction is truly androgynous here; he uses a neuter pronoun (*touto*) to modify
a masculine noun (*tokos*) that has as its primary meaning a feminine act, "a
bringing forth, birth, the time of delivery," according to the abridged version of Liddell and Scott.

26. *Theatetus*, trans. Cornford, in *Collected Dialogues of Plato*.

27. Page duBois, *Sowing the Body*, 169–83. My brief discussion of the
Theatetus is particularly indebted to duBois.

28. See particularly Lewis Farnell's pages on the profusion of local Artemises during the pre-classical period in his section on that goddess in *Cults
of the Greek States*, vol. 2.

29. Marylin Arthur, "Early Greece," 24.

30. *Theogony*, trans. Athanassakis.

31. Joseph Fontenrose discusses the events narrated in the Homeric
Hymn and makes this suggestion (*Python*, 13–14).

32. Ibid., 15.

33. Nilsson, *Minoan-Mycenaean Religion*, 467–68; Fontenrose, *Python*,
418.

34. Fontenrose, *Python*, 418.

35. Aeschylus, *Eumenides*, trans. Lattimore, in *Complete Greek Tragedies*,
vol. 1.

36. Arthur, "Early Greece," 13.

37. Ibid., 14. Occasionally, however, Homer *does* show a woman being
excluded, as when Telemachos (11.356–59 and 12.350–53) formulaically tells
his mother to go to her room and attend to her own work rather than to
the work of men, which concerns war.

38. The standardization is thought to have occurred in the time of Pei-
sistratos and his sons in Athens, ca. 530–10 B.C.E.; see Stanford's introduction to the Greek text, xxvii.

39. This and the following quotations are taken from the Pandora passage, ll. 42–105, of *Works and Days*, trans. Lefkowitz in *Women's Life in Greece and Rome,* ed. Lefkowitz and Fant.

40. Sarah B. Pomeroy, *Goddesses, Whores,* 49.

41. Xenophon, *Oeconomicus,* 7.5, trans. Lord, in *Xenophon's Socratic Discourse.*

42. Readers and scholars for generations have been puzzling over this paradox. How could a society so repressive of women produce such strong female dramatic characters? We need to remember that the tragedies are set in the distant, mythic past—which may be eternal in the unconscious or in the imagination, but which is not eternal in social customs. Philip Slater's convincing thesis in *The Glory of Hera* is that this mythic past was also within the individual memory, repressed or unrepressed, of every Athenian male who was dominated at the beginning of his life by a much stronger woman, his mother. Slater further argues that the more repressive of women a society is, the more likely a woman is to find an outlet for her frustrated sense of personal power in the domination of her children, who then grow up with extremely ambivalent feelings toward her. The dramatist, he believes, is gifted with intuitive access to this primal material and awakens the audience to its reality.

43. Euripides, *Medea,* ll. 230–34, 241–47, trans. Warner in *Complete Greek Tragedies,* vol. 3.

44. Freud's harsh dictum that "anatomy is destiny" holds true, I believe, for the lives of most women in most pre-twentieth century societies. Without reliable birth control, a sexually active woman lived at the mercy of her reproductive system.

45. Jean Pépin, *Mythe et allégoire,* 97.

46. Ibid., 96. According to Iamblichus, Pythagoras believed that he himself had once been Euphorbos, a character from the *Iliad,* in a former life (*Life of Pythagoras,* 41). Diogenes Laertius, however, reports that Pythagoras, in one of his journeys to the Underworld, saw Homer being tormented for lies he had told about the gods; Cynthia Thompson, "Stoic Allegory," 36.

47. All information in this paragraph is from Thompson, "Stoic Allegory," 21–22.

48. Felix Buffière, *Les mythes d'Homère,* 237.

49. Pépin, *Mythe et allégoire,* 107.

50. Ibid.

51. Quoted by Pépin, 110. This and other translations from the French, unless otherwise indicated, are mine.

52. Diogenes, quoted by Dion Chrysostrom, *Oratio,* 24–25; in Pépin, 110–11.

53. Not Heraclitus of Ephesus, but a later group of writers known collectively as Heraclitus the Mythographer; Thompson, "Stoic Allegory," 4–5.

54. Zeno, *Stoicorum Veterum Fragmenta*, 1.146; quoted by Dodds, *Greeks and the Irrational*, 238.

55. Heraclitus [Mythographer], *Allégories d'Homère*, 1.1, ed. Buffière.

56. See, for instance, Hugo Rahner's *Greek Myths and Christian Mystery*, 181–222.

57. Lamberton, *Homer the Theologian*, 41.

58. Pseudo–Plutarch, *Life and Poetry of Homer*, 126.

59. Translated by Lamberton in *Homer the Theologian*, 116.

60. Ibid., 115–16. Lamberton leaves the word *genesis* untranslated because it is a technical term in later Platonism, referring to the entire cycle of coming-to-be and passing away that is the existence of the sublunary realm. His translation of *kykeon* as "witch's brew" rather than as "mixture" or simply "brew" seems a liberty that Porphyry may not have intended.

61. Ibid., 117.

62. Erich Kahler, "Persistence of Myth," 3.

63. Lewis, *Allegory of Love*, 78.

Chapter 4: The Legacy of Allegory

1. Alcman, frag. 28 in *Lyrica Graeca Selecta*, ed. Page, 23.

2. Apollonius's location of Circe's domain on the coast of Italy is indicative of his century, for by that time the focus of Greek exploration and trade had switched from East to West.

3. Virgil, *The Aeneid*, 7.10–24, trans. Robert Fitzgerald. All other quotations from the *Aeneid* will be from the Fitzgerald translation, with line references given to the Latin text.

4. A point made by Charles Segal in "Circean Temptations," 425.

5. Charles H. Taylor, Jr., "Obstacles to Odysseus' Return," 50, 579.

6. Adam Parry, "Two Voices of Virgil," 92.

7. Christine Perkell, "On Creusa, Dido," 8, 204.

8. Brooks Otis, *Virgil*, 385.

9. Michael Putnam, *Poetry of the Aeneid*, 200–201.

10. That the *Aeneid* as we have it did not satisfy Virgil is proved by his deathbed instruction to his friend Varius to burn the manuscript. Fortunately, Augustus ordered this wish disregarded (*Oxford Classical Dictionary*, 2d ed., 1124).

11. Ovid, *Amores* (2.1.14–20) in *The Erotic Poems*, trans. and ed. Peter Green. All subsequent quotations from the *Amores* and the *Remedia* will be from Green's translation.

12. Marylin Arthur, "'Liberated' Women," 81.

13. Green, "Notes and References," in Ovid, *Erotic Poems*, 277.

14. Ibid., 290.

15. *Metamorphoses,* 14.403–15, trans. Horace Gregory.

16. For discussions of this earlier myth see Amaury de Riencourt, *Sex and Power in History* (37), and Joseph Campbell, *The Power of Myth* (47–48). Merlin Stone's chapter on "Unraveling the Myth of Adam and Eve" in *When God Was a Woman* also traces and documents the twists that the patriarchal Hebrews gave to a much older myth.

17. Campbell, *Power of Myth,* 48.

18. Aristotle, *Politics,* 1254b3, trans. Lefkowitz, *Women's Life,* 63.

19. Plutarch, "Advice to Bride and Groom," 142E in *Moralia,* vol. 2, trans. Babbitt.

20. Tertullian, "On the Apparel of Women" in *Ante-Nicene Fathers,* vol. 4, trans. and ed. Coxe, 14.

21. Clement of Alexandria, *Stromateis,* vol. 7, 16.95, in *Alexandrian Christianity,* trans. and ed. Oulton and Chadwick.

22. Lamberton, *Homer the Theologian,* 261; Peter Brown, *Augustine of Hippo,* 36.

23. St. Augustine, *City of God,* 18.17, trans. Sanford and Green.

24. John J. O'Meara, "St. Augustine's Attitude to Love," 56. Also see Brown, *Augustine of Hippo,* 389. Augustine's views on the relationship of the spirit to the flesh were also influenced by Neo-Platonism. He read a Latin translation of Plotinus *before* he converted to Christianity and was moved by this reading to change his mode of life.

25. Brown, *Augustine of Hippo,* 390. More precisely, Augustine says the married act rightly in procreation, but wrongly if they seek pleasure in the act.

26. Boethius, *Consolation of Philosophy,* 4.3, trans. Watts.

27. Arnobius, "Adversus Gentes," in *The Ante-Nicene Fathers,* vol. 6, ed. Roberts and Donaldson, 466.

28. Athanasius, "Contra Gentes," in *Nicene and Post-Nicene Fathers,* vol. 4, ed. Schaff and Wace, 9.

29. E. K. Rand, *Ovid and His Influence,* 135.

30. *Ovide Moralisé,* ed. de Boer, 5:70.

31. Servius, *Servii Grammatici,* vol. 2, ed. Thilo, 127, trans. Phyllis Stanley.

Chapter 5: Renaissance Circes

1. The school of Chrysoloras, a Greek teacher attracted to Florence by a group of her citizens around the turn of the Quattrocentro, was operating decades before these scholars arrived. But Chrysoloras's pupils Bruni and Niccoli concentrated on translating Plato and Aristotle, rather than Homer. See Hans Baron, *Crisis of the Early Italian Renaissance.*

2. W. B. Stanford, "Introduction" to *The Odyssey of Homer,* xxix.

3. Henry Green, ed., "Introduction" to Whitney's *A Choice of Emblemes,* xxvi.

4. According to Natalie Zemon Davis, "husband dominators are everywhere in popular literature [of early modern Europe]. . . . The point about such portraits is that they are funny and amoral: the women are full of life and energy, and they win much of the time" ("Women On Top," in *Society and Culture,* 134–35). Davis admits, however, that "in the early modern period, up to the late eighteenth century, the patriarchal family is not challenged as such even by the most searching critics of relations between the sexes" (ibid., 142).

Why, then, was the woman-on-top *topos* so prevalent? Probably because it expresses a truth that is the shadow side of patriarchy: that men are vulnerable to women. Louis Montrose's statement that "patriarchal norms are compensatory for the vulnerability of men to the powers of women" expresses this relationship succinctly. See *"A Midsummer Night's Dream* and the Shaping Fantasies of Elizabethan Culture," in *Rewriting the Renaissance,* ed. Ferguson, 77.

5. For an incisive discussion of Amazonian mythology, which was "ubiquitous in Elizabethan texts," see Montrose's article.

6. Renaissance women helped run family businesses, occasionally dressed in men's clothing, and were socially active in villages and at court. Although the desirability of women's modesty and silence is stressed in text after text of the times, this does not seem to have been an era in which women routinely complied with that desire. Renaissance Europe was not Periclean Athens. See particularly Davis's *Society and Culture in Early Modern France,* and Linda Woodbridge's *Women and the English Renaissance.*

7. Even in the otherwise thoroughly renovated society of Thomas More's *Utopia,* traditional patterns of sexual hierarchy are preserved. The equality between the sexes professed and practiced by seventeenth-century English Quakers was truly innovative.

8. Whitney, *Choice of Emblemes,* 82.

9. This speaker is Gryllus, who inspired Spenser's Grill in the Bower of Bliss. Plutarch's dialogue was also the dominant source for Gelli's *Circe,* shortly to be discussed. Plutarch, "Beasts Are Rational," in *Moralia,* vol. 12.

10. Whitney, *Choice of Emblemes,* 10.

11. H. Kramer and J. Sprenger, *Malleus Maleficarum,* trans. Summers, 127.

12. Burton, *Anatomy of Melancholy* 3:55–56.

13. This myth offers a slick explanation for Circe's change of locale between the composition of the *Odyssey* and the composition of Apollonius Rhodius's *Argonautica.*

14. Sarmatia was an ancient term for what would now be the steppes region of Russia; at its southern edge it verged on the Black Sea and overlapped with the region known as Scythia.

15. Comes, *Mythologieae*, 174–75; this and other quotes from Comes are translated by Phyllis Stanley.

16. Ibid., 174.

17. Golding, trans., *Shakespeare's Ovid*, p. 6, ll. 276–77.

18. Alan Macfarlane's search of legal records reveals that witch prosecutions reached their height in the county of Essex during 1580–99, the period that also marked the height of Elizabeth I's power. See Macfarlane, *Witchcraft in Tudor and Stuart England*, 28–29.

19. Sandys, trans., *Ovid's Metamorphosis Englished*, 655.

20. Augustine's ideas on nature and sexuality, which reached their final development during the Pelagian controversy in his old age, are very lucidly discussed by Elaine Pagels in *Adam, Eve, and the Serpent*, 130–34.

21. Gelli, *Circe*, trans. Robert Adams, 59. Further references to this work will appear in the text.

22. This speech seems to be intended as a rebuttal of passages such as the following from Aristotle's *On the Generation of Animals* 2:3, 737a (trans. A. L. Peck): "Just as it sometimes happens that deformed offspring are produced by deformed parents, and sometimes not, so the offspring produced by a female are sometimes female, sometimes not, but male. The reason is that the female is as it were a deformed male; and the menstrual discharge is semen, though in an impure condition; i.e., it lacks one constituent, and one only, the principle of Soul."

23. Agrippa, in *De nobilitate et praecellentia Foemenei sexus* (written in 1509 and translated into English in 1542) begins by asserting the complete spiritual and intellectual equality of women. He then reminds his readers, "with a near-anthropological modernity, that women's social and political inferiority . . . has not, at other times and in other cultures, invariably obtained." See Woodbridge, *Women and the English Renaissance*, 39–41.

24. In the pamphlet war known as the Controversy about Women, male writers often defended women for their modesty and good behavior, sometimes citing patient Griselda as a model. The outspoken, feisty figures whom the attackers of women used in their polemics as negative examples are far more admired by modern feminists.

25. Merritt Y. Hughes mentions Cristoforo Landino's interpretation of Virgil's Circe as the embodiment of spiritual evil and Pico della Mirandola's warnings against lust (Circe) in a letter to his nephew ("Spenser's Acrasia," 387–88).

26. Bruno, *Giordano Bruno's The Heroic Frenzies*, trans. Paul Memmo, Jr., 25.

27. Ibid., 261.

28. Felton Gibbons, *Dosso and Battista Dossi*, 114.

29. Berenson, *Study and Criticism of Italian Art*, 31–32.

30. Gibbons, *Dosso and Battista Dossi*, 200.

31. Lodovico Ariosto, *Orlando Furioso*, trans. Harington, 8.13.7.

32. John Rupert Martin, *Farnese Gallery*, 3.

33. Ibid., 33.

34. Ibid., 39.

35. George Chapman, trans., *Chapman's Homer*, ed. Nicoll, 2:14.

36. George Lord, *Homeric Renaissance*, 21.

37. The Latin translation in de Sponde's edition, published in Basel in 1583, was actually that of Andreas Divus. For information about Chapman's use of this text see R. S. Ide, "Exemplary Heroism in Chapman's Homer," *Studies in English Literature* 22 (1982): 121–36.

38. *Ligurei*, the word Homer uses in 12.44 to describe the quality of the Sirens' songs, is a variation of the one he uses to describe Circe's own voice. In his note to the Greek text, Stanford says that these words "describe the kind of sound the Greeks like best: it is defined by Aristotle in *De Audibilibus* 804a,25ff. as consisting of sharpness and precision."

39. Lord, *Homeric Renaissance*, 92.

40. Quoted by Kenneth Charlton in *Education in Renaissance England*, 209.

41. Ascham, *English Works*, ed. Wright, 225.

Chapter 6: Spenser, the Witch, and the Goddesses

1. In his letter to Ralegh about the poem, Spenser states that Gloriana represents "the most excellent and glorious person of our soueraine" (*The Faerie Queene*, ed. A. C. Hamilton, 737). He thus bases the structure of his poem upon the courtly convention of tribute.

2. More than twice as many witches were prosecuted at the Essex Assizes during 1580–99 than during any other twenty year period. Alan Macfarlane, *Witchcraft in Tudor and Stuart England*, 28.

3. Ibid., 14. The Witchcraft Act of 1563 put the crime within the jurisdiction of the secular courts.

4. Dekker, Ford, and Rowley, *The Witch of Edmonton* 2.1; quoted by Antonia Fraser, *Weaker Vessel*, 118.

5. Reginald Scot, *Discoverie of Witchcraft*, 29. Scot's book attacks both the "flat and plaine knaverie . . . practised against these old women" and the *Demonology* of Jean Bodin, published four years earlier.

6. Ibid., 37.

7. In *Politics* 1254b3, Aristotle emphasizes the necessity of the rational

element in human nature ruling over the passionate one and draws an analogy to the proper rule of one sex over the other: "again, the male is by nature superior, and the female inferior, and the one rules, and the other is ruled; this principal of necessity extends to all mankind." In *The Generation of Animals*, 729a, 741a, he states that the child's soul derives from its male parent, the matter of its body from the female parent.

8. Stephen Greenblatt, *Renaissance Self-Fashioning*, 175.

9. Camille Paglia, *Sexual Personae*, 191.

10. The raging beasts that guard the way to the enchantress appear in both Tasso and Virgil. There is no suggestion in Tasso, however, that the beasts are her erstwhile lovers, as they clearly are in *The Faerie Queene* and as—if we choose to believe Servius—they are in the *Aeneid*. The beasts in the *Odyssey*, who may or may not be Circe's former favorites, are placid and fawning. Only Spenser and Virgil emphasize the rage of male creatures under the enchantress's control.

11. Greenblatt, *Renaissance Self-Fashioning*, 172.

12. Joan Larsen Klein, "From Errour to Acrasia," 41, 199.

13. Lewis wonders, apropos of the painted ivy, "whether those who think that Spenser is secretly on Acrasia's side, themselves approve of metal vegetation as a garden ornament, or whether they regard this passage as a proof of Spenser's abominable bad taste." Lewis, "*The Faerie Queene*," in Hamilton, ed., *Essential Articles*, 6.

14. One of the details Spenser retains is the comparison of the bathers rising from the water to the morning star. Ironically, he has already used this comparison to praise Gloriana in 2.9.4.

15. Greenblatt, *Renaissance Self-Fashioning*, 173.

16. A. C. Hamilton, "Introduction to Book III" of *The Faerie Queene*, 299.

17. Spenser's ideal of Chastity is not celibacy, but faithful married love. In this respect, he was very much a man of the Reformation, who no longer gave credence to the post-Augustinean Catholic ideal of sexual asceticism.

18. Jonathan Goldberg briefly and insightfully discusses the connection between the conventions of chivalry in Elizabeth's court and the conventions of discourse in Spenser's goddess cantos. "Like Venus's Temple," he remarks, "Elizabeth's court was a place of endless courting, where 'all doe learne to play the Paramoure'" (*Endlesse Work*, 139, 152–53). Goldberg also remarks on Spenser's successful poetic "courting" of the Queen, causing him to be granted the "respectable salary" of fifty pounds a year after the publication of the first half of *The Faerie Queene* (171).

19. Lewis, *Allegory of Love*, 312–13.

20. Goldberg, *Endlesse Work*, 26.

21. One has only to check Spenser's idea of Artegall's heroic mission against historic fact—i.e., Ireland's conversion to Catholic Christianity in

the fifth century—to realize that the poet's imagination here is corrupted and partisan.

22. Louis Montrose, "*Midsummer Night's Dream,*" 78.

Chapter 7: The Lovelorn Temptress

1. See the end of act 3 of "Ulisse et Circe," in *Le théâtre italien,* ed. Gherardi, vol. 3.

2. Jean Rousset, *La littérature de l'âge Baroque,* 255–57, 262.

3. Sometimes the reigning authorities were characters within the masques, as when Charles I's queen, Henrietta Maria, played Divine Beauty in Aurelian Townshend's *Tempe Restored* or James I's queen, Anne of Denmark, took one of the leading roles in Ben Jonson's 1609 *Masque of Queenes.*

4. Browne, *Whole Works of William Browne,* ed. Hazlitt 2:244–45.

5. Townshend, *Aurelian Townshend's Poems and Masks,* ed. Chambers. When *Tempe Restored* was published later in 1631, Townshend followed its text with a paragraph overtly stating its allegorical meaning.

6. Ibid., 97.

7. Masques in the early seventeenth-century Stuart courts were not merely innocuous entertainments. They had an important ideological function, flattering the king who sat in the choice seat in the audience through onstage idealizations of his role. Neo-Platonic philosophy was an important element in this idealization. Stephen Orgel describes the masque as "the triumph of the aristocratic community." "At its center," he remarks, "is a belief in the hierarchy and a faith in the power of idealization. Philosophically, it is both Platonic and Machiavellian; Platonic because it presents images of the good to which the participants aspire and may ascend; Machiavellian because its idealizations are designed to justify the power they celebrate" (*Illusion of Power,* 40). The influence of Neo-Platonic philosophy on the English masque can be discerned as early as Ben Jonson's *Masque of Blacknesse* in 1605. See "The Imagery of Ben Jonson's *Masques of Blacknesse and Beautie*" in D. J. Gordon, *The Renaissance Imagination.*

8. Townshend, *Poems and Masks,* 91.

9. Ibid., 99.

10. Peter Mendes, "Appendix" to *Comus,* in John Milton, *Odes, Pastorals, Masques,* 166.

11. A point made by Orgel in *Illusion of Power,* 52.

12. Mendes, "Appendix," 163.

13. Rosemond Tuve, "Image, Form, and Theme," 140. Tuve maintains that Circe is "the hinge upon which Milton's whole invention moves" in *Comus* and that "he has caught and deepened every important phase of the significance she had borne."

14. The Egerton family would have been exceedingly anxious to avoid all appearance of scandal, since they were related to the family of Lord Castlehaven, who had recently been executed for various sexual crimes. The Castlehaven case was a major scandal of the early 1630s. Christopher Hill, *Milton and the English Revolution*, 43.

15. The fact that Sabrina comes up rather than down is mechanically as well as symbolically important. Her appearance required contraptions much simpler and less costly than those, for instance, in *Tempe Restored*.

16. In a well-known article, "The Action of *Comus*," E. M. W. Tillyard argues that Milton's belated reference to the Garden of Adonis does provide an effective resolution to the masque's debate. He holds that "the Attendant Spirit by mentioning the Garden of Adonis, the very workshop of nature, gives the solution. This garden has all the bounty described by Comus and all the comeliness and order insisted on by the Lady." See *Maske At Ludlow*, ed. Diekhoff, 53. Tillyard's argument, however, is very fragile because it overlooks the location of Milton's garden.

17. The brief narrative interlude between Eve's taste of the fruit and her consciousness of sin might be regarded as a return to the original myth of the Garden, before it was given the Hebraic interpretation we find in Genesis; see my discussion of the myth of the Fall in chapter 4, "The Legacy of Allegory." The Genesis myth's secondariness, its insistence upon the creation of a female body out of a male one, can be proved against every human being's experience. Just as Zeus swallows Metis in order to give birth to Athene, so Adam also (but rather more vaguely) appropriates feminine procreative power.

18. The penitent, well-instructed Adam refers to death as "the Gate of Life" in 12.571.

19. Alan S. Trueblood, *Experience and Artistic Expression*, 191–94.

20. Lope de Vega, *La Circe con otras Rimas y Prosos*, trans. Martha Rivera and Julia Alvarez.

21. The English titles of these plays are *Love, the Greatest Enchantment* and *The Sorceries of Sin*. All quotations will be taken from *Love the Greatest Enchantment, The Sorceries of Sin, The Devotion of the Cross*, trans. Denis MacCarthy; the plays will hereafter be cited as *LGE* or *SS*.

22. MacCarthy, "Introduction" to *LGE*, 5–6.

23. J. Richards LeVan, "Theme and Metaphor," 191.

24. Manuel Duran probes the playwright's attitudes toward authority and his despair about earthly life. He believes that "Calderón's plays reconcile Plato and the New Testament to an extent that is . . . much more complete and meaningful than any attempt by Erasmus, Pico della Mirandola, and the numerous Renaissance scholars who attempted this task" ("Toward a Psychological Profile," 27).

25. Sigmund Freud, *Civilization and Its Discontents,* in *Complete Psychological Works,* trans. Strachey, 21:84.

Chapter 8: Whore and Femme Fatale

1. Quoted by W. B. Stanford in *Ulysses Theme,* 11.

2. For treatments of this image in nineteenth-century British and/or American literature, see Sandra M. Gilbert and Susan Gubar, *Madwoman in the Attic;* Elizabeth Hardwick, *Seduction and Betrayal;* and Leslie Fiedler, *Love and Death in the American Novel.* For a thorough discussion of the image in fin-de-siècle visual art, see Bram Dijkstra, *Idols of Perversity,* and Patrick Bade, *Femme Fatale.*

3. In the Circe chapter of *Ulysses* Joyce makes clear how these two stereotypes reflect and depend upon each other. Bella-Bello, the threatening, aggressive man-woman, disappears only when the pure nymph springs to life out of the engraving hanging above Bloom's bed.

At least one nineteenth-century woman, Charlotte Brontë, was outspokenly aware that these polarized stereotypes had nothing to do with the real nature of women. The protagonist of her novel *Shirley* explains that "the cleverest, the acutest men are often under an illusion about women . . . their good woman is a queer thing, half doll, half angel; their bad woman is almost always a fiend. Then to hear them fall into ecstasies with each other's creations, worshipping the heroine of such a poem, novel, drama, thinking it fine, divine. Fine and divine it may be, but often quite artificial." Brontë's use of the neuter pronoun here seems entirely appropriate.

4. Quoted by Dijkstra in *Idols of Perversity,* 321.

5. Frank Budgen, *Making of Ulysses,* 17.

6. Ibid. Joyce thought Odysseus's delicate behavior with Nausicaa earned him this title.

7. James Joyce, *Ulysses,* 703. Further references will be included in the text.

8. W. B. Stanford, "Notes" to the *Odyssey,* ed. Stanford, 1:215 and 2:328.

9. The scar from this wound enables his old maidservant Eurycleia to identify him when he has returned to Ithaca in beggar's disguise and she is bathing his feet. The wound also connects Odysseus with his grandfather, who named him. It was received when the two were hunting on the slopes of Parnassos.

10. Robert Newman, "Left-Handed Path of Circe," 23, 226.

11. This clarifying observation regarding space, time, and text is Hugh Kenner's in his *Ulysses,* 120.

12. Joyce, *Letters,* ed. Ellmann, 2:191–92.

13. The 1909 correspondence between Joyce and his wife reveals his de-

sire to be dominated and flogged, at least in fantasy, by Nora, who "with a full bosom and big fat thighs, would rip off his trousers and beat him as if he were a naughty child." Both Joyces experimented in these letters with casting aside all verbal sexual inhibitions; for Joyce this correspondence must have been good practice for the composition of "Circe." For a thorough discussion of it, see Brenda Maddox, *Nora*, 105ff.

14. Quoted by Dijkstra in *Idols of Perversity,* 393.

15. Ibid.

16. A point made by Mark Shechner in *Joyce in Nighttown,* 113.

17. Quoted by Budgen, *Making of Ulysses,* 230–31.

18. Maddox also suggests that Joyce named Molly after moly (*Nora*, 198). The fact that Joyce himself sometimes carried around a pair of Nora's soiled drawers as a talisman against evil adds plausibility to this suggestion (Shechner, *Joyce in Nighttown,* 121).

19. Stephen's vision of his dead mother is indisputably *his* vision, and not just a fantastic figure provided by Joyce as a result of his authorial rummaging in the contents of Stephen's unconscious. Stephen speaks to this ghost and reacts to her—as Hamlet behaves toward his father's ghost, as Bloom is later to speak and react to his vision of Rudy. Bloom's dramas with Bello, the nymph, and Mrs. Bellingham et al. are of a different order. They have no effect upon his actions or speech in the moment.

20. Ellmann, *Ulysses on the Liffey,* 146.

21. Ellmann, in his essay "*Ulysses:* A Short History," which is appended to the Penguin edition of the novel, discusses Joyce's rescue by Alfred Hunter and its effect on the conception of *Ulysses;* see 707–10.

22. This is a phrase from Yeats's poem. It appears in Joyce's first episode and earlier in the Circe chapter, spoken by Mrs. Dedalus when she appears to Stephen in the brothel.

23. Ellmann, *Ulysses on the Liffey,* 148.

24. The phrase "psychic release" is somewhat misleading. Bloom, whose fantasies take up most of the chapter, never acts them out. Stephen, with his chandelier-bashing, does, but his acting out seems intended as a sign of his relative immaturity. The primary purgation is literary: Joyce lets down the walls between his characters' inner impulses and the reader.

However, as mentioned before, Joyce brings the Everyman concept to bear upon the laws of psychodynamics. Though Bloom and Stephen do not become conscious of their unconscious wishes in the way that a patient in psychotherapy might, they nevertheless seem to benefit from the psychic *Walpurgisnacht* of "Circe."

25. Marilyn French, *Book as World,* 250.

26. Joyce, *Letters* 1:170; both phrases are translated from German.

27. French, *Book as World,* 249. This observation provides a good argu-

ment for emphasizing the archetypal rather than personal aspects of Molly's identity. Bonnie Kime Scott concludes that "interpreted as a realistic being, Molly has been found offensive repeatedly" (*Joyce and Feminism,* 159).

28. It is unlikely that Molly has acted on these other attractions. As Ellmann says, "the book makes clear that this first relationship [with Boylan] is something new" (*Ulysses on the Liffey,* 165).

29. Joyce, *Letters* 2:311.

30. This is Joyce's description of the movement of Molly's monologue in a letter to Budgen; *Making of Ulysses,* 262–63.

Chapter 9: Her Voice

1. The most notable exceptions are visual artists: George Braques, Marc Chagall, and Romare Bearden. Bearden includes several scenes in which Circe appears within his series of twenty "Odysseus Collages," first exhibited in 1977. "Circe's Domain" is the most striking of these; it shows the enchantress seated, with sharp teeth and long, sharp sword. She is attended by a much tamer looking male palace guard. Bearden's Circe is fiercer than Homer's; perhaps it was also inspired by legends of the warrior women of Dahomey.

2. Porter, "Defense of Circe," 138–39.

3. Welty, *Eye of the Story,* 114.

4. Ibid., 81.

5. Welty, "Circe," in *Collected Stories,* 533. Further references will be included in the text.

6. This detail recalls both Apollonius Rhodius's Circe, with her cemetery of male corpses hung in willows, and the Çatal Hüyük practice of exposing their dead for vultures to pick clean.

7. Reprinted in Atwood, *Selected Poems,* 141.

8. Atwood, "Circe/Mud Poems," in *You are Happy,* 47–49. Further page references will be included in the text.

9. Estella Lauter's phrase in *Women as Mythmakers,* p. 69.

10. Atwood's perception that the old goddess powers are embattled and vengeful (shaped in a fist) might have been prompted by Circe's nasty behavior at the beginning of Homer's version of the myth. It is probably no accident that the original Circe turned Odysseus's men into swine, the sacred animals of the vegetation goddess. See my discussion of "The Ritual Significance of Pigs" in chapter 2.

11. Quoted by Linda Schierse Leonard in *On the Way to the Wedding,* 109.

12. Atwood would, I believe, agree with William Blake on the potentiality of the moment as both an escape from and a redirection of time:

Every Time less than a pulsation of the artery
Is equal in its period & value to Six Thousand Years.
For in the Period the Poets Work is Done: and all the Great
Events of Time start forth & are conceived in such a Period
Within a Moment: a Pulsation of the Artery.
                                          (*Milton,* plates 28 and 29)

13. Jane Lilienfeld points out that the victim's posture during the sacrifice parallels that of Circe as Odysseus takes her for the first time, "thus aligning her firmly with the victims of the priestly elite." See "Silence and Scorn in a Lyric of Intimacy," 192.

Conclusion

1. Dorothy Dinnerstein, *Mermaid and the Minotaur,* 124.
2. Quoted by Dinnerstein, 120.
3. The gist of Plutarch's thought (see chapter 4 of this book) was repeated less gracefully in the early seventeenth century by Thomas Tuke and in the sixteenth century by Juan Luis Vives (who, however, saw the husband as representing reason). Tuke and Vives are quoted by Diane Kelsey McColley in *Milton's Eve,* 11.
4. Carol Christ, *Laughter of Aphrodite,* 213, 215.

Bibliography

Aelian. *On the Characteristics of Animals.* Trans. A. F. Scholfield. Loeb Classical Library. Cambridge: Harvard University Press, 1959.

Aeschylus. "Eumenides." Trans. Richmond Lattimore. In *The Complete Greek Tragedies.* Vol. 1. Ed. David Grene and Richmond Lattimore. Chicago: University of Chicago Press, 1959.

Akurgal, Ekrem. *The Art of the Hittites.* London: Thames and Hudson, 1962.

Alciati, Andrea. *Emblemata Cum Commentariis.* 1621; rpt. New York: Garland Publishing, Inc., 1976.

———. *Emblemata.* Leiden, 1551.

Alpers, Paul J. *The Poetry of the Faerie Queene.* Princeton: Princeton University Press, 1967.

Apollonius Rhodius. *Argonautica.* Ed. George W. Mooney. London: Longmans, Greene, 1912.

———. *Argonautica.* Trans. E. V. Rieu. Harmondsworth: Penguin Books Ltd., 1959.

Aptekar, Jane. *Icons of Justice: Iconography and Thematic Imagery in The Faerie Queene V.* New York: Columbia University Press, 1969.

Apuleius. *The Golden Ass.* Trans. Robert Graves. Harmondsworth: Penguin Books Ltd., 1950.

Ariosto, Lodovico. *Orlando Furioso.* Trans. Sir John Harington. Ed. Graham Hough. London: Centaur Press, 1962.

Aristophanes. "Lysistrata." In *Five Comedies of Aristophanes.* Trans. Benjamin Bickley Rogers. Garden City, N.Y.: Doubleday, 1955.

———. "Thesmophoriazusae." In *Aristophanes.* Vol. 3. Trans. Benjamin Bickley Rogers. Cambridge: Harvard University Press, 1969.

Aristotle. *On the Generation of Animals.* Trans. A. L. Peck. Loeb Classical Library. Cambridge: Harvard University Press, 1942.

———. *Politics.* Trans. H. Rackham. Loeb Classical Library. Cambridge: Harvard University Press, 1932.

Arnobius. "Adversus Gentes." In *The Ante-Nicene Fathers.* Vol. 6. Ed. Alexander Roberts and James Donaldson. Buffalo: Christian Literature Co., 1886.

Arthur, Marylin. "Early Greece: The Origins of the Western Attitude Towards Women." *Arethusa* 6 (1973): 7–58.

———. "'Liberated' Women: The Classical Era." In *Becoming Visible,* ed. Renate Bridenthal and Claudia Koonz, 60–89. Boston: Houghton Mifflin, 1977.

Ascham, Roger. *English Works.* Cambridge: Cambridge University Press, 1905.

Astour, Michael C. *Hellenosemitica: An Ethnic and Cultural Study of West Semitic Impact on Mycenaean Greece.* Leiden: E. J. Brill, 1965.

Athanasius. "Contra Gentes." In *Nicene and Post-Nicene Fathers,* 2d ser., vol. 4. Ed. Philip Schaff and Henry Wace. New York: Christian Literature Co., 1892.

Atwood, Margaret. *Selected Poems.* Toronto: Oxford University Press, 1976.

———. *Surfacing.* Don Mills, Ont.: General Publishing Co., Ltd., 1973.

———. *You Are Happy.* New York: Harper and Row, 1974.

Augustine, St. *The City of God.* Vol. 5. Trans. Eva Sanford and William Green. Loeb Classical Library. Cambridge: Harvard University Press, 1965.

Bade, Patrick. *Femme Fatale: Images of Evil and Fascinating Women.* New York: Mayflower Books, 1979.

Baker, David J. "Some Quirk, Some Subtle Evasion: Legal Subversion in Spenser's *A View of the Present State of Ireland." Spenser Studies* 6 (1986): 147–63.

Balpinar, Belkis, Udo Hirsch, and James Mellaart. *The Goddess from Anatolia,* 4 vols. Milan: Eskenazi, 1989.

Barnett, R. D. "Early Greek and Oriental Ivories." *Journal of Hellenic Studies* 68 (1948): 1–25.

Baron, Hans. *The Crisis of the Early Italian Renaissance.* Princeton: Princeton University Press, 1966.

Berenson, Bernhard. *The Study and Criticism of Italian Art.* London: G. Bell and Sons Ltd., 1912.

Beye, Charles R. *The Iliad, the Odyssey and the Epic Tradition.* Garden City, N.Y.: Doubleday, 1972.

Blake, William. *The Complete Poetry and Prose of William Blake.* Ed. David V. Erdman. New York: Doubleday, 1982.

Bly, Robert. *Sleepers Joining Hands.* New York: HarperCollins, 1985.

Boethius. *The Consolation of Philosophy.* Trans. and ed. V. E. Watts. Harmondsworth: Penguin Books Ltd., 1969.

Bradford, Ernle. *Ulysses Found.* New York: Harcourt, Brace and World, Inc., 1963.

Brand, C. P. *Torquato Tasso.* Cambridge: Cambridge University Press, 1965.

Bridenthal, Renate and Claudia Koonz, eds. *Becoming Visible: Women in European History.* Boston: Houghton Mifflin, 1977.

Briganti, Guliano. *Il manierismo e Pellegrino Tibaldi.* Rome: Cosmopolita, 1945.

Brown, Peter. *Augustine of Hippo.* Berkeley: University of California Press, 1967.

———. *Society and the Holy in Late Antiquity.* Berkeley: University of California Press, 1982.

Brown, Robert, Jr. *The Myth of Kirke.* London: Longmans, Greene, 1883.

———. *Semitic Influence in Hellenic Mythology.* London, 1898.

Browne, William [of Tavistock]. "The Inner Temple Masque." In *The Whole Works of William Browne,* ed. W. Carew Hazlitt. London: Roxburghe Library, 1869.

Bruno, Giordano. *Giordano Bruno's The Heroic Frenzies.* Trans. Paul Memmo. Chapel Hill: University of North Carolina Press, 1966.

Budgen, Frank. *James Joyce and the Making of Ulysses.* Bloomington: Indiana University Press, 1960.

Buffière, Felix. *Les mythes d'Homère et la pensée grecque.* Paris, 1956.

Burkert, Walter. *Greek Religion.* Trans. John Raffan. Cambridge: Harvard University Press, 1985.

Burton, Robert. *The Anatomy of Melancholy.* Vol. 3. New York: Dutton, 1932.

Butterworth, E. A. *Some Traces of the Pre-Olympian World.* Berlin: De Gruyter, 1966.

Calderón de la Barca, Pedro. *Love the Greatest Enchantment, The Sorceries of Sin, and The Devotion to the Cross.* Trans. Denis F. MacCarthy. London: Longman, Greene, Longman and Roberts, 1861.

Caldwell, Mark L. "Allegory: The Renaissance Mode." *English Literary History* 44 (1977): 580–600.

Calepino, Ambrogio. *Ambrosii Calepini Dictionarium Octolinguae.* Coloniae Allobrogum: Sumptibus Caldaorianae Societatis, 1609.

Campbell, Joseph. *Occidental Mythology.* New York: Viking, 1970.

———. *The Power of Myth.* New York: Doubleday, 1988.

Carpenter, Rhys. *Folk Tale, Fiction, and Saga in the Homeric Epics.* Berkeley: University of California Press, 1946.

Cartari, Vincenzo. *Le Imagini . . . degli Dei.* 1571; rpt. New York: Garland Publishing, Inc., 1976.

Chapman, George, trans. *Chapman's Homer: Volume Two, The Odyssey and the Lesser Homerica.* Ed. Allardyce Nicoll. New York: Pantheon Books, 1956.

Charlton, Kenneth. *Education in Renaissance England.* Toronto: University of Toronto Press, 1965.

Christ, Carol P. *The Laughter of Aphrodite.* San Francisco: Harper and Row, 1987.

Clark, Stephen R. L. "Aristotle's Woman." *History of Political Thought* 3 (1982): 177–91.

Clement of Alexandria. "Stromateis." In *Alexandrian Christianity,* trans. and ed. John Oulton and Henry Chadwick. Philadelphia: Westminster Press, 1954.

Cole, Susan G. "Could Greek Women Read and Write?" In *Reflections of Women in Antiquity,* ed. Helene P. Foley, 219–45. New York: Gordon and Breach Science Publishers, 1981.

Comes, Natalis. *Mythologiae.* 1567; rpt. New York: Garland Publishing, Inc., 1976.

Cook, J. M. *The Greeks in Ionia and the East.* New York: Frederick A. Praeger, 1963.

Cooper, Thomas. *Thesaurus Linguae Romanae et Brittanicae.* London, 1573.

Curran, Leo C. "Transformation and Anti-Augustanism in Ovid's *Metamorphoses.*" *Arethusa* 5 (1972): 71–92.

Curtius, Ernst Robert. *European Literature and the Latin Middle Ages.* Trans. Willard R. Trask. New York: Harper and Row, 1953.

Dauber, Antoinette B. "The Art of Veiling in the Bower of Bliss." *Spenser Studies* 1 (1980): 163–75.

Davis, Natalie Zemon. *Society and Culture in Early Modern France.* Palo Alto: Stanford University Press, 1975.

de Armas, Frederick A. "Metamorphosis in Calderón's *El mayor encanto, amor.*" *Romance Notes* 22 (1981): 208–12.

Demetrakopoulos, S. A. "Eve as a Circean and Courtly Fatal Woman." *Milton Quarterly* 9 (1975): 99–106.

de Riencourt, Amaury. *Sex and Power in History.* New York: Dell Publishing Company, 1975.

Dijkstra, Bram. *Idols of Perversity.* New York: Oxford University Press, 1986.

Dinnerstein, Dorothy. *The Mermaid and the Minotaur: Sexual Arrangements and Human Malaise.* New York: Harper and Row, 1977.

Dodds, E. R. *The Greeks and the Irrational.* Berkeley: University of California Press, 1951.

duBois, Page. *Sowing the Body: Psychoanalysis and Ancient Representations of Women.* Chicago: University of Chicago Press, 1988.

————. "'The Devil's Gateway': Women's Bodies and the Earthly Paradise." *Women's Studies* 7:43–58.

Dunbar, Henry. *A Complete Concordance to the Odyssey and the Hymns of Homer.* Oxford: Clarendon Press, 1880.

Duran, Manuel. "Towards a Psychological Profile of Pedro Calderón de la Barca." In *Approaches to the Theater of Calderón,* ed. Michael D. McGaha, 17–32. Washington, D.C.: University Press of America, 1982.

Eisler, Riane. *The Chalice and the Blade.* San Francisco: Harper and Row, 1987.

Eliade, Mircea. *Myth and Reality.* Trans. Willard. R. Trask. New York: Harper and Row, 1963.

Elias, Norbert. *Power and Civility.* New York: Pantheon Books, 1982.

Ellmann, Richard. *James Joyce.* New York: Oxford University Press, 1962.

————. *Ulysses on the Liffey.* New York: Oxford University Press, 1972.

Elyot, Sir Thomas. *Bibliotheca Eliotae.* Ed. Thomas Cooper. 1548; rpt. Delmar, N.Y.: Scholars' Facsimiles and Reprints, 1975.

Epic of Gilgamesh. Trans. and ed. N. K. Sandars. Harmondsworth: Penguin Books Ltd., 1972.

Euripides. "Medea." Trans. Rex Warner. In *The Complete Greek Tragedies.* Vol. 3. Ed. David Grene and Richmond Lattimore. Chicago: University of Chicago Press, 1959.

Famous Pictures Reproduced. Chicago: Stanton and Van Vliet, 1917.

Farnell, Lewis R. *The Cults of the Greek States.* Vols. 2 and 3. Oxford: Clarendon Press, 1896, 1907.

Fauth, W. "Gyges und die 'Falken.'" *Hermes* 96 (1968): 257–64.

Ferguson, Margaret W., Maureen Quilligan, and Nancy J. Vickers, eds. *Rewriting the Renaissance.* Chicago: University of Chicago Press, 1986.

Fiedler, Leslie. *Love and Death in the American Novel.* New York: Criterion Books, 1960.

Finley, John H., Jr. *Homer's Odyssey.* Cambridge: Harvard University Press, 1978.

Fletcher, Angus. *Allegory: The Theory of a Symbolic Mode.* Ithaca: Cornell University Press, 1964.

Florio, John. *A World of Words.* 1598; rpt. Hildesheim, N.Y.: G. Olms, 1972.

Foley, Helene P. "Reverse Similes and Sex Roles in the *Odyssey.*" *Arethusa* 11 (1978): 7–25.

————. "The Conception of Women in Athenian Drama." In *Reflections of Women in Antiquity,* ed. Helene P. Foley, 127–65. New York: Gordon and Breach Science Publishers, 1981.

Fontenrose, Joseph. *Python: A Study of Delphic Myth and Its Origins.* Berkeley: University of California Press, 1959.

Fränkel, Hermann. *Ovid, a Poet Between Two Worlds.* Berkeley: University of California Press, 1945.

Frankfort, Henri. *The Art and Architecture of the Ancient Orient.* Baltimore: Penguin Books, 1955.

Fraser, Antonia. *The Weaker Vessel.* New York: Alfred A. Knopf, 1984.

French, Marilyn. *The Book as World: James Joyce's Ulysses.* Cambridge: Harvard University Press, 1976.

Freud, Sigmund. "Civilization and Its Discontents." In vol. 21 of *The Standard Edition of the Complete Psychological Works of Sigmund Freud.* Trans. James Strachey. London: Hogarth Press, 1961.

Froula, Christine. "When Eve Reads Milton: Undoing the Canonical Economy." *Critical Inquiry* 10 (1983): 321–47.

Gelli, Giovanni Battista. *The Circe of Giovanni Battista Gelli.* Trans. and ed. Robert Adams. Ithaca: Cornell University Press, 1963.

Germain, Gabriel. *Génèse de l'Odyssée.* Paris, 1954.

Giamatti, A. Bartlett. *The Earthly Paradise and the Renaissance Epic.* Princeton: Princeton University Press, 1966.

Gibbons, Felton. *Dosso and Battista Dossi: Court Painters at Ferrara.* Princeton: Princeton University Press, 1968.

Gilbert, Sandra M. and Susan Gubar. *The Madwoman in the Attic: The Woman Writer and the Nineteenth-Century Literary Imagination.* New Haven: Yale University Press, 1979.

Gimbutas, Marija. *The Gods and Goddesses of Old Europe, 7000 to 3500 B.C.* Berkeley: University of California Press, 1974.

———. *The Language of the Goddess.* San Francisco: Harper and Row, 1989.

Gohlke, Madelon S. "Embattled Allegory: Book II of *The Faerie Queene.*" *English Literary Renaissance* 8 (1978): 123–40.

Goldberg, Jonathan. *Endlesse Work: Spenser and the Structures of Discourse.* Baltimore: Johns Hopkins University Press, 1981

———. "The Mothers in *Faerie Queene* III." *Texas Studies in Literature and Language* 17 (1975): 5–26.

Golden, Mark. "Male Chauvinists and Pigs." *Echos du Monde Classique* 32:1–12.

Golding, Arthur, trans. *Shakespeare's Ovid: Golding's Translation of the Metamorphoses.* Ed. W. H. D. Rouse. Carbondale: Southern Illinois University Press, 1961.

Gombrich, E. H. *Symbolic Images: Studies in the Art of the Renaissance.* New York: Phaidon Publishers Inc., 1972.

Gordon, D. J. *The Renaissance Imagination.* Ed. Stephen Orgel. Berkeley: University of California Press, 1975.

Graves, Robert. *The Greek Myths.* 2 vols. Harmondsworth: Penguin Books Ltd., 1960.

Greenblatt, Stephen. *Renaissance Self-Fashioning.* Chicago: University of Chicago Press, 1980.

Gsänger, Hans. *Ephesos, Zentrum der Artemis-Mysterien.* Schaffhausen, Switzerland: Novalis Verlag, 1974.

Gurney, O. R. *The Hittites.* London, 1952.

Guthrie, W. K. C. *Orpheus and Greek Religion.* London: Methuen and Co., Ltd., 1952.

Hamilton, A. C., ed. *Essential Articles for the Study of Edmund Spenser.* Hamden, Conn.: Archon Books, 1972.

Hardwick, Elizabeth. *Seduction and Betrayal.* New York: Random House, 1974.

Harrison, Jane. *Myths of the Odyssey in Art and Literature.* London, 1882.

———. *Prologomena to the Study of Greek Religion.* 1907; rpt. London: Merlin Press, 1962.

Hawkins, Peter S. "From Mythography to Myth-Making: Spenser and the Magna Mater Cybele." *Sixteenth Century Journal* 12 (1981): 51–64.

Heraclitus [Mythographer]. *Allégories d'Homère.* Ed. Felix Buffière. Paris, 1962.

Herodotus. *Histories.* 4 vols. Loeb Classical Library. Cambridge: Harvard University Press, 1925.

Herr, Cheryl. "'One Good Turn Deserves Another': Theatrical Cross-Dressing in Joyce's Circe Episode." *Journal of Modern Literature* 2 (1984): 263–76.

Hesiod. *Theogony.* Trans. Apostolos N. Athanassakis. Baltimore: Johns Hopkins University Press, 1983.

Hill, Christopher. *Milton and the English Revolution.* New York: Viking Press, 1977.

Hillman, James. *Anima: An Anatomy of a Personified Notion.* Dallas: Spring Publications, 1985.

Hobson, Anthony. *The Art and Life of J. W. Waterhouse, R.A.* New York: Rizzoli, 1980.

Hogarth, David George. *Excavations at Ephesus: The Archaic Artemesia.* London: British Museum, 1908.

Homer. *Odyssey.* Ed. W. B. Stanford. 2 vols. New York: St. Martins Press, 1959.

———. *The Odyssey.* Trans. Robert Fitzgerald. Garden City, N.Y.: Doubleday, 1963.

The Homeric Hymns. Trans. Apostolos N. Athanassakis. Baltimore: Johns Hopkins University Press, 1976.

Horapollo. *Hieroglyphics.* Trans. and ed. Alexander Turner Cory. London: William Pickering, 1840.

Hughes, Felicity A. "Psychological Allegory in *The Faerie Queene* III.11–12." *Review of English Studies* 29 (1978): 129–46.

Hughes, Merritt Y. "Spenser's Acrasia and the Circe of the Renaissance." *Journal of the History of Ideas* 4 (1943): 381–99.

Hughes-Hallett, Lucy. *Cleopatra: Histories, Dreams and Distortions.* New York: Harper and Row, 1990.

Iamblichus of Chalcis. *Life of Pythagoras.* Trans. Thomas Taylor. London: A. J. Valpy, 1818.

Jacobsthal, Paul. "The Date of the Ephesian Foundation-Deposit." *Journal of Hellenic Studies* 71 (1951): 85–95.

Jaeger, Werner. *Paideia.* Trans. Gilbert Highet. Vol. 1. New York: Oxford University Press, 1969.

James, E. O. *The Cult of the Mother Goddess.* London: Thames and Hudson, 1959.

Jayne, Sears. "Ficino and the Platonism of the English Renaissance." *Comparative Literature* 4 (1952): 214–38.

———. "The Subject of Milton's Ludlow *Mask.*" In *A Maske at Ludlow,* ed. John S. Diekhoff, 165–87. Cleveland: Case Western Reserve University Press, 1968.

Johnson, Buffie. *Lady of the Beasts.* San Francisco: Harper and Row, 1988.

Joyce, James. *The Letters of James Joyce.* Ed. Richard Ellmann. Vol. 2. New York: Viking Press, 1966.

———. *Ulysses.* Harmondsworth: Penguin Books Ltd., 1969.

Jung, Carl. "Archetypes of the Collective Unconscious." In vol. 9 of *Collected Works.* New York: Pantheon, 1959.

———. "The Transcendent Function." In vol. 8 of *Collected Works.* Princeton: Bollingen, 1960.

Kahler, Erich. "The Persistence of Myth." *Chimera* (Spring 1946): 2–11.

Kanta, Katherine G. *Eleusis.* Trans. W. W. Phelps. Athens, 1979.

Karabaş, Seyfi. "The *Odyssey* and the Turkish Quatrains." *Journal of Human Sciences* 1 (1983): 139–55.

Kenner, Hugh. *Ulysses.* London: George Allen and Unwin, 1980.

Kerenyi, Karl. *Goddesses of the Sun and Moon.* Trans. Murray Stein. Irving, Texas: University of Dallas, 1979.

———. *Hermes, Guide of Souls: The Mythologem of the Masculine Source of Life.* Zurich, 1976.

Keuls, Eva C. *The Reign of the Phallus: Sexual Politics in Ancient Athens.* New York: Harper and Row, 1985.

Klein, Joan Larsen. "From Errour to Acrasia." *Huntington Library Quarterly* 41 (1978): 173–99.

Kleinbaum, Abby. *The War against the Amazons.* New York: New Press, 1983.

Kors, Alan C. and Edward Peters, eds. *Witchcraft in Europe, 1100–1700.* Philadelphia: University of Pennsylvania Press, 1972.

Kramer, H. and J. Sprenger. *Malleus Maleficarum*. Trans. Montague Summers. New York: Arrow Books, 1971.

Kramer, Samuel N. *The Sacred Marriage Rite*. Bloomington: Indiana University Press, 1961.

———, ed. *Mythologies of the Ancient World*. New York: Doubleday, 1961.

Lamberton, Robert. *Homer the Theologian: Neoplatonist Allegorical Reading and the Growth of the Epic Tradition*. Berkeley: University of California Press, 1986.

Lauter, Estella. *Women as Mythmakers: Poetry and Visual Art by Twentieth-Century Women*. Bloomington: Indiana University Press, 1984.

——— and Carol Schreier Rupprecht, eds. *Feminist Archetypal Theory*. Knoxville: University of Tennessee Press, 1985.

Lederer, Wolfgang. *The Fear of Women*. New York: Grune and Stratton, 1968.

Lefkowitz, Mary R. and Maureen B. Fant, trans. and eds. *Women's Life in Greece and Rome*. Baltimore: Johns Hopkins University Press, 1982.

Leonard, Linda Schierse. *On the Way to the Wedding: Transforming the Love Relationship*. Boston: Shambhala, 1987.

Lerner, Gerda. *The Creation of Patriarchy*. New York: Oxford University Press, 1986.

Leslie, William H. "The Concept of Woman in the Pauline Corpus in Light of the Social and Religious Environment of the First Century." Ph.D. Diss., Northwestern University, 1976.

Lethaby, W. R. "The Earlier Temple of Artemis at Ephesus." *Journal of Hellenic Studies* 38 (1917): 1–16.

LeVan, J. Richards. "Theme and Metaphor in the *Auto Historial:* Calderón's *Los encantos de la Culpa.*" In *Approaches to the Theater of Calderón*, ed. Michael D. McGaha, 187–98. Washington, D.C.: University Press of America, 1982.

Lewis, C. S. *The Allegory of Love*. Oxford: Oxford University Press, 1936.

Lilienfeld, Jane. "Silence and Scorn in a Lyric of Intimacy: The Progress of Margaret Atwood's Poetry." *Women's Studies* 7 (1980): 185–94.

Lord, George de F. *Heroic Mockery: Variations on Epic Themes from Homer to Joyce*. Newark: University of Delaware Press, 1977.

———. *Homeric Renaissance: The Odyssey of George Chapman*. New Haven: Yale University Press, 1956.

Lyrica Graeca Selecta. Ed. D. L. Page. Oxford: Clarendon Press, 1968.

McColley, Diane Kelsey. *Milton's Eve*. Urbana: University of Illinois Press, 1983.

Macfarlane, Alan. *Witchcraft in Tudor and Stuart England*. London: Routledge and Kegan Paul, 1970.

Maddox, Brenda. *Nora: The Real Life of Molly Bloom*. Boston: Houghton Mifflin, 1988.

Mandl, Betty. "Images of Transformation: Joyce's Ulysses in Midlife." *Journal of Mental Imagery* 10, no. 2 (1986): 79–86.

Martin, John Rupert. *The Farnese Gallery.* Princeton: Princeton University Press, 1965.

Mellaart, James. "Excavations at Çatal Hüyük, 1961." *Anatolian Studies* 12 (1962): 41–66.

———. "Excavations at Çatal Hüyük, 1962." *Anatolian Studies* 13 (1963): 43-103.

———. "Excavations at Çatal Hüyük, 1963." *Anatolian Studies* 14 (1964): 39–119.

———. "Excavations at Hacilar, 1960." *Anatolian Studies* 11 (1961): 39–76.

Mellink, Machteld. "Comments on a Cult Relief of Kybele from Gordion." In *Beitrage Zur Attertumskunde Kleinasiens,* 349–60. Mainz: 1983.

Merchant, Carolyn. *The Death of Nature: Women, Ecology, and the Scientific Revolution.* San Francisco: Harper and Row, 1980.

Milton, John. "Comus." In *Odes, Pastorals, and Masques.* Ed. David Aers et al. Cambridge: Cambridge University Press, 1975.

———. *Paradise Lost.* Ed. Merritt Y. Hughes. New York: Odyssey Press, 1962.

Montrose, Louis. "*A Midsummer Night's Dream* and the Shaping Fantasies of Elizabethan Culture." In *Rewriting the Renaissance,* ed. Margaret W. Ferguson et al., 65–87. Chicago: University of Chicago Press, 1986.

Morrison, Toni. *Song of Solomon.* New York: Knopf, 1977.

Mylonas, George. *Eleusis and the Eleusinian Mysteries.* Princeton: Princeton University Press, 1961.

Nellist, B. "The Allegory of Guyon's Journey: An Interpretation." *English Literary History* 30 (1963): 89–106.

Neumann, Erich. *The Great Mother.* New York: Pantheon, 1955.

———. *The Origins and History of Consciousness.* Princeton: Princeton University Press, 1973.

Newman, Robert D. "The Left-Handed Path of Circe." *James Joyce Quarterly* 23:223–26.

Nilsson, Martin P. *Greek Piety.* Trans. Herbert Rose. Oxford: Clarendon Press, 1948.

———. *Homer and Mycenae.* London: Methuen and Co., Ltd., 1933.

———. *The Minoan-Mycenaean Religion and Its Survival in Greek Religion.* Lund: C. W. K. Gleerup, 1950.

O'Faolain, Julia and Lauro Martines, eds. *Not In God's Image.* New York: Harper and Row, 1973.

Okerlund, Arlene N. "Spenser's Wanton Maidens: Reader Psychology and the Bower of Bliss." *PMLA* 88 (1973): 62-68.

O'Meara, John J. "St. Augustine's Attitude to Love in the Context of His Influence on Christian Ethics." *Arethusa* 2 (1969): 46–60.

Orgel, Stephen. *The Illusion of Power.* Berkeley: University of California Press, 1975.

Otis, Brooks. *Virgil: A Study in Civilized Poetry.* Oxford: Clarendon Press, 1963.

Otto, Walter F. *The Homeric Gods.* Trans. Moses Hadas. New York: Pantheon Books, 1954.

Ovid. *Metamorphoses.* Trans. Frank Justus Miller. 2 vols. Loeb Classical Library. London: William Heinemann, 1916.

———. *The Erotic Poems.* Trans. and ed. Peter Green. Harmondsworth: Penguin Books Ltd., 1982.

———. *The Metamorphoses.* Trans. Horace Gregory. New York: New American Library, 1958.

Ovide Moralisé. Vol. 5. Ed. C. de Boer. Wiesbaden: Sändig, n.d.

The Oxford Classical Dictionary. 2d ed. Ed. N. G. L. Hammond and H. H. Scullard. Oxford: Clarendon Press, 1970.

Paetz, Bernhard. *Kirke und Odysseus.* Berlin: Walter de Gruyter, 1970.

Pagels, Elaine. *Adam, Eve, and the Serpent.* New York: Random House, 1988.

———. *The Gnostic Gospels.* New York: Vintage Books, 1981.

Paglia, Camille. *Sexual Personae.* New York: Random House, 1991.

Parrot, André. *The Arts of Assyria.* Trans. Stuart Gibbons and James Evans. New York: Golden Press, 1961.

Parry, Adam M. "The Two Voices of Virgil's *Aeneid.*" In *The Language of Achilles and Other Papers,* 78–96. Oxford: Clarendon Press, 1989.

Pépin, Jean. *Mythe et allégoire.* Paris, 1976.

Perkell, Christine G. "On Creusa, Dido, and the Quality of Victory in Virgil's *Aeneid.*" *Women's Studies* 8 (1981): 201–23.

Perrot, Georges and Charles Chipiez. *History of Art in Phrygia, Lydia, Caria, and Lycia.* London: Chapman and Hall, Ltd., 1892.

Picard, Charles. *Éphèse et Claros, Réchèrches sur les sanctuaires et les cultes de l'Ionie du Nord.* Paris, 1922.

Plato. "Phaedo." In *Great Dialogues of Plato.* Trans. W. H. D. Rouse. New York: New American Library, 1956.

———. "Symposium." In *Great Dialogues of Plato.* Trans. W. H. D. Rouse. New York: New American Library, 1956.

———. *The Collected Dialogues of Plato.* Ed. Edith Hamilton and Huntington Cairns. Princeton: Princeton University Press, 1961.

———. *The Republic.* Trans. B. Jowett. New York: Modern Library, n.d.

Plutarch. "Advice to Bride and Groom." In *Moralia.* Vol. 2. Trans. F. C. Babbitt. Loeb Classical Library. London: William Heinemann, 1928.

————. "Beasts Are Rational." In *Moralia*. Vol. 12. Trans. W. C. Helmbold. Loeb Classical Library. London: William Heinemann, 1968.

————. "Of Isis and Osiris." In *Moralia*. Vol. 5. Trans. Frank Cole Babbitt. Loeb Classical Library. London: William Heinemann, 1969.

————. "The Dialogue on Love." In *Moralia*. Vol. 9. Trans. W. C. Helmbold. Loeb Classical Library. London: William Heinemann, 1961.

Pocket Interlinear New Testament. Trans. and ed. Jay P. Green, Sr. Lafayette, Ind.: Associated Publishers and Authors, Inc., 1981.

Pollack, Zailig. "Concupiscence and Intemperance in the Bower of Bliss." *Studies in English Literature, 1500–1900* 20 (1980): 43–58.

Pomeroy, Sarah. *Goddesses, Whores, Wives, and Slaves*. New York: Schocken Books, 1975.

Porter, Katherine Anne. "A Defense of Circe." In *The Collected Essays and Occasional Writings of Katherine Anne Porter*. New York: Delacorte Press, 1970.

Pseudo-Plutarch. "The Life and Poetry of Homer." In Plutarch, *Moralia*. Vol. 7. Ed. G. N. Bernadakis. Leipzig: Teubner, 1896.

Putnam, Michael C. J. "*Aeneid* VII and the *Aeneid*." *American Journal of Philology* 91 (1970): 408–30.

————. *The Poetry of the Aeneid*. Cambridge: Harvard University Press, 1966.

Rahner, Hugo. *Greek Myths and Christian Mystery*. Trans. Brian Battershaw. New York: Harper and Row, 1963.

Rand, E. K. *Ovid and His Influence*. Boston: Marshall Jones Co., 1925.

Renfrew, Colin. *Before Civilization*. New York: Alfred A. Knopf, 1972.

————. *The Emergence of Civilization: The Cyclades and the Aegean in the Third Millenium B.C.* New York, 1972.

Roberts, Gareth. "Three Notes on Uses of Circe by Spenser, Marlowe, and Milton." *Notes and Queries* 25 (1978): 433–35.

Roche, Thomas P., Jr. *The Kindly Flame: A Study of the Third and Fourth Books of Spenser's Faerie Queene*. Princeton: Princeton University Press, 1964.

Rogers, Katherine M. *The Troublesome Helpmate: A History of Misogyny in Literature*. Seattle: University of Washington Press, 1966.

Rohde, Erwin. *Psyche*. Trans. W. B. Hillis. London: Routledge and Kegan Paul, 1950.

Rousset, Jean. *La littérature de l'age Baroque en France: Circé et le Paon*. Paris: Librairie José Corti, 1953.

Rudat, Wolfgang E. H. "Milton, Freud, St. Augustine: *Paradise Lost* and the History of Human Sexuality." *Mosaic* 15 (1982): 109–21.

————. "'Thy Beauty's Heavenly Ray': Milton's Satan and the Circean Eve." *Milton Quarterly* 19 (1985): 17–19.

Sandys, George, trans. *Ovid's Metamorphosis Englished, Mythologized, and Represented in Figures*. Ed. Karl K. Hulley and Stanley T. Vandersall. Lincoln: University of Nebraska Press, 1970.

Scot, Reginald. *The Discoverie of Witchcraft*. 1584; rpt. Carbondale: Southern Illinois University Press, 1964.

Scott, Bonnie Kime. *Joyce and Feminism*. Bloomington: Indiana University Press, 1984.

Segal, Charles. "Circean Temptations: Homer, Vergil, Ovid." *Transactions and Proceedings of the American Philological Association* 99 (1968): 419–42.

Servius. *Servii Grammatici Qui Feruntur in Vergilii Carmina Commentarii*. Vol. 2. Ed. George Thilo. Leipzig: B. G. Teubner, 1883.

Shechner, Mark. *Joyce in Nighttown*. Berkeley: University of California Press, 1974.

Shumway, Nicolas. "Calderón and the Protestant Reformation." *Hispanic Review* 49 (1981): 329–48.

Siegel, Carol. "'Venus Metempsychosis' and *Venus in Furs:* Masochism and Fertility in *Ulysses*." *Twentieth Century Literature* 33 (1987) 179–95.

Slater, Philip. *The Glory of Hera*. Boston: Beacon Press, 1968.

Smalley, D. "The Ethical Bias of Chapman's Homer." *Studies in Philology* 36 (1939): 169–91.

Snell, Bruno. *The Discovery of the Mind*. Trans. T. C. Rosenmeyer. Oxford: Clarendon Press, 1953.

Spelman, Elizabeth. "Woman as Body: Ancient and Contemporary Views." *Feminist Studies* 8:109–31.

Spenser, Edmund. "A View of the Present State of Ireland." In *The Works of Edmund Spenser, A Variorum Edition*. Vol. 9. Ed. Edwin Greenlaw et al. Baltimore: Johns Hopkins University Press, 1943.

———. "The Shepheardes Calender." In *The Works of Edmund Spenser, A Variorum Edition*. Vol. 7. Ed. Edwin Greenlaw et al. Baltimore: Johns Hopkins University Press, 1943.

———. *The Faerie Queene*. Ed. A. C. Hamilton. London: Longman Group Ltd., 1977.

Spretnak, Charlene. *Lost Goddesses of Early Greece*. Boston: Beacon Press, 1978.

Stanford, W. B. *The Ulysses Theme*. Oxford: Clarendon Press, 1961.

——— and J. V. Luce. *The Quest For Ulysses*. New York: Praeger, 1974.

Stone, Merlin. *When God Was a Woman*. New York: Dial Press, 1976.

Strong, Roy. *The Cult of Elizabeth*. London: Thames and Hudson, 1977.

Tasso, Torquato. *Godfrey of Bulloigne: A Critical Edition of Edward Fairfax's Translation of Tasso's Gerusalemme Liberata*. Ed. Kathleen M. Lea and T. M. Gang. Oxford: Clarendon, 1981.

Tate, J. "On the History of Allegorism." *Classical Quarterly* 28 (1934): 105–15.

———. "The Beginnings of Greek Allegory." *Classical Review* 31 (1927): 214–15.

Taylor, Charles H., Jr. "The Obstacles to Odysseus' Return: Identity and Consciousness in the *Odyssey*." *Yale Review* 50 (1961): 569–80.

Tertullian. "On the Apparel of Women." In *The Ante-Nicene Fathers*. Vol. 4. Ed. A. Cleveland Coxe. Boston: Christian Literature Publishing Co., 1885.

Thomas, Thomas. *Dictionarium Linguae Latinae et Anglicanae*. 1587; rpt. Menton: The Scolar Press Ltd., 1972.

Thompson, Cynthia. "Stoic Allegory of Homer: A Critical Analysis of Heraclitus' *Homeric Allegories*." Ph.D. Diss., Yale University, 1973.

Thompson, M. S. "The Asiatic or Winged Artemis." *Journal of Hellenic Studies* 29 (1909): 286–307.

Thomson, George D. *The Prehistoric Aegean*. New York: Citadel Press, 1965.

Tillyard, E. M. W. "The Action of *Comus*." In *A Maske At Ludlow*, ed. John S. Diekhoff, 43–57. Cleveland: Case Western Reserve University Press, 1968.

Townshend, Aurelian. "Tempe Restored." In *Aurelian Townshend's Poems and Masks*, ed. E. K. Chambers. Oxford: Clarendon Press, 1912.

Trueblood, Alan S. *Experience and Artistic Expression in Lope de Vega*. Cambridge: Harvard University Press, 1974.

Tuve, Rosamond. "Image, Form, and Theme in *A Mask*." In *A Maske At Ludlow*, ed. John S. Diekhoff, 126–64. Cleveland: Case Western Reserve University Press, 1968.

———. *Allegorical Imagery: Some Medieval Books and Their Posterity*. Princeton: Princeton University Press, 1966.

Tyrrell, William Blake. *Amazons: A Study in Athenian Mythmaking*. Baltimore: Johns Hopkins University Press, 1984.

"Ulisse et Circe." In *Le theâtre italien*. Vol. 3. Ed. Evaristo Gherardi. Paris: Cusson and Witte, 1700.

Vande Kieft, Ruth M. *Eudora Welty*. Boston: Twayne Publishers, 1987.

Vega, Lope de. *La Circe con otras Rimas y Prosos*. Madrid: Alonso Martin, 1624; rpt. San Sebastian, 1935.

Verdenius, W. J. "*Odyssey* 10, 398." *Mnemosyne* 25 (1975): 418.

Vermaseren, *Cybele and Attis*. London: Thames and Hudson, 1977.

Virgil. *Aeneid*. Ed. R. D. Williams. 2 vols. New York: St. Martins Press, 1972.

———. *The Aeneid*. Trans. Robert Fitzgerald. New York: Random House, 1984.

Vivante, Paolo. "On Homer's Winged Words." *Classical Quarterly* 25 (1975): 1–12.

————. *The Homeric Imagination.* Bloomington: Indiana University Press, 1970.

Walker, Susan. "Women and Housing in Classical Greece: The Archaeological Evidence." In *Images of Women in Antiquity,* ed. Averil Cameron and Amélie Kuhrt, 81–91. Detroit: Wayne State University Press, 1983.

Wardropper, Bruce W. "The Standing of Calderón in the Twentieth Century." In *Approaches to the Theater of Calderón,* ed. Michael D. McGaha, 1–16. Washington, D.C.: University Press of America, 1982.

Webster, T. B. L. *From Mycenae to Homer.* London: Methuen and Co., Ltd., 1958.

Wehr, Demaris. *Jung and Feminism: Liberating Archetypes.* Boston: Beacon Press, 1987.

Welty, Eudora. "Circe." In *Collected Stories of Eudora Welty,* 531–37. New York: Harcourt Brace Jovanovich, 1980.

————. *The Eye of the Story: Selected Essays and Reviews.* New York: Random House, 1979.

Wheelwright, Phillip. *Metaphor and Reality.* Bloomington: Indiana University Press, 1962.

Whitman, Cedric H. *Homer and the Heroic Tradition.* Cambridge: Harvard University Press, 1958.

Whitney, Geffrey. *A Choice of Emblemes.* Ed. Henry Green. New York: Benjamin Blom, 1967.

Willey, Basil. *The Seventeenth-Century Background.* Garden City, N.Y.: Doubleday, 1953.

Wilson, A. N. *The Life of John Milton.* Oxford: Oxford University Press, 1983.

Wind, Edgar. *Pagan Mysteries in the Renaissance.* New Haven: Yale University Press, 1958.

Woodbridge, Linda. *Women and the English Renaissance: Literature and the Nature of Womenkind, 1540–1620.* Urbana: University of Illinois Press, 1984.

Xenophon. "Oeconomicus." In *Xenophon's Socratic Discourse,* trans. Carnes Lord, ed. Leo Straus. Ithaca: Cornell University Press, 1970.

Zamboni, Giuseppe. *Ulisse nell'isola di Circe.* Naples: Dalla Tipografia Flautina, 1819.

Index

Judith Yarnall teaches writing and literature at Johnson State College in Vermont. She holds degrees in history and English from Bates College, the University of Virginia, and McGill University. The mother of three adult daughters, she has published poetry in various journals and traveled extensively in Greece and Turkey, where she lived for a year.